PRENTICE-HALL HISTORY OF MUSIC SERIES

H. WILEY HITCHCOCK, editor

MUSIC IN THE MEDIEVAL WORLD, 2ND ED., *Albert Seay*

MUSIC IN THE RENAISSANCE, 2ND ED., *Howard Mayer Brown*

BAROQUE MUSIC, *Claude V. Palisca*

MUSIC IN THE CLASSIC PERIOD, 2ND ED., *Reinhard G. Pauly*

NINETEENTH-CENTURY ROMANTICISM IN MUSIC, 2ND ED., *Rey M. Longyear*

TWENTIETH-CENTURY MUSIC: AN INTRODUCTION, 2ND ED., *Eric Salzman*

FOLK AND TRADITIONAL MUSIC OF THE WESTERN CONTINENTS, 2ND ED., *Bruno Nettl*

MUSIC CULTURES OF THE PACIFIC, THE NEAR EAST, AND ASIA, 2ND ED., *William P. Malm*

MUSIC IN THE UNITED STATES: A HISTORICAL INTRODUCTION, 2ND ED., *H. Wiley Hitchcock*

MUSIC OF LATIN AMERICA, *Gerard Béhague*

MUSIC IN INDIA: THE CLASSICAL TRADITIONS, *Bonnie C. Wade*

MUSIC IN INDIA: THE CLASSICAL TRADITIONS

BONNIE C. WADE

Department of Music
University of California, Berkeley

PRENTICE-HALL, INC., ENGLEWOOD CLIFFS, NEW JERSEY 07632

Library of Congress Cataloging in Publication Data

WADE, BONNIE C
Music in India.

(Prentice-Hall history of music series)
Bibliography: p.
Discography: p.
Filmography: p.
Includes index.
1. Music—India—History and criticism. I. Title.
ML338.W32 781.7'54 77-28488
ISBN 0-13-607028-0 pbk.
ISBN 0-13-607036-1

Printed in the United States of America

10 9 8 7 6 5 4 3 2 1

PRENTICE-HALL INTERNATIONAL, INC., *London*
PRENTICE-HALL OF AUSTRALIA PTY. LIMITED, *Sydney*
PRENTICE-HALL OF CANADA, LTD., *Toronto*
PRENTICE-HALL OF INDIA PRIVATE LIMITED, *New Delhi*
PRENTICE-HALL OF JAPAN, INC., *Tokyo*
PRENTICE-HALL OF SOUTHEAST ASIA PTE. LTD., *Singapore*
WHITEHALL BOOKS LIMITED, *Wellington, New Zealand*

FOR INDIAN MUSIC WALLAHS

CONTENTS

FOREWORD

Students and informed amateurs of the history of music have long needed a series of books that are comprehensive, authoritative, and engagingly written. They have needed books written by specialists—but specialists interested in communicating vividly. The Prentice-Hall History of Music Series aims at filling these needs.

Six books in the series present a panoramic view of the history of Western music, divided among the major historical periods—Medieval, Renaissance, Baroque, Classic, Romantic, and Contemporary. The musical culture of the United States is viewed historically as an independent development within the larger Western tradition, and a similar approach is accorded to the music of Latin America. A book devoted to the traditional music of India draws comparisons with Western music. In another pair of books, the rich yet neglected folk and traditional music of both hemispheres is treated. Taken together, the eleven volumes of the series will be a distinctive and, we hope, distinguished contribution to the history of the music of the

Foreword, continued

world's peoples. Each volume, moreover, may be read singly as a substantial account of the music of its period or area.

The authors of the series are scholars of national and international repute—musicologists, critics, and teachers of acknowledged stature in their respective fields of specialization. In their contributions to the Prentice-Hall History of Music Series their goal has been to present works of solid scholarship that are eminently readable, with significant insights into music as a part of the general intellectual and cultural life of man.

H. WILEY HITCHCOCK, *Editor*

PREFACE

Music in India encompasses a vast panoply of instruments, forms, performers, principles, and history in the religious, folk, tribal, "hybrid," film-dance-theater, and classical traditions. Since it is not possible to treat all of these aspects in a single volume with the thoroughness they deserve, this book focuses on the two classical traditions: North Indian, or Hindustānī, and South Indian, or Karnatak. This is the Indian music most familiar to Western audiences and most readily available through live and recorded performances.

This introductory text is written for the uninitiated Westerner, and tries to achieve a balance between technical and nontechnical discussion. I have provided transcriptions from good available recordings so that the reader may follow the music referred to and learn what to listen for.

A chapter each is devoted to the listener and Indian music, melody, melody instruments, rhythm and meter, rhythm instruments and drumming, and performance genres of the Hindustānī and the Karnatak traditions.

A historical map is provided for reference. Photographs and musical examples are given throughout. The appendix contains bibliographic sources, a discography, and a filmography. A glossary and index are also provided.

In the preparation of this book I have benefited enormously from the suggestions of innumerable friends, to whom I owe many thanks. First, to my teachers of Indian music (mentioned in the order they came into my musical life): Shaikh Hasan, my instructor in *sitār* during my residency in Pakistan; M. Giersarz, who first instructed me in the Karnatak tradition and *vīṇā* at the University of California, Los Angeles; Sumati Mutatkar, my advisor at Delhi University and an invaluable source on Hindustānī classical vocal forms; Pandit Pran Nath of the Kirana *gharānā*, my teacher in Delhi of Hindustānī vocal music, particularly *khyāl*; and Shri Sita Ram of the Delhi bāj, my instructor in Delhi on the *tablā*. Special thanks are extended to Pandit Sharda Sahai of the Benares bāj, who for the past several years has been my teacher in tablā and Hindustānī rhythmic theory and drumming.

I am deeply grateful to Professors Prem Lata Sharma of Benares Hindu University, and Harold S. Powers of Princeton University, who were provocative and exacting taskmasters at various stages in my development as a scholar of Indian music. Special thanks are also due to Professor Nazir Jairazbhoy of UCLA, who read the manuscript in various stages and offered invaluable advice.

The idea for this book was born and developed during the years when I taught at Brown University, and I am beholden to that institution's resources, students, and faculty for helping it bear fruit. I have benefited from my students in the general Asian Music survey and, in particular, the Music of India courses at Brown University, and most recently at UC Berkeley, and from my teacher-students in the National Endowment for the Humanities 1975 Summer Seminar for College Teachers. Discussions with four graduate students—Shirish Korde, Amy Catlin, Frances Shepherd, and Sharon Woodruff—clarified the form of presentation and lent fresh perspectives.

A number of friends and colleagues who teach Indian music and who shared my need for an introductory text have provided valuable information and advice: Peter Row, *bīnkār* and *sitārist*, on tunings and instrumental practice; Charles Capwell on the *sarod* and its tradition; Robert Brown on instruments and forms of the Karnatak tradition. I have also taken many useful suggestions from Harold Powers, Sudesh Aurora, Regula Qureshi, Bruno Nettl, Kamala Vendanthan, and Sara Stalder.

I am especially indebted to David Schonfeld for his advice and help on South Indian notations and transcriptions, as well as transnotations and translations from Tamil and Telugu. To my friend Dr. Stanley Summers of Providence, Rhode Island, I express thanks for his interest in the project and his excellent photographs.

Prentice-Hall editors Norwell F. Therien, Jr. and Ted Jursek, who recognized the necessity for such a book, prodded and encouraged me all the way. H. Wiley Hitchcock has been a thoughtful and thorough general editor, and his counsel is greatly appreciated. My final debt, as always, is to P., who was helpful with every facet of the preparation. The errors are mine alone.

BONNIE C. WADE

LIST OF PLATES

LIST OF MUSICAL EXAMPLES

LIST OF CHARTS

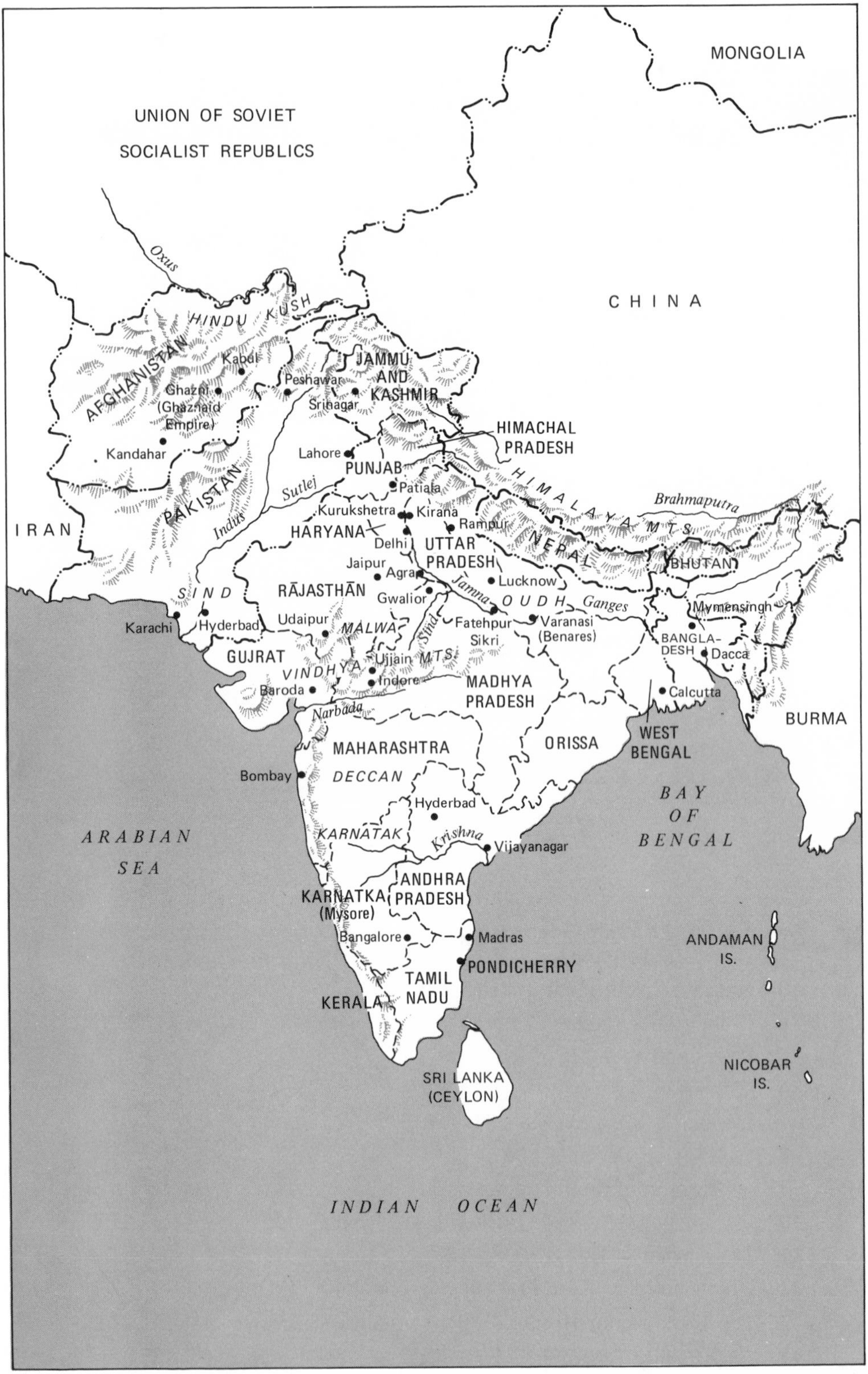

MONGOLIA
UNION OF SOVIET
SOCIALIST REPUBLICS
CHINA
Oxus
HINDU KUSH
AFGHANISTAN
Kabul
Ghazni
(Ghaznaid
Empire)
Kandahar
Peshawar
JAMMU
AND
KASHMIR
Srinagar
HIMACHAL
PRADESH
Lahore
PUNJAB
Patiala
HIMALAYA MTS.
Brahmaputra
PAKISTAN
Sutlej
Indus
IRAN
Kurukshetra
Kirana
Rampur
HARYANA
Delhi
UTTAR
PRADESH
NEPAL
BHUTAN
Jaipur
Agra
Lucknow
RĀJASTHĀN
Jamna
Gwalior
SIND
OUDH
Ganges
Karachi
Hyderbad
Udaipur
MALWA
Sind
Fatehpur
Sikri
Varanasi
(Benares)
Mymensingh
BANGLA-
DESH
Dacca
GUJRAT
VINDHYA
Ujjain
MTS.
Indore
MADHYA
PRADESH
Baroda
Calcutta
Narbada
BURMA
WEST
BENGAL
ORISSA
MAHARASHTRA
Bombay
DECCAN
Hyderbad
BAY
OF
BENGAL
ARABIAN
SEA
KARNATAK
Krishna
Vijayanagar
ANDHRA
PRADESH
KARNATKA
(Mysore)
Bangalore
Madras
PONDICHERRY
ANDAMAN
IS.
TAMIL
NADU
KERALA
NICOBAR
IS.
SRI LANKA
(CEYLON)
INDIAN OCEAN

INTRODUCTION

Until the last two decades, most Westerners were secure in their belief that there was but one sophisticated system of music in the world, and that it was theirs. But in the wake of Sputnik came a flood of federal and foundation monies for foreign-language and area studies, which exposed Americans to worlds outside of Europe and demonstrated the power and near timelessness of the great civilizations of Asia, Africa, and pre-Columbian America. Slowly, we have become aware of the complexities and majesty of the arts of those continents, one of which is their music.

Yet we are still at the threshold of understanding non-Western musics, for knowledge of a musical system requires much of the person who wishes to acquire it, not the least of which are access to the music itself and guidance to understanding the cultural and historical values of a non-Western society. These requirements are perhaps no better demonstrated than with the classical music of India.

The avenues to the study of Western music are diverse, and certainly readily available. One can learn to play an instrument or join a chorus, check books out of a library and read for oneself, or enroll in classes for more personally guided learning. Think of the literature available on Western classical music alone—the volumes upon volumes devoted to the history of musical styles, the editions of compositions, the theoretical treatises and histories of theory, the biographies of great and not-so-great composers, the studies of musical instruments and their builders, and the like. The number of authors is large: several generations of scholars have worked in many European and American countries, and all of them have been interested in facets of the art and liturgical music of Western civilization through time.

The avenues in the West for studying Indian classical music—an at least equally enormous subject—are practically the same (except joining a choral organization), but they certainly are not as readily available. Instrumental instruction can now be found only in some major urban centers and at a few universities scattered throughout the country. Instruments on which to practice have similarly sparse distribution.

The literature on Indian music is small, relatively speaking, and much of it is in Sanskrit, Hindi, Marathi, Tamil, Telugu, and other Indian languages. Many of the remaining sources are in English, the lingua franca in India since the mid-eighteenth century. But most of these have been written by Indian scholars and have been geared to the thought patterns of Indians who have recourse to other sources for checking unexplained terminology and who do not need the same type of framework established for them that Westerners do. Unfortunately, such sources confuse rather than clarify matters for beginning Western students.[1]

Most of the other older sources in English were written by British colonial administrators who lived in India for an extended time. Many of these writers evince warmth and respect for Indian civilization and often an understanding of it. But their level of awareness of Indian music was not that of the trained observer, and their works were written for an audience prone to consider Indian music a cacophony of primitive screeches.

Several books were produced as a result of the fad for Indian music in this country during the 1960's. Unfortunately, these are couched in West-centric terms and thus evince little real understanding of the complexities of India's cultures. A few are "sing-along-with-the-*sitār*" types. And only occasionally has the growing desire to learn about the musics of India been helped by concert-program notes and record-liner notes (the most impressive of these are the notes by Robert Brown and Jon Higgins on several Nonesuch recordings).

[1] A notable exception is *My Music, My Life* (New York: Simon & Schuster, 1968), by Ravi Shankar, the great sitārist who has aroused widespread interest in Indian classical music in America and who has become adept at explaining his music to us.

Indian classical music deserves much more. In recent years, a small number of good dissertations on specific features of Indian classical music have been produced by young scholars, most of them in the United States, and this demonstrates the seriousness with which the study of Indian music is being undertaken here. We who write about India's music try to transmit an empathy and respect for Indian cultures similar to that of Fox-Strangways, Day, and Clements, but we do not have to write for the same audience. We write for a public who are not only receptive to learning about what they already respect, but who also have Indian music to listen to after a visit to a record shop and a flip of a switch. In order to understand a music, one must be able to know what to listen for in it and also to learn in the thought patterns of the culture. These are the avenues, first and foremost, that this book hopes to provide.

The challenge in writing such a volume is that it must range—if I may make a cross-cultural comparison—from a book comparable to one on basic Western theory to a sophisticated analysis of musical masterpieces. The problem is exacerbated in that *two* classical-music traditions, the Hindustānī and the Karnatak, have flourished simultaneously in the Indian subcontinent since about the sixteenth and seventeenth centuries. Phonograph records containing music from both traditions are available in the United States, but very often listeners do not realize they are hearing two different traditions.

One of the usual tasks of ethnomusicologists who specialize in Indian music is to learn about both traditions, although most choose one or the other tradition on which to concentrate their research. This volume undertakes to explain each tradition and to compare and contrast them.

The musical repertoire of India is mammoth: it includes far more than the Hindustānī and Karnatak traditions of Indian classical music. It also includes folk-music traditions—both rural and urban—that are as vast and as varied as the thousands of cultures and subcultures within the subcontinent. Yet until recently there has been relatively little comprehensive research on Indian folk-music traditions and, thus, limited access to sources of folk music. This has led me to decide not to include a discussion of these traditions in this volume. The same problems exist for tribal, "hybrid," film-dance-theater, religious, and ritual musics.

In light of these considerations, it seems best to make the intent of this volume to acquaint the reader with the theory of India's two classical-music traditions and to provide a practical manual for learning to listen to and appreciate Indian classical music. A discussion of all Indian music is better left to another and entirely different type of book.

The reader who is looking primarily for the emphasis on cultural context that one might expect from an ethnomusicologist may conclude that this is a heavily musicological study. It is and it is not. This volume is first and foremost an introduction to the principles, ideas, and systems of the two traditions of Indian classical music. As in any introduction to a highly theorized system of music, it is necessary to speak to the theory. In doing so, I am taking the approach of Indian musicologists by trying to speak to the theory through the ideas of those Indians who have dealt with it—the conceptualizers, articulators, and connoisseurs, as well as the performers. It must be stressed that Indian classical music, at least in remembered time, has been the province of the elites and not the masses in Indian society, whether North or South. It is the elites who have made Indian classical music a highly theorized system, and to the greatest extent possible this discussion takes their approaches to their music.

This volume is geared to the listener as well as the performer. Chapter One concerns the listener and the effect of music, both of which lie at the heart of the Indian theory of aesthetics, *rasa*. The chapter also describes performance situations in both North and South India and in both the past and the present. In order to show how theory is put into practice, Chapter One concludes with a discussion of who becomes a performer and who remains a listener. Since this is one major difference between the musical spheres of North and South India, the fact of the two traditions of classical music and the reasons (in brief) why there are two such traditions within one musical system are presented.

In Chapters Two and Three I begin the task of comparing concepts in Indian and Western classical musics. More often when I am teaching Indian music than the music of any other culture I am asked to compare it with Western music.[2] For some reason, persons with a working knowledge of Western music seem to have more difficulty coming to terms with Indian classical music than do the musically uninitiated. To counter what seems to be an inevitable attempt to compare Western and Hindustānī music, I have designed a format that is based on comparison but that should result in contrast. Hindustānī *rāga*, or melodic, concepts are contrasted with Western concepts by means of a right- and left-hand-page arrangement.[3] Then the melodic concepts of Karnatak music are presented.

[2]In most universities today, music departments that employ an ethnomusicologist call upon him or her to teach a course on "The Musics of the World." Aiming for the most effective research and teaching, the eight to thirty or so other members of the faculty divide Western classical music among themselves. If the department also offers Western folk musics, then that too is most often the purview of the ethnomusicologist. That responsibility, which is far too comprehensive for any one scholar, will be relieved when music departments get in step with other academic departments and realize that the numerous sophisticated systems throughout the world (in this case, musical systems) require the expertise that only additional specially trained staff can give.

[3]The presentation of Western music in this book is geared only to the purpose at hand—the instruction of beginning students. It certainly is not my final approach to the study of Western music theory. Both the Western and the Indian systems are explained in terms that are as simple as possible.

Since musical notation is the primary means of providing examples in this book, notational systems used in the Indian tradition are explained in Chapter Two. Also discussed in that chapter are the melodic drone and the *tāmbūra*, the principal instrument on which the drone is produced in performance.

Chapter Three includes a section on the classification of melody types in the Hindustānī and Karnatak traditions. The chapter ends with a discussion of the origin and classification of rāgas and the naming of rāgas. The latter is especially important in North India, since performances are referred to by the name of the rāga rather than the name of the composition.

To provide a break from the fairly technical information in Chapters Two and Three, I describe in Chapter Four the primary melody-producing instruments used in North and South India: the Hindustānī *sitār*, *sarod*, flute, *shehnai*, and *sāraṅgī*; and the Karnatak *vīṇā*, flute, and violin. I point out the relationships between the construction of the instruments and the melodic systems. Finally, I develop historical perspective by commenting on the preference for different instruments at different times in the history of the music, and by discussing the reasons for those preferences.

In Chapter Five, contrasts are again drawn—this time, between the Hindustānī and Western systems of *tāla*, or rhythm and meter. The discussion of the same elements in the Karnatak tradition follows. The chapter concludes with information on general performance practices, such as the approaches to speed—for instance, levels of speed and acceleration—in the Hindustānī and Karnatak traditions.

Chapter Six, a counterpart to Chapter Four, is devoted to rhythm instruments: the Hindustānī *tablā* and *pakhāvaj*; and the Karnatak *mṛdaṅga*, *ghaṭam*, *kanjīra*, and *tālam*. Several types of compositions for drums are illustrated and explained.

Performance genres of Hindustānī and Karnatak music are the next topics of discussion. Chapters Seven and Eight concern those performance genres that can be heard on readily available recordings. Chapter Seven treats the Hindustānī *ālāp-dhrupad*, *ālāp-joṛ-jhālā-gat*, and *khyāl*, in which rāga is of prime importance, and then the "light classical" forms *ṭhumṛī* and *dhun*. Chapter Eight discusses the Karnatak *varṇam*, *kriti*, and *rāgam-tānam-pallavi*; the difference between *kriti* and *kirtana*; the "light classical" genre *tillānā*; the organizational principle of *rāgamālikā*; and the instrumental form *tānam*.

Chapter Nine combines all of these various elements by commenting on what is required of a musician—that is, what is expected of a good performer and how the listener should judge "good" and "less good." The interrelationships between performers in performance and the interaction of performer with audience are also discussed. Comments by Indian critics and writers about the "superstars" of Indian music conclude the volume.

ONE
THE LISTENER AND INDIAN MUSIC

THE SETTING

India is a land of extremes, where one may see the opulence of mahārājas and the abjectness of untouchables, the beauty of the Tāj Mahāl shimmering in silver moonlight and the hovels of the multitude of poor. Sun-scorched valleys are fed by the eternal Ganges and guarded by the majestic, snow-capped Himālayas. India is a country of diverse geography, peoples, religions, and musics (see Plate 1).

India is a subcontinent in South Asia, bordered by the Arabian Sea on the west and the Bay of Bengal on the east. Her population of more than 600,000,000 is a mixture of many culture groups, the two most populous of which claim origin from either the invader Aryan or indigenous Dravidian peoples. The northern "third" of the country—commonly referred to as Hindustān, after the River Sind—and parts of the central area are in many respects different culturally from the southern reaches of the subcontinent.

Plate 1
Ethnic Variety in India

The North has endured waves of invading forces who stayed to influence and to modify the prevailing culture; the South appears to have been influenced less by foreign currents.[1]

Since 1947, India has appeared to the West as a kaleidoscope of cultural change and continuity. Not much of India's diverse land or countless ethnic and religious groups have been blessed with material riches; these have been the province of the few. Yet today, mahārājas and their heirs have been shorn of their titles, and of their purses and privileges as well. India is now a democracy, with a president, a prime minister, a cabinet, and two houses of

[1] The contemporary subcontinent is known to us by its political divisions of Pakistan (bordered by Iran, Afghanistan, and India), India (bordered by Pakistan, China, Nepal, Bangladesh, Burma, and, to its south, Sri Lanka, formerly Ceylon), and Bangladesh (East Bengal prior to 1947 and East Pakistan prior to 1971; bordered by India and Burma). I use the term "classical 'Indian' music" to refer to the musical system of the political entities of India, Pakistan, Bangladesh, and Sri Lanka, although I shall focus on the modern nation-state of India as exemplary of all four areas. For an excellent, short, and readable introduction to India, see Bernard Cohn, *India: The Social Anthropology of a Civilization* (Englewood Cliffs, N.J.: Prentice-Hall, 1971).

Parliament. The many princely states have melded into federal states, and much of the pomp and circumstance, the rituals of royalty that sparked the imagination of the populace, are gone, preserved only in scattered pockets by supporters of tradition. With the fading of princely privilege has gone royal patronage of the arts. Court centers have become metropolises where wealthy merchants invest for profit rather than in poetry and song.

In recent years, the ethnic and religious strife that once bloodied the country seems to have been quelled. Although basically Hindu in worldview, India proclaims herself a secular state, and her political parties run the gamut of political and religious beliefs, and ethnic identities. India has sought to allay the fears of her Muslim minority by seeing to the election and appointment of Muslims to high public office.

Also in recent years, India has become to the West more than a distant exotic land. We import her textiles and decorate our walls with exquisitely designed and colored cloths. Cashmere shawls from Kashmīr, brass vases, trays, tables, and lamps from Rājasthān are as familiar to us as Chinese lanterns. This is due partly to the philosophical turmoil among America's youth, who in the 1960's turned eastward for inspiration, and to the paths of yoga and transcendental meditation. We see the devout enthusiasm of Hare Krishna groups, who have found in Krishna a believable human transfiguration of God (and whose dress and form of worship seem more outlandish in this country than those of Christian missionaries have seemed in many other lands, because it is Westerners who are so adorned). It is in keeping with India's spiritual heritage that the West has been taking from her not industrial, mass-produced objects but rather the finest treasures of her artisans, her philosophical-religious heritage, and, not least of all, her musical genius.

The West has been fortunate to have had Indian classical music brought to it by a handful of accomplished artists, who have performed before live audiences and explained to them the meaning, the context, and the content of their music. Finally, we have learned that this music must be listened to in terms of itself—not as exotic, meandering sound, but as exquisite, expressive art.

THE RELATIONSHIP BETWEEN LISTENER AND PERFORMER

The important relationship between listener and performer in Indian music is illustrated in the folk ballad recounted below.[2] This ballad, sung

[2]This narrative is taken from the Preface to the ballad "Kenaram, the Robber-Chief" and from the ballad itself, which appear in *Eastern Bengal Ballads: Mymensingh*,

originally by the poetess Chandravati, daughter of Bangshi Das, is set sometime between 1575 and 1590 in the Mymensingh district of Bangladesh. It is a true story, but several of its elements are shared by various types of folklore of the vast Indian subcontinent. When music is mentioned in a narrative, it is an integral part of the tale and not just incidental. Moreover, the performers of the music are integral to the story; the listener is central to the story; and an intense listening situation is important to the outcome.

The mid-sixteenth century was an uneasy time in many villages in Bangladesh (see map). With local leaders busily contesting with one another to increase their territory and with the reigning sovereign preoccupied with fighting off the advancing Mughal armies, the lands and people were at the mercy of marauding bands of thieves. One of the most notorious bands was that of Kenaram, the robber-chief.

Kenaram's early life was unsettled. He was the son and only child of a Brahmin couple who lived in the village of Bakulia, situated at the edge of a wide, wild, jungly stretch—the Jalia hawor. Kenaram had been an eagerly awaited child, for after several years of childless marriage his parents lived in shame, withdrawn from the villagers. Kenaram's birth was attributed to the mercy of the goddess Manasa Devi. His mother was not to enjoy her son for long, however, for she died when Kenaram was seven months old. Overcome with grief, the father set out to visit shrines, never to return, and the child was left with his maternal uncles in the village of Devpur in Mymensingh.

When Kenaram was three years old, the district of Mymensingh was visited by one of the most cruel famines ever recorded in Bengal history. In final desperation, parents sold their children for money or food. Little Kenaram was sold by his uncles for a quantity of rice to a man of the Kaivarta caste.[3] Each of the seven sons of this Kaivarta man was the leader of a gang.

---

ed. and comp. Dinesh Chandra Sen (Calcutta: University of Calcutta, 1923), Vol. I, pp. 165–79.

[3]The term "caste" is an English translation of *casta*, which the Portuguese used to describe the various separate groups with which they came in contact in the sixteenth century. Since that time, Westerners have used the word caste to describe a Hindu social group, although there are similar castes within other religious and ethnic groups in the subcontinent. In the eighteenth and nineteenth centuries, the term came to be applied indiscriminately to the four *varṇa*, which are groupings (akin to classes in the Western sense but which are *not* classes) into which Hindu society became divided. Today, the Western term "class" is loosely applied to varṇa, and the Western term "caste" is loosely equivalent to *jāti*, the thousands of groupings and subgroupings that make up Indic society. As A. L. Basham explains in a defense of the extraordinary flexibility of the Indian system, some jātis die out and new ones appear, but the four great varṇa—the framework of Indian society—remain stable. Previously, varṇa and jāti were thought to have been a discriminatory system introduced into India by the Aryans, but evidence increasingly indicates that a very sophisticated system of ordering society was present in the subcontinent before the arrival of the Aryans. For a most succinct and, to the layman, understandable discussion of Indic civilization, see Cohn's *India*, specifically pp. 111–17 and 124–41.

Their mode of operation was to emerge from the dense jungle of long reeds—the Jalia hawor—to plunder the villages and to strangle any wayfarers they should happen upon. Kenaram grew up among such people and became an expert in robbing and killing. Though a Brahmin by birth, he was never taught to distinguish virtue from vice and he had no idea of the concept of sin. His delight in life was robbing, not for booty to spend on himself but for the sake of burying it under the earth; he killed men for sport. Kenaram became the most dreaded man in the district, and his band the most dreaded in the area.

One day Bangshi Das, the poet and a devotee of Manasa Devi, happened to pass through the dismal Jalia hawor with his band of singers. Their minds were so filled with devotion that they danced as they went. While Bangshi Das sang the praises of the goddess to the music of his one-stringed *ektāra*, the band played on drums and cymbals, oblivious to their surroundings. Just as they reached the outskirts of the Jalia hawor they heard the frightening cry, "Victory to Kali," and before them appeared the dreaded Kenaram with his men. Like the very god of death, Kenaram demanded that Bangshi Das and his followers surrender their lives and their money.

With dignity and aplomb, Bangshi Das replied that Kenaram and his men certainly were welcome to the few possessions that he and his group had—some torn clothing and a few *seers* of rice.[4] Bangshi Das then admonished Kenaram: "It is a sad thing to reflect that you do not care for real treasure, which is devotion to Manasa Devi, but commit heinous crimes for temporal riches, which will not last."

Kenaram assured Bangshi Das that there was no way to dissuade him from what he had done and enjoyed for so many years. Through conversation, the band of singers came to realize that they faced the most feared of all

---

The varṇa are a hierarchy comprising, from top to bottom, *Brāhmaṇs*, the prestigious learned class, not all of whom are priests (the priests are members of the jāti(s) called Brahmin); *Kṣatriyas*, the warrior and governing groups; *Vaisya*, or mercantile elements; and *Śūdras*, all other working groups (primarily peasants). It is suggested that the Āryans did develop another category, known then as *Pañcama* (fifth category), whose function was to keep the indigenous peoples out of the varṇa social order, which the Āryans had subsumed. This fifth group was the untouchable or depressed group, popularized more recently by Mohandas Gandhi as *Harijan* (literally, "children of God"). It is crucial that the Western reader understand these groupings and do so in terms of the Indian "varṇa" and "jāti" rather than the Western "class" and "caste." Probably the best historical discussion of varṇa and jāti is to be found in A. L. Basham, *The Wonder that was India* (New York: Grove Press, Evergreen Books, 1959 pp. 137–55). See also Louis Dumont, *Homo Hierarchicus: The Caste System and its Implications* (London: Weidenfeld & Nicolson, 1970), for probably the best discussion of the religious and philosophical underpinnings of social stratification in Indic cultures. For a fine and succinct analysis by a historian of religions, see Kees W. Bolle, "Views of Class, Caste, and Mankind," *Studia Missionalia*, 19 (1970), pp. 165–75.

[4]A *seer* (or *sīr*) is a measure of grain, equal to about 2 pounds.

dacoits, Kenaram. But Bangshi Das remained calm, facing the robber as if nothing had happened. Kenaram finally asked, "What is your name? I ask this because I see you are a very bold fellow to speak to me in this way."

"I am Bangshi Das."

"Are you that celebrated man whose songs are said to melt even a stone?"

"Yes, they may melt a stone but not the stony heart of a robber."

Indeed, Kenaram was not moved. He instructed his captives to prepare themselves for death. Then Bangshi Das made a request. He wished to sing for the last time those songs about Manasa Devi that throughout his life had given his soul the joys of the other world. Kenaram hesitated for a moment, decided to honor the request, saying, "Listen to me. Here do I sheathe my sword. I give you permission to sing the songs as long as I do not unsheathe it again."

Settling themselves in the green grass, and surrounded by lighted torches, the musicians began. Full of a devotion intensified by the thought of his approaching end, Bangshi Das sang, assisted by his chorus. The story of Behula, the faithful young bride, was the subject of the song.[5] In the bridal chamber, Behula's husband had been bitten by a snake and had died. The maids in attendance called Behula a witch, saying it was not the snake but her evil eye that had killed him. Behula ignored both the abuse and the sympathy that were offered her. When the corpse was about to be taken away for cremation, she stepped forward and said that she would carry it on a raft until she reached the regions of death, in order to restore her husband to life. To the thousands who remonstrated with her from the shore, Behula appeared to be the very angel of love, prepared for all risks and sacrifices, and for martyrdom.

At this point in the story, the fierce Kenaram threw away his sword and began to weep aloud. He entreated the Brahmin to sing again what he had sung, offered him all his wealth, and implored the ascetic to tell him how he might be saved from sin. When Bangshi Das refused the riches, Kenaram was distraught. He thought back on his life. He ordered his men to dig up his riches, which were brought to him in pitchers. These he flung one by one into the river that flowed by. He then threatened to kill himself to atone for his sins. Seeing that the thief was sincerely repentant, Bangshi relented and offered advice.

Eventually, Kenaram became a disciple of the man whose songs had touched him, and he too lived by singing songs about Manasa Devi. Those to whom he had once been a terror approached him with requests to sing, and

[5]This song about Behula is part of a lengthy ballad about Manasa Devi. The ballad is rich in vignettes such as the birth of Manasa Devi and the goddess Durga's quarrel with the god Shiva. See Sen, *Eastern Bengal Ballads*, p. 176, n.1.

they often burst into tears at the feeling he evoked as he sang and danced, lost in reveries. Thus did the music of a saintly man turn a stone into a soft-hearted man.

Centuries ago in India, this receptivity to artistic expression was discussed by *pandits* (learned men or teachers).[6] These individuals were primarily grammarians and poets who were concerned with words, what they can and do express, and how they express what they do. The pandits believed that the words in poetry are logically meant to convey meaning, whether that meaning is obvious or implicit. And, of course, the words are used to express that meaning to someone—to a reader.

Arguments raged as to the meaning poetry conveyed, and how it was conveyed. It became generally agreed upon that "poetry was not the mere clothing of agreeable ideas in agreeable language; emotion (as opposed to mere knowledge) plays an important part in it."[7] There were several schools of thought as to how meaning and emotion were conveyed. One prominent school held that emotion cannot be stated; it can only be suggested. But however it was conveyed, emotion would be effective only if it were aroused in the reader.

Not just any reader can understand. According to theory, it must be someone who has "latent impressions" of feelings that may be aroused, and who also has a particular state of mind in which the "relish of the emotion" is possible. He must have the capacity to transcend ordinary emotion and experience the true enjoyment of poetic sentiment (*rasa*) in a state of bliss, to forsake empirical feeling for pure intuition. Such a person is then a *rasika:* "Those who do not possess this intuition can never relish the spiritual state, and theorists are merciless in their satire on dull grammarians and mere dialecticians, who are incapable of sustaining the aesthetic attitude."[8] As a poem from the so-called medieval period of Indian history puts it:

> A poet's song
>
> Sings in the hearts of poets: the common
> throng
>
> Does not respond.

[6]This discussion appears in various Sanskrit works dating back to at least the sixth century A.D. Among these is Bharata's *Nāṭya Śāstra*, the oldest extant treatise on the fine arts.

[7]S. K. De, *Sanskrit Poetics as a Study of Aesthetics* (Berkeley and Los Angeles: University of California Press, 1963), p. 10.

[8]*Ibid.*, p. 13. Another scholar adds, "An emotion is recognized as Rasa if it is a sufficiently permanent major instinct of man, if it is capable of being delineated and developed to its climax with its attendant and accessory feelings and if there are men of that temperament to feel imaginative emotional sympathy at the presentation of that Rasa." (V. Raghavan, *The Number of Rasa-s* [Madras: Adyar Library and Research Centre, 1967], p. 17).

The ocean's swell

Wakes to the moon: do tides rise
in a well

Or muddy pond?[9]

This appreciation for the experience of aesthetic bliss, first expressed elaborately by poets and grammarians, was taken up in time by musicians. Their art too is an emotive one, and it too elicits an aesthetic response from a listener.

Other ideas in ancient Indian culture put music on a special plane. Music was viewed as a creation of divine agency. It was the finest of the arts, it was the ultimate synthesis of intuition and expression, and it was given the status of *Adhyatma Vidya*, a pathway to self-realization.[10] The following statements from Indian texts reiterate these ideas about music.

> Out of this complex fabric of subtle sound arose the concept of Pranava, Omkara, as the source of all sound. Sound and life being inseparable, the former was identified with god, . . . the latter with life. . . . Herein lay the unity of spirit and matter. As the word of God, the Vedas and the Upaveda, music, were part of Him. They were derived from Pranava. . . . [Lord Shiva] taught the science of Music to his consort, Parvati. She passed it on to other celestial beings like Tumburu, Narada, Nandikeshwara and Saraswati.[11]

> Oh mind! Attain the bliss of Brahman [magical force or potency, especially of words] by losing yourself in Nāda, with all its Rāgas composed of the seven notes. . . .

> Is there any bliss greater than this—to deem it sufficient to dance, to sing divine music, to pray for His presence and to be in communion with him in mind. . . .[12]

Thus, in the ballad we have recounted, the making of music is an act of devotion and the path to self-realization for the wandering ascetic Bangshi Das and his band. And for Kenaram, a murderer and a thief who turns into a *rasika*, the expression of devotion through song is so effective that he too chooses that path to God: "He sang and danced, lost in reveries."

[9]This poem appears in *Poems from the Sanskrit*, edited and translated by John Brough (Penguin Classics 1968), p. 74. Copyright © John Brough, 1968. Reprinted by permission of Penguin Books Ltd.

[10]R. Rangaramanuja Ayyangar, *History of South Indian (Carnatic) Music From Vedic Times to the Present* (Madras: R. Rangaramanuja Ayyangar, 1972), p. 11.

[11]*Ibid.*, pp. 10–11.

[12]Cited in C. Ramanujachari and V. Raghavan, *The Spiritual Heritage of Tyāgarāja*, 2nd ed. (Madras: Sri Ramakrishna Math, 1966), pp. 511 and 508, respectively. These two song texts are excerpts from kriti by Tyāgarāja entitled "Nada Loludai" and "Intakanna Yanandameni."

DIVERSITY: A CHARACTERISTIC OF INDIAN CULTURES

It might seem an unrealistic jump from the rarefied theoretical writings of learned pandits to the oral recounting of historical vignettes of folk life in ballad. But in India, the two are somehow not so unrelated as they might seem. The *Mahābhārata* and the *Rāmāyana*, the two great Indic epics composed in the earliest centuries of Aryan India, were oral lore, and they remain so for the bulk of the population, retold in myriad forms of drama, dance, and song. Many cultural ideas, heroic ideals, and patterns of daily life are reinforced through these epics. This is due, in part, to the close relationship that seems to have existed, at least in earlier times, between the learned and the unlettered. The courts, the centers of education, and the residences of the pandits have always been close to the villages, the cities, and the towns. Pandits and populace together revere and share a respect for "the tradition." In this way, as in others, the "classical" is the "folk" and the "folk" is the "classical."

The thousands of years between the ancient and modern periods might seem to imply an impossibility of continuity, especially if measured in the Western concepts of time and space. But again, in Indian terms the gap is not impossible; there is continuity. Even in the twentieth century, scarcely a book on Indian music does not reiterate the divine origins of music and the details of melodic theory given in Bharata's *Nāṭya Śāstra*, written sometime between the second century B.C. and the sixth century A.D.[13] (To Indians, whose civilization encompasses millenia, a few centuries are but a flick of time.) Even though the theoretical details of such ancient treatises cannot be precisely related to melodic practice today, the effort is made continually to find evidence of continuity of these treatises throughout Indian musical history, and when we read so frequently about those long-ago times, they begin to seem like yesterday.

Not that things remain unchanged. Since the second millenium B.C., when a group of related tribes known as the *Āryas* began to settle among the original Dravidian peoples and other indigenous tribes on the then sparsely settled land, the subcontinent has been populated by Aryan and Dravidian ethnic offshoots. These agricultural and pastoral groups moved constantly, searching for land, security, and riches. As the various groups settled down, India began to resemble a giant ethnic patchwork quilt, for it housed an incredible variety of local and regional cultures. The Aryan influence gradually became the dominant one; even the Dravidian peoples, who were pushed south by the more aggressive Aryans, adopted elements of the Indo-European

[13]Ayyangar describes this work as "a survey of the ancient Indian music up to 500 B.C. Part of it is legend." (*History of South Indian Music*, p. 22)

culture and language (more so than we tend to realize). Almost the entire subcontinent became Sanskritized, which provided a homogeneous environment for the effective dissemination of philosophy and custom.

Music played a sacred role in Aryan India (1500–500 B.C.), for sacrificial rites were recited and sung. It appears that women were among the singers in the earliest of these times: "Formerly wives of Sāma-vedic priests were entrusted with the sweet singing of difficult Sāma-chants; afterwards this task was transferred to the male priests or Udgātṛs."[14] Women continued as dancers and singers in the religious sphere, however, for in the so-called medieval period and especially around the ninth century A.D., when temples became cultural centers, special groups of women were trained to dance and sing as part of their service to God.

The performing arts were fostered also in homes and courts. In the dramas of Kālidāsa of about 400 A.D., members of the elite (particularly women) are depicted as students of music:

> KING (*smiling*): Well, let us sit down. (They seat themselves and the retinue arranges itself. A lute is heard behind the scenes.)
>
> CLOWN (*listening*): My friend, listen to what is going on in the music-room. Someone is playing a lute, and keeping good time. I suppose Lady Hansavati is practising.
>
> KING: Be quiet. I wish to listen.[15]

In Kālidāsa's plays *Mālavikā and Agnimitra* and *The Dynasty of Raghu*, we read of a music school in which teachers of the highest order imparted training in the arts of music and dancing, acting, and painting to pupils of the royal household and to others.[16]

Three hundred years later, in the eighth century A.D., one of India's most famous writers, Daṇḍin, spoke of urban and elite life in Ujjain, the old capital of Malwa (see map).[17] Sophistication, luxury, and gaiety pervaded this culture, which, of course, included substantial patronage of the arts:

> The salubrious means of entertainment popular with the urban people in general and the nobility in particular were the various *goṣṭhīs* or clubs which

[14]Quoted from the *Śatapatha Brahmaṇa* 14-3-1-35, in Jogiraj Basu, *India of the Age of the Brāhmaṇas* (Calcutta: Sanskrit Prstak Bhandar, 1969), pp. 40, 51–52.

[15]Kālidāsa, *Shakuntalā and Other Writings*, trans. Arthur W. Ryder (New York: Dutton, 1959), p. 52. Kālidāsa, considered India's greatest poet and dramatist, probably flourished during the reigns of the Buddhist Gupta emperors Chandra Gupta II and Kumarā Gupta I (A.D. 375–455), when ancient Indian courtly culture was at its zenith (Basham, *Wonder that was India*, p. 418). He was probably patronized by King Vikramaditya in the city of Ujjain in western central India (Kālidāsa, *Shakuntalā*, p. ix).

[16]Bhagwat Saran Upadhya, "Some of the Fine Arts Depicted by Kālidāsa," *Indian Historical Quarterly*, XIV (1939), pp. 376–77.

[17]Scholars disagree about Daṇḍin's dates. De (in his "Tentative Chronology," *Sanskrit Poetics*, p. 117) places him in the first half of the eighth century. Basham (*Wonder that was India*, p. 442) places him in the Gupta Period, late sixth and early seventh centuries.

> were largely connected with scholastic and artistic accomplishment. . . . These were periodically convened in a public hall or at the residence of one of the *nāgarakas* [artists] or even at the house of a courtesan, and were attended by the members of the same age, wealth, learning and temperament. . . . The *saṁgītagoṣṭhī*, one of the most popular amongst such cultural gatherings, was convened by the kings and the nobles in recurring periodicity, wherein were presented performances, either group or individual, of *saṁgīta*, the triple symphony of song, instrumental music, and dancing.[18]

The kings and nobles also organized dance performances, which attracted much popular attention. The accomplished courtesans and the dancing girls of the palace performed at these events.

So close were the two arts of music and dance that both were included in the Sanskrit word *saṅgīta*—the arts of singing, playing musical instruments, and dancing. For each of the three aspects of saṅgīta there is a specific word—*gīta* for singing, *vādya* for playing instruments, *nāṭya* for dancing—but the concept of saṅgīta combines them all into one thought. This conception of the performing arts continued through the centuries and is maintained today. The National Academy of the Performing Arts, for instance, is called by two descriptive words only—*Saṅgīt Nāṭak* Akademi (*nāṭak* referring to drama).

In the twelfth and thirteenth centuries, life on the subcontinent again underwent change as a result of external influences. Through the Himalayan passes of the Northwest, historically India's Achilles' heel, poured wave after wave of Afghan, Turki, Persian, and central Asian followers of Islam, some coming to proselytize, many others to plunder. Mainly, they were seeking new lands from which to wield sovereignty over the extensive Asian trade routes and political peripheries.

But this was only the second of three Islamic intrusions into the subcontinent. The first had occurred in the early eighth century, immediately on the heels of the outward expansion of Mohammed's faith. The Arabs, who arrived on the subcontinent in A.D. 712, moved mainly in Pakistan's coastal areas of Sind, and pockets in the South, and stayed only for a short while. Three centuries later, from A.D. 1001 on, warlike tribes from Afghanistan began systematic raids into the subcontinent. In the thirteenth century, these incursions culminated in the establishment of a sultanate at Delhi (A.D. 1206). This made permanent the presence of Islam in the subcontinent. For three centuries, Muslim Afghans, Turki, and Indian sultans extended a rather lavish, if phlegmatic, control over their subjects, mainly in the northern areas of the subcontinent. Then, grown flabby and dissolute, they fell prey in 1526 to the aggressive Muslim Mongol leader Babar, who came from the stark plains of central Asia. The Mughals, as the Muslim Mongols came to be

[18]Dharmendra Kumar Gupta, *Society and Culture in the Time of Dandin* (Delhi: Mekarchand Lachhmandas, 1972), pp. 275–77.

known from that time on, were the final wave of Muslims to enter the subcontinent. They unified almost all of northern India and much of the Deccan (central India), building an empire the likes of which had not been seen since the Guptas, more than a millenium earlier.[19]

Islam was a new experience for the subcontinent, and it marked the first real and enduring threat to Hinduism since Buddhism challenged Brahmanism (560 B.C.–c. 300 A.D.). Although the subcontinent was politically and ethnically diverse, for thousands of years it had been united by a shared religious culture, the basis of Hinduism. The presence of Islam and its status as the belief system of the subcontinent's new rulers made it an attractive alternative to the Indian masses, for social and economic as well as political reasons.

The Mughals were unable to stretch their hegemony across the entire subcontinent, however. South of the Deccan, several Hindu states and the last of the great Hindu empires, the Vijayanagara (A.D. 1335–1565), continued to flourish. Extending south from the Krishna River to the tip of the peninsula (see map), the Vijayanagara Empire rivaled the sultanates at Delhi and remained a formidable imperial challenge for the early Mughal emperors.

We have descriptions from numerous foreign travelers of life in the villages, towns, and courts of North and South India. Many Europeans provided such accounts—particularly of Vijayanagara—especially after the arrival of the Portuguese on the western coast of India. One of the earliest accounts is that of the Italian Nicolo di Conti, who visited the southern empire in the early fifteenth century. The splendor of the court and the wealth of the capital that impressed di Conti were still there a century later to intrigue the Portuguese visitors Paes and Nuñiz.

Music seemed constant at court. Paes reported women playing "trumpets and drums and pipes (but not like ours) and viols, and many other kinds of music."[20] Nuñiz reported that among the more than 4,000 women who lived within the gates of the King's palace were dancing girls and also "women . . . who play instruments and sing." Most important, Nuñiz remarked, "Even the wives of the King are well versed in music."[21]

A major musical event that occurred in the court of Raghunatha Nāyaka in the southern region of Tanjore (see map) was recounted by Rāmabhadrāmba, a female writer in the Vijayanagara court. Raghunatha

[19]The Vindhya Mountains (see map) have tended to form a natural barrier between the North, formerly called Hindustān, which is part of the land mass of Asia, and the peninsula, often called the Deccan, which simply means "south." Nowadays, the term Deccan is used sometimes for the whole peninsula, but more often for its northern and central portions. The southeastern part of the peninsula forms a large plain, the land of the Tamils.

[20]Quoted in Robert Sewell, *A Forgotten Empire* (*Vijayanagar*) (London: Swan Sonnenschein, 1900), pp. 273–74.

[21]Quoted in Sewell, *A Forgotten Empire*, pp. 382–83.

convened an assembly of learned persons, who were to examine the accomplishments of the ladies at his court. The women were found to be able to compose metric poetry in eight languages, to sing very sweetly, and to play the vīṇā, the rāvanahasta, and other musical instruments. Some of the rāgas that were sung were designed by Raghunatha Nāyaka himself, who was a master of the art of music.[22] Apparently, it was commonplace for reigning monarchs to be proficient musicians.

The temple also remained a center for the arts in this Hindu Kingdom. Paes confirmed that during festivals, dancing girls "remained dancing in front of the temple and idol for a long time."[23] That these women were held in high regard according to old Hindu tradition and were rewarded for their talents is suggested by a stone inscription dated A.D. 1356: "Among the dancing-girls of the temple (at Tēkkaḷ), Malaiyāttai Śrīraṅga Nāyakiyār Māṇikkam, daughter of Śeṇḍikkā-dēvī, was granted the first turn in the temple of Aruḷāla-nādan, and certain lands (specified), and her sister Varadi, the first turn in the temple of the consort of the above god and certain land."[24] The Vijayanagara kings also continued the tradition of providing for vocal and instrumental music in the temples by giving grants or providing players. Thus, Hindu ideas and customs regarding music were maintained in the great kingdom until 1565, when its ruler was defeated by a coalition of Muslim sultans from the northern Deccan and the empire came to an end.

In Islamic monotheistic thought, music is not believed to be of divine origin; nor do a host of gods and goddesses entertain themselves or desire to be entertained with song and dance. No mosque is a center for the arts; even chanting in the services is not considered music. Even secular music is frowned upon by some groups of orthodox Muslims. Nonetheless, conflict between Muslim rulers and their orthodox religious advisers was usually decided in favor of the ruler, and almost invariably, Muslim rulers in India were lavish patrons of the arts in their courts. For religious reasons, however, music was regarded not as a path to self-realization for anyone who might pursue it (as in Hindu belief), but as entertainment. In court sessions (*darbārs*) and in private living quarters, troupes of dancers and musicians were retained for the enjoyment of the royal households. We read less frequently that the Muslim sovereigns themselves learned to play an instrument or sing, or even that their wives and daughters did so. More and more, the performing was left to certain families and to any others whom such families might agree to teach.[25]

[22]B. A. Saletore, *Social and Political Life in the Vijayanagar Empire, 1346–646* (Madras: B. G. Paul, 1934), Vol. II, p. 164.

[23]Quoted in Sewell, *A Forgotten Empire*, p. 267, and n. 1.

[24]Quoted in Saletore, *Vijayanagar Empire*, Vol. II, p. 226.

[25]The attitude of the musicians themselves, many of whom were high-caste Hindus who had converted to Islam, is difficult to ascertain. Today, the Hindu reverence for music and music making seems to be shared by many Muslim musicians.

Whichever role the patron took (listener and/or performer), and for whatever reasons, one belief seems to have been shared by Hindu and Muslim alike: listeners were expected to know a great deal about what they were hearing and to respond to the performer accordingly. This capacity was not the intuitive receptivity to emotion suggested by the music that is involved in rasa; it was the empirical "I know what you are doing every moment that you are doing it, and why." It was an expectation that kept performers on their toes and made the listener-performer relationship an intensely personal one. The result was an elitist ideal of a musical sort. And, indeed, Indian classical music has been mainly for the elite.

During the eighteenth century, with the British presence first in economic and then in political affairs, the patronage of music waned in the disintegrating Mughal Empire. The last of the Delhi sultans to make lavish outlays of funds for the arts was Muhammad Shah, who ascended the Delhi throne in 1719. Musicians clustered at the courts that could afford to support them, including the still splendid courts of Hindu rājas in Gwalior, Baroda, Rampur, Indore, Udaipur, and Jaipur. Other local sovereigns assumed British customs and spent their monies on British leisure pursuits.

In the South however, music flourished in the eighteenth and nineteenth centuries, particularly at the courts of Tanjore, in southeastern India, and Travancore, a small state in the southwestern corner of India (see map). The South Indian writer Ayyangar considers the eighteenth century "the crimson dawn" and the nineteenth century "the golden age." The nineteenth century was vibrant with the music of many composers, among them three masters: Muttuswāmi Dīkshitar (1775–1835), Syāma Śastri (1763–1827), and Tyāgarāja (1767–1817), the last of whom is revered as a saint.

By the twentieth century, patronage had almost become a thing of the past in many northern and southern courts. Musicians turned to urban centers and a wider public in order to support themselves. However, the growing sense of nationalism in the late nineteenth and early twentieth centuries was accompanied by a renaissance of cultural spirit among performing artists and teachers throughout India. Since Independence (1948), in particular, there has been an increased interest in the traditional arts. Throughout the country, more people are learning music and more public concerts are being held. The musical sphere is being revitalized.

But there are significant differences between today's musical milieus and those of the past, as we know them. Contemporary audiences are not always well tutored in the music they are hearing. Consequently, the performer-audience give-and-take falls short of the ideal and is often different from the practice of the past. In addition, the Indian audience today is frequently much larger than the audience in the days of select court patronage. Large numbers of people at weekend-long festivals hear types of performances that formerly were meant for the ears of relatively few persons.

Public-address systems rob the occasion of intimacy and deprive the performance of many subtleties.

For better or worse (depending on whose opinion you hear) artists respond to their audiences by tailoring their music to them. Indian musicians now produce phonograph records and perform in the radio studios, frequently to an imaginary audience. Indian universities are establishing departments of music; private schools of music are opening everywhere, making musical training available to many. This in turn is bound to create further change.

If we consider the number of years, decades, even centuries that have passed since Indian history and thought were first recorded, giving us proof that music flourished in the subcontinent, the continuity of Indian music over time is truly remarkable. But also given that time span, and the cultural variety and geographical diversity of India, it is not surprising that regional differences have developed even within the sphere of classical music. At some undocumented time between the twelfth and the sixteenth centuries, differences developed to the extent that two traditions of classical music could be distinguished: the Hindustānī and the Karnatak, each a variation of the ancient system. The details of melodic theory (rāga) differ, as do those of meter (tāla). The instruments used also differ, as do the genres performed. Understanding each of these two traditions, distinguishing between them, but also perceiving what they share, should be the aim of the reader of this book.

TWO

THE SHARED TRADITION: ENSEMBLE, PITCH, NOTATION, AND DRONE

INTRODUCTION

On a public stage, or in a deeply carpeted (and probably slightly raised) space in private quarters, a concert of Indian classical music is about to begin. The artists number at least two, and probably three or more. Applause or expectant rustling greets them as they come to the fore. Lifting hands folded together in the traditional motion, each artist nods to return the greeting. The musicians then sit in their proper places and begin checking their instruments for proper tuning.

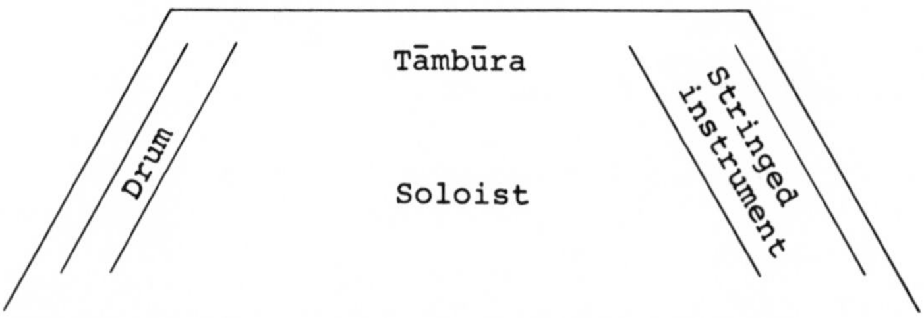

The ensemble will vary from performance to performance, depending on the type of music to be made, and the seating arrangement will vary accordingly. In Plate 2, a vocal performance in North India, the ensemble consists of, from left to right, tablā, tāmbūra, vocalist, tāmbūra and sāraṅgī (a stringed instrument). In Plate 3, a *nagasvaram* performance in South India, the ensemble consists of mṛdañga on the left, nagasvaram soloist in the center, tāmbūra behind, and violin to the right. Plate 4 shows an ensemble for a vocal performance in South India. The vocalist is in the center, behind him to the left and right are ghaṭam and tāmbūra, in foreground left, mṛdañga, and right, violin.

Plate 2
A Vocal Performance in North India

Plate 3
A Nagasvaram Performance in South India

Plate 4
A Vocal Ensemble in South India

The basic team in any performance of classical music anywhere in India consists of a melody-producing instrumentalist, a percussionist, and the keeper of the drone. The melody-producing artist is the soloist, except in a percussion concert—for instance, a North Indian tablā concert—where he fulfills an accompanying role. The drone is usually played on a stringed instrument called the tāmbūra.

It is clear from the seating arrangement of the performers and from the sequence of events that the soloist is "in command." He rechecks the fine tuning necessary for the tāmbūra, then hands the instrument back to the player. If further tuning of the drum is needed, it is done by the drummer, often with the approval of the soloist. If an accompanying stringed instrument is present, it too is tuned for the ensemble. When all is well, the soloist signals the tāmbūra player to begin, and then he himself begins.

When artists in any culture perform, they bring to their performance a wealth of musical knowledge and skill. This knowledge may include traditional concepts and details, which the artist pulls together in ever fresh ways (as in improvisation). Or it may include compositions in which those concepts and details have already been captured. An artist of Indian classical music must be comfortable with both these possibilities for performance, since much of the music he makes, whether it is Hindustānī or Karnatak, is improvised. An improvisatory performance is a musical "moment" that has never existed before and will never exist again in the same form. The shaping of a performance lies largely with the soloist; his is an enormous responsibility.

What does his knowledge consist of? The two basic elements in Indian music are melody and rhythm. Harmony, as it developed in the West, with chords of three or more simultaneous pitches progressing in a logical succession, has never appealed to the Indian ear. For the Indian musician, chords create too much sound at once, and one cannot concentrate on what is most important: the melody line and the rhythm.

In Indian classical music, melody takes priority. And only one melody is developed at a time. Because Indian music makers have never tied melody and rhythm to the restrictive base that harmony is (in many respects), and because they have avoided multiple simultaneous melodies (as in Western polyphony), they have been free to concentrate on subtleties of melody and intricacies of rhythm that can boggle the Western musical imagination.

The melodic conceptual system as a whole is called rāga (in the South it is called *rāgam* and in the North *rāg*, due to language differences). Rāga is a Sanskrit word derived from the verb *rānj*—"to color, to tinge with emotion." (To be consistent, I shall use the Sanskrit term rāga throughout the discussion of both Hindustānī and Karnatak music.) The rāga system is ancient, and many authors have elucidated its development across the millenia. I shall discuss rāga primarily as it exists today. Before beginning this discussion, however, I must describe the manner in which materials are presented in the chapters to come, and I must introduce the basic vocabulary with which to talk about rāga.

HINDUSTĀNĪ NOTATION

Throughout this book, Western notation is used as a medium for demonstrating musical points. Admittedly, this is a method alien to the subject matter, not only because it is Western notation rather than Indian, but also because notation does not play a meaningful part in Indian music. A miniscule number of pieces of Indian music have been notated, and most of these are traditional songs.

Consider for a moment why notational systems develop, and for what purposes they are used. In the West, one reason notation proliferated was that it was needed to show the coordination among the parts in multi-part music. In India, that necessity has never arisen, since one melody at a time is preferred. Notation is also a means of transmitting musical materials. But in

India, written transmission has been seen as unnecessarily restrictive: since improvisation is the heart of the tradition, classical music (as well as folk music) has always been transmitted orally.

Another facet of written transmission is the number of people with whom one wishes to share the material, for that number is potentially increased when music is notated, not to mention published. In North India, many artists have taken pains to be certain that their knowledge is transmitted to only a few, if any, successors. They are extremely possessive of their traditions, which include not only specific songs but also individualistic ways of rendering a rāga. Tales are even told of artists purposely singing a rāga incorrectly in order to hide its true nature from all but their own disciples. The musicologist who gathered the largest collection of notated songs in North India, Pandit Vishnu Narayan Bhaṭkhande of Bombay, complained that many artists refused to sing their songs for him and allow him to notate them. Furthermore, he was refused permission to publish already notated music held in private collections. A recent example of the same sentiment, expressed about the South Indian tradition and in regard to dance, may be noted in Jon Higgins's study of the music of Bhārata Nāṭyam. Higgins explains why he did not include full choreography with the musical examples: "The *aḍavus* learned by a dancer constitute an intimate and somewhat closely guarded aspect of her art. Thus, Balasaraswati has stipulated that the *nṛtta* compositions of her teacher Kandappa Pillai not be represented in this study."[1]

More music has been notated in the Karnatak tradition than in the Hindustānī tradition. One reason for this is perhaps that music education has been more systematic and more widespread for a longer time in the South. The systematic approach to learning music apparently originated in one man, Purandara Dasa (1484–1564), who was accordingly dubbed the "father of Karnatak music." Purandara Dasa devised graded exercises (*alankāra*) for practicing rāga and tāla, and he composed many songs specifically for learning purposes. Such a long-standing tradition of systematizing musical training may have contributed to the South Indian receptivity to notation for educational purposes, if for no other purpose. In addition, a repertoire of songs such as *varṇam* (see Chapter Eight) has provided a body of music that is relatively notatable.

Notation is also a means of preservation, and the use of notation would presumably imply a desire for preservation. In the South, the desire is strong to know who composed what, and composers themselves publish their compositions in notated form. The "composer," as distinguished from the

[1] Jon Higgins, *The Music of Bharata Naṭyam* (Ann Arbor, Mich.: University Microfilms, 1973), p. 52, n.1. *Aḍavu* is the coordination of hands, torso, and feet, and is represented in notation by one or more dance syllables; *nṛtta* is "pure dance," in which the interpretive element is entirely absent (*Ibid.*, pp. 339, 342).

"performer" (though they may be the same person during that individual's lifetime), is on the whole more significant in the Karnatak tradition than in the Hindustānī. In the North, there does not seem to be this desire to remember who composed songs. The sense of ownership of drum compositions seems to be stronger there than that of songs, and memory rather than notation is counted on as a means of preserving the compositions. This is probably another reason why far less music is notated in North than in South Indian classical music.

By "notated," a far different degree of exactness is implied for Indian classical music than for its Western counterpart. One may find a melody notated and published in a collection in North India, but the notated form is unlikely to be the source from which a performer learned the melody. And even if he had learned it from that notation, his performance would most likely deviate drastically from the notated version. There does not seem to be a desire to render songs as they were originally composed or learned. Karnatak notations of *kriti* (see Chapter Eight) are rather like Western folk-song variants: performers publish their own variant of a song, and although two variants might be quite different, they are regarded as the same song. Notations of Karnatak *varṇa* are more standardized, but even with varṇa the profuse ornamentation in performance style is an element supplied by the performer from his own knowledge rather than implied or written out in the notation. For these and other reasons, melodies in notated form bear little resemblance to their realization in performance. The notation gives only a skeletal outline, paring the music to its melodic and rhythmic essentials.

A close parallel in Western music is popular song. A popular song is likely to be rendered very differently when performed by two different singers. The tempo may be changed, notes added or omitted, the rhythm almost totally altered. Yet both singers start with basically the same melody. That melody has been notated and copyrighted, and the copyrighted form is the only form in which we ordinarily find the melody notated.

Using Western notation for Indian music necessitates a clear drawing of contrasts and the introduction of some terminology. To counter the seemingly inevitable attempts to find similarity between the Indian and Western musical systems, I have divided the following material geographically in such a way as to stress their differences. However, I should emphasize that readers who *do not* wish to use this material contrastively can simply ignore the pages of Western material; those who *do* wish to see contrasts will have the material in front of them with which to do so. This device can also be useful for Indian teachers of music. Three points should be clearly understood here. One is that the materials on each musical system, Western and Hindustānī, are presented in an extremely basic way, so as to assure that the elementary principles of both systems are understood. Second, both systems are given in order to provide points of reference, should they be desired by the reader. Finally, if comparisons are to be made between systems, it is the author's intent that Western music be compared with Hindustānī, not vice versa. That is, the Western system should be perceived as if the reader had learned the Hindustānī system first.

The following two right-hand pages are for those readers who know nothing of Western music and who wish to read solely for Indian concepts. The following two left-hand pages are on Western concepts and are coordinated with the Hindustānī material. To understand the differences between the two musical systems, compare the Western material with its counterpart in the Indian material. Differences between Karnatak and Hindustānī music are discussed in the next section.

Western

In Western music, a pitch may be referred to either by a specific name (a, b, c, d, e, f, g), or in relative terms by a *solfège* syllable (do, re, mi, fa, sol, la, ti). (Solfège is the use of syllables for pitch names.)

A specific pitch name refers to a standardized pitch measurement based on "concert pitch," which is typically set at 440 cps (cycles per second) for pitch *a*. This principle applies whether a pitch is referred to orally or is written in notation.

In the West, the means of naming pitch registers is traditionally by groups of eight (*octaves*). Within an octave there are seven basic pitches (as given above). The eighth begins the cycle again. Some attempts have been made to achieve uniformity in the naming of pitch registers. Nevertheless, although there is consensus about the pitch "middle C" on the piano being taken as a specific point of reference, there is no uniformity in Western music in references to pitch registers.

EXAMPLE 2-1 Pitch Registers in Western Music

The different levels of pitch in Western music are not named uniformly. There is consensus about the absolute pitch referred to as "middle C," but otherwise there is no uniformity in Western music in references to absolute pitches. ("Middle B" means nothing, for example.) Some attempts have been made to achieve uniformity of pitch nomenclature, however. Three different systems (and there are others) are shown below.

EXAMPLE 2-2 Western Nomenclature of Pitch Registers

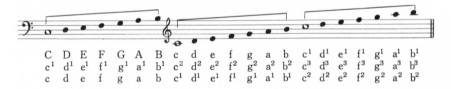

C	D	E	F	G	A	B	c	d	e	f	g	a	b	c^1	d^1	e^1	f^1	g^1	a^1	b^1
c^1	d^1	e^1	f^1	g^1	a^1	b^1	c^2	d^2	e^2	f^2	g^2	a^2	b^2	c^3	d^3	e^3	f^3	g^3	a^3	b^3
c	d	e	f	g	a	b	c^1	d^1	e^1	f^1	g^1	a^1	b^1	c^2	d^2	e^2	f^2	g^2	a^2	b^2

Hindustānī

In North Indian music a pitch (*svara*) is referred to in relative terms by the solfège syllables Sa, Re, Ga, Ma, Pa, Dha, Ni. (Some Hindustānī musicians use Ri instead of Re.)

There is no standardized "concert pitch" in Hindustānī melodic practice. The pitch Sa is relative: it varies with the natural range of a singer's voice, or with the dimensions of a particular musical instrument. Whether referred to orally or in notation, therefore, a pitch syllable indicates no precise pitch.

In India, the means of naming pitch registers is traditionally by groups of seven (*saptak*). The saptak includes seven basic pitches (as given above). Relative levels are used for referring to pitch registers—low, middle, and high (plus very low and very high). Low register is called *maṅdra saptak*; middle register is *madhya saptak*; high register is *tār saptak*.

EXAMPLE 2-3 Pitch Registers in Hindustānī Music

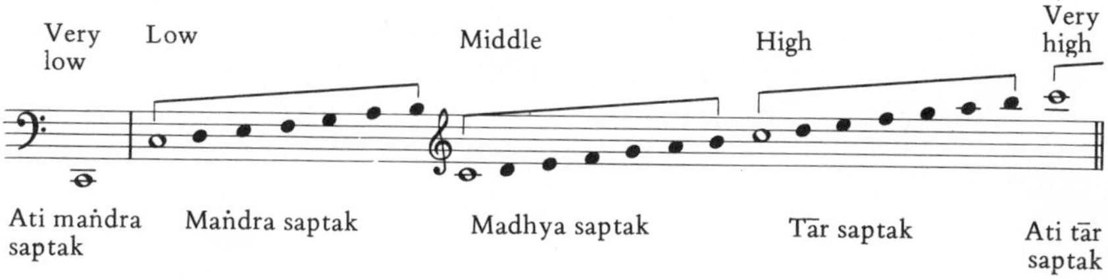

The different levels of pitch in Indian music are named uniformly: middle Pa is always referred to as madhya Pa, low Pa is referred to as maṅdra Pa, and high Pa as tār Pa. In notation, a dot above the syllable Sa (Sȧ) indicates high Sa (or tār Sa), a dot below the syllable (Sạ) means low Sa (or maṅdra Sa), and two dots below means very low Sa or ati maṅdra Sa (Sa̤). No dot indicates middle Sa (or madhya Sa).

EXAMPLE 2-4 Hindustānī Nomenclature of Pitch Registers

The pitches Sạ, Sa, and Sȧ are relative, of course. One could transcribe the phrase Sȧ Re Nị Sa as

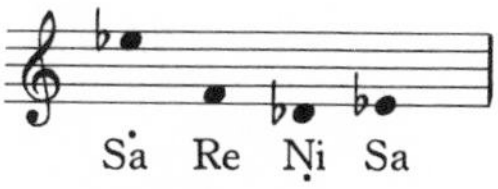

or as

since the absolute pitches depend on the individual instrument or singer.

Western

A person familiar with Western music theory knows that pitches other than the basic seven can be used—the five additional pitches of a chromatic scale. To the basic pitch names can be added signs that indicate a pitch a half step lower (♭—flat) or a half step higher (♯—sharp); either of these may be canceled with a natural sign (♮). Each of the five additional pitches can be notated as either sharp or flat: C♯ and D♭ are the same pitch in the tempered tuning system, D♯ and E♭ are the same pitch, and so forth.

EXAMPLE 2-5 Western Chromatic Pitches

Sizes of intervals between pitches are standardized in the tempered tuning system. This permits ensembles of instruments to play together without tuning problems.

Hindustānī

A person familiar with Hindustānī musical theory knows that pitches other than the basic seven can be used. Five additional pitches—a second Re, Ga, Ma, Dha, and Ni (Sa and Pa are invariable)—can be used. These five pitches and the seven original ones can be written as follows: Sa Re Re Ga Ga Ma Ma̍ Pa Dha Dha Ni Ni. The line underneath the syllables Re, Ga, Dha, and Ni indicates a pitch approximately a half step lower (*komal*); the small vertical line above Ma indicates a pitch approximately a half step higher (*tivra*). The twelve pitches notated above are then called Sa, komal Re, Re, komal Ga, Ga, Ma, tivra Ma, Pa, komal Dha, Dha, komal Ni, and Ni. The unaltered basic pitches are called *shuddh* ("natural"), as in Re shuddh.

Sizes of intervals (*śruti*) between pitches are not standardized. The interval from Sa to Re (komal Re) may equal a half step in Western music, or it may be smaller than that. Traditional musicians consider flexibility of intonation one of the most precious of Hindustānī musical practices. This flexibility causes no problem in ensemble performance, because the soloist on a melodic instrument sets the intonation, and any other melodic instrument accompanying him must match that intonation.

Many articles and books on Indian music state that an octave is divided into twenty-two intervals, or *śrutis*. This conclusion derives from early music-theory treatises that spoke of two parent scales, Sa *grama* and Ma *grama*, distinguished from each other by interval sizes measured in śrutis. According to these treatises, there were three sizes of intervals between pitches: two śrutis, three śrutis, and four śrutis. The interval arrangement in the Sa grama scale was as follows: Sa_3 Ri_2 Ga_4 Ma_4 Pa_3 Dha_2 Ni_4 (Sa); the interval arrangement of the Ma grama scale was this: Sa_3 Ri_2 Ga_4 Ma_3 Pa_4 Dha_2 Ni_4 (Sa). The total number of śrutis in each scale was twenty-two. From this it was apparently concluded that in modern practice there are twenty-two pitches within each octave—an assertion that is probably seen as a partial explanation for microtonal variations in pitch intonation. But it seems certain that ancient theory treated a single śruti as the basic unit of existing intervals and not as a musical tone in its own right.[2]

In an article on intonation in present-day North Indian classical music, Nazir Jairazbhoy and A. W. Stone report having measured the intonation of the intervals in performances of the same rāga by several different musicians. They found that the rāga varied considerably in intonation from one performance to another, at least as far as sizes of "seconds" and "thirds" were concerned. Furthermore, they found that intonation varied even *within* a performance. The authors concluded:

> With this divergence between musicians, it would appear that intonation is a matter of personal choice, perhaps influenced by the teacher's intonation but not bound to it. . . . Under these circumstances it would seem pointless [at this point] to consider applying the ancient 22 śruti system, or for that matter, any system of exact intonation, to North Indian classical music.[3]

In an article published in 1975 (see note 2), Jairazbhoy again tackled the subject of śruti theory. This is a topic in Indian music theory that will be addressed from time to time by various scholars. It will probably never be laid to rest, because of the difficulties of understanding ancient theory in terms of present-day performance practice.

The information on melody given in the previous pages forms the basis of the notation system most widely used in North India.[4] It was advocated at the end of the nineteenth century and early in the twentieth century by the Indian musicologist V. N Bhaṭkhande, a scholar whose influence was enormous. Examples 2-6, 2-7, and 2-8 are the notation, transliteration, and

[2]Nazir Jairazbhoy, "An Interpretation of 22 Śrutis," *Asian Music*, 6, nos. 1 and 2 (1975), p. 54.

[3]Nazir Jairazbhoy and A. W. Stone, "Intonation in Present-Day North Indian Classical Music," *Bulletin, School of Oriental and African Studies*, 26 (1963), pp. 130–31.

[4]This system is explained in greater detail in Walter Kaufmann, *Musical Notations of the Orient* (Bloomington, Ind.: Indiana University Press, 1967), pp. 185–200.

transnotation of a song according to Bhatkhande's method. Examples 2-7 and 2-8 have been left incomplete so that the reader can continue them if desired. This particular melody ("Phula van kī geṅda") was chosen because it has been recorded by one of the great artists in Hindustānī vocal music, Ustād Faiyaz Khan, and, thus, the notated version can be compared with the sung version.[5] The lack of similarity between the two is eloquent and demonstrates why notation means so little to Hindustānī performers.

In Hindustānī notation, the pitches of the melody are aligned vertically above the song text. Sanskrit letters are used to indicate pitches:

स रे (रि) ग म प ध नि

Sa Re (Ri) Ga Ma Pa Dha Ni

To indicate a flat (♭—*komal*), one draws a line underneath the letter; to indicate a sharp (♯—*tivra*), one places a mark above it:

स रे̲ रे ग̲ ग म म॑ प ध̲ ध नि̲ नि

Sa Re♭ Re Ga♭ Ga Ma Ma♯ Pa Dha♭ Dha Ni♭ Ni

Grace notes are placed just over the main pitch. A glide (*meend* or *mīnd*) between two pitches is indicated by a slur above them. In the first full line of Example 2-6, Pa is a grace note to komal Dha, Ma is a grace note first to Pa and then to komal Ga, and Sa is a grace note to Re. In the same line, komal Dha is joined to Ma by a glide. These are the only two types of ornamentation that appear in Example 2-6. In Indian music, the connecting of pitches and the use of additional pitches such as grace notes are considered ornamentation. Pitch register is shown by a dot underneath the syllable for low, a dot over the syllable for high, and the absence of a dot for middle. Example 2-6 consists of pitches in the middle and high registers.

The first two counts of the melody in Example 2-6 appear by themselves at the upper right corner of the example. Each syllable receives one count, and four counts are grouped together, separated by a vertical bar. (For a full explanation of the metric significance of the notation, see Chapter Five.) Durations beyond one count are shown by a dash to the right of the letter. Subdivisions of a count are shown by a slur underneath the letters. In the second line of the second section (*aṅtarā*) of the song in Example 2-6, the first four counts demonstrate both of these conventions: Ṙe—Ṡa Ṙe Ġa, 𝅗𝅥 ♫ ♩.

As the song text is given in musical notation, there is no indication of where a word begins and ends. The symbol S is used to show that a syllable is prolonged for another unit of time. A comma is used for a breath mark in

[5]Example 2-6 is performed on Odeon recording MOAE 131; the notation is found in V. N. Bhaṭkhande, *Krāmik Pustak Mālikā* (Hathras: Sangit Karyalaya, 1963), Vol. III, pp. 664–65. This would not have been a notation Khansahib learned from; undoubtedly, he learned from rote.

the text line For example, in the first complete line of Example 2-6, the last subdivision includes first a tie of the text-syllable *ri* from the preceding subdivision, then a breath mark between the second and third counts:

रि | ऽ मा, फु ल

ri - - - - mā, Phu-la

The subdivisions of each line in Example 2-6, shown by vertical bars, are also labeled by means of notational symbols that appear below the line: ० ३ × २ . These symbols are indications of the meter. × marks the first count in the meter, ० marks the middle of the meter, and the arabic numerals २ and ३ indicate further metrical subdivisions. The meter has a structural framework of 4 + 4 + 4 + 4 counts (this is explained fully in Chapter Five).

A second notation of "Phula van kī geṅda" appears in Example 2-9; this style of notation differs mostly in its indication of rhythm and meter.[6] The repetition of the first line is suggested by the text word "vana" (वन) written at the end of the line, rather than by the rewriting of the line, as in Example 2-6. A count is shown by o ; a half count is ◡; and two counts is —. The subdivisions of the meter are shown as follows: + (count 1), ७ (count 5), ९ (count 9), and ३ (count 13). Barlines are drawn between counts 8 and 9 only. The indication for pitch register is also different. Tār saptak is indicated by a slight vertical line above the syllable. सा॑ equals सां in the Bhatkhande notation.

Although these notations are perfectly viable, they bear little relation to the music in performance. They present only the skeleton of a piece, which is always fleshed out in performance. They can also serve as the basis for a long improvisation.

EXAMPLE 2-6 Bhaṭkhande Notation of "Phula van kī geṅda"

राग जौनपुरी–त्रिताल (मध्यलय)

स्थायी

															प	सा
															फु	ल
							प	म	म		सा					
Melody:	नि	ध	प	ध	म	म	ध	प	ग	–	रे	म	–	प	प	सां
Text:	व	न	की	गें	ऽ	द	मे	का	मा	ऽ	ऽ	रि	ऽ	मा,	फु	ल
	०				३				×				२			

[6]N. V. Patwardhan, *Rāg Vignān* (Poona: Timalepor, 1960), Part II, p. 98.

EXAMPLE 2-6 (Cont.)

प म | म सा
नि ध प ध | म प ध प | ग – रे म | म प प सां
व न की गें | ऽ द मैं का | मा ऽ ऽ ऽ | री मा, फु ल
० | ३ | × | २
Antarā
अन्तरा
प | नि सां | | सां
म – प प | ध – – नि | सां – सां सां | नि सां सां –
ना ऽ म न | जा ऽ ऽ नूँ | कौ ऽ म न | जा ऽ नूँ ऽ
० | ३ | × | २
० | ३

EXAMPLE 2-7 Transliteration of "Phula van kī geṅda"

Rāg Jaunpurī—Trītāl (Madhya laya)

Sthāī

														Pa	Sȧ
														Phu	la
						Pa	Ma	Ma		Sa					
Ni	Dha	Pa	Dha	Ma	Ma	Dha	Pa	Ga	–	Re	Ma	–	Pa	Pa	Sȧ
va	na	kī	gen	– – –	da	mai	kā	mā – – – –			ri	–	mā,	Phu	la
o				३				×				२			
						Pa	Ma	Ma		Sa					
Ni	Dha	Pa	Dha	Ma	Pa	Dha	Pa	Ga	–	Re	Ma	Ma	Pa	Pa	Sȧ
va	na	kī	geṅ	– –	da	mai	kā	mā – – – – – –				ri	mā,	Phu	la
o				३				×				२			

Antarā

EXAMPLE 2-8 Transnotation (to Western) of "Phula van kī genda"

Rāg Jaunpurī   Odeon recording MOAE 131, Side B, band 4

Sthāī

Phu - la   va - na   kī   geṅ - - da   mai - kā   mā - - ri - - mā, phu - la

va - na   kī   geṅ - - da   mai - kā   mā - - - ri - mā, phu - la

Aṅtarā

nā   ma - n   jā - nūṅ   kau - ma - n   jā - nūṅ

kā - soṅ_____   ka - hi - ye   pu - kā - - - - -

Sthāī returns

- - - - ra,   Phu - la   va - na   kī   geṅ - - da   mai - kā

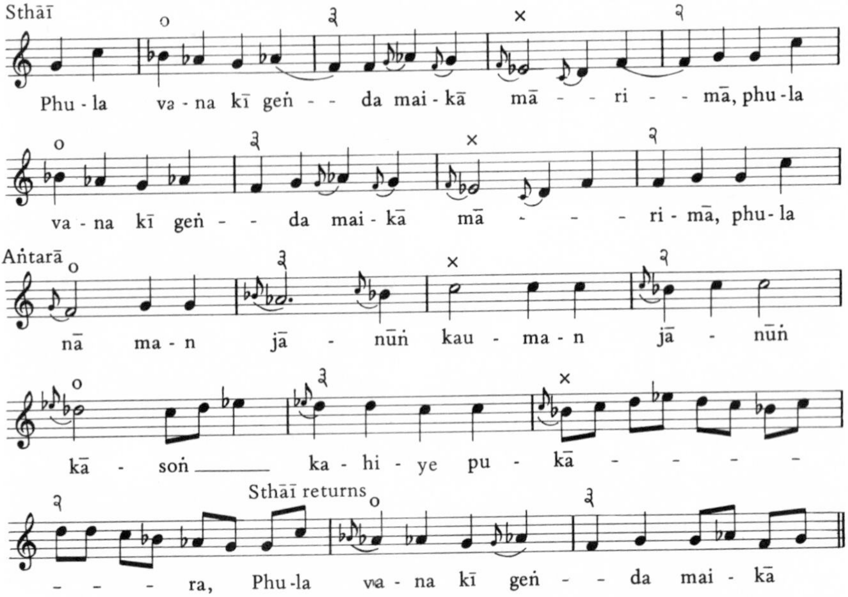

EXAMPLE 2-9 *Rāg Vignān* Notation of "Phula van kī genda"

क्र. ८१ राग–जौनपुरी, तीनताळ (मध्यळय)

फुलवनकी गेंद मैका मारिमा ॥ ध्रु० ॥ ना मन जानूं कोमन जानूं कासो   Text
कहिये पुकारे ॥ १ ॥

प म प सां नि सां प प म प ध प | म गृ सा रे म प म
० ० ० ० ० ० ० ० ० v v ऽ v | – ०० – ०० ०
फु ळ व न की गैं . द मै . का . | मा . रि मा फु ळ वन   vana
  +   ७   १   ३

॥ अंतरा ॥   Aṅtarā

म प प नि ध नि | सां सां सां नि रे सां रे सां रे म गृ रे रे सां सां |
– ०० – – | – ० ० ० ० – v v v ० ० ० ० |
ना मन जा नूं | को म न जा . नूं कासो . . क हि ये पु
+   ७   १   १   +   ७

नि सां रे गृ रे सां नि सां रे रे सां नि ध प प म
v v v v v v v v v v v v v v v v
का . . . . रे . . . . . फु ळ ववकी
१   ३

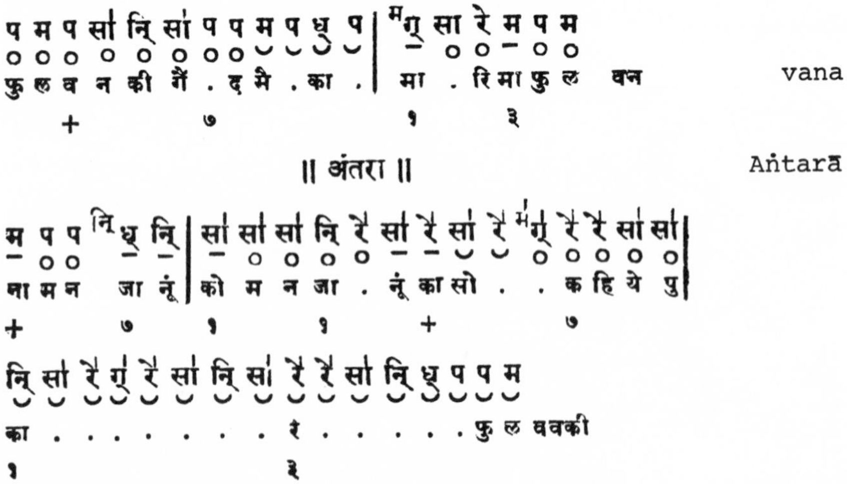

Sthāī: Tossing a ball of flowers at me.
Aṅtarā: Not knowing the heart ....
          Who called loudly?

The Karnatak melodic tradition, which stems from the same ancient system as the Hindustānī tradition, shares with that tradition a corpus of similar ideas and nomenclature. It also utilizes seven basic pitches (svara)—Sa, Ri (instead of the Hindustānī Re), Ga, Ma, Pa, Dha, and Ni. These syllables are abbreviations for words, as follows:

Sa	Śadja			Pa	Panchama
Ri	Riśabha	Ma	Madhyama	Dha	Dhaivata
Ga	Gāṅdhāra			Ni	Niśāda

"Sa" is the abbreviation for the Sanskrit word "śadja." As it is written in Sanskrit, the "ś" is pronounced *sh*. In music, however, it is pronounced *s*. In Sanskrit, words formed with "śat" or "śad" have the meaning "six," as in "śaddarshan"—the six schools of Hindu philosophy, and "sadrāga"—the six main rāgas of an early classification system. In music, however, Sa is the syllable and "śadja" the word for "the first pitch"; the reason for this divergence in meaning is unknown.

Ri (or Re, as it is usually said in the North) is short for "riśabha"—"the second pitch." Ga is short for "gāṅdhāra," a word that refers to the area west of the Sindhu River; it is not known why this word is used to refer to a musical pitch. "Ma" is from "madhyama," or "middle"; it refers to the middle pitch in a saptak. "Madhyama" and the short Hindi form "madhya" are terms used in several different musical contexts, such as "madhya saptak" (middle register) and "madhya laya" (middle speed). "Pa" is short for "panchama," which means "fifth"; it is the fifth pitch in a saptak. "Dha" stands for "dhaviat," "the sixth pitch. "Ni" is from "niśāda" —the name of a non-Aryan tribe in India.

The use of syllables to refer to musical pitches is very old in India. According to one source, svara nomenclature first appears in the *Ṛkpratisakhya*, a grammatical treatise that was current around 600 B.C.[7] At some undocumentable time in the Vedic period (roughly 1500–500 B.C.), older names for the pitches were dropped in favor of the ones now used.[8] Another source suggests that a solfège system is referred to in the *Narada Parivājaka*

[7] R. Rangaramanuja Ayyangar, *History of South Indian (Carnatic) Music from Vedic Times to the Present* (Madras: R. Rangaramanuja Ayyangar, 1972), p. 7.

[8] *Ibid.* Such periods are only approximate, A. L. Basham, in *The Wonder that was India* (New York: Grove Press, Evergreen Books, 1959), p. xix, gives 1500 to 500 B.C. as the dates of the "Proto-Historic" or Vedic age. William Theodore de Bary, in *Sources of Indian Tradition* (New York: Columbia University Press, 1964), Vol. I, p. xx, notes the Vedic period as 1200 to 600 B.C., although he puts the composition of the *Ṛg Veda* in the period 1500–1200 B.C.

Upanishad (which dates, along with other Upanishads, from circa 600 B.C.).[9] According to yet another source, "In the Kudimiyamalai inscriptions of the Pallava period (7 th cent. A.D.) there are whole passages written in Sa ri ga ma notation, though with vowel variations. The *Saṅgīta Ratnākara* (13th cent. A.D.) gives some songs in Sa ri ga ma notation."[10]

In Karnatak music, the number of pitches available in addition to the basic seven is the same as in Hindustānī music. However, when they are named there seems to be more. As in the Hindustānī tradition, Sa and Pa are invariable. And there are two Mas. But there are three categories each of Ri, Ga, Dha, and Ni, rather than two categories each, as in Hindustānī music. The lowest of each of the variable pitches is considered the natural form (*suddha*). The generic name of the remaining forms is *vikrita svaras*. The total selection of Karnatak pitches is given in Chart 1, which includes both the pitch names and the corresponding solfège syllables.

	PITCHES	SOLFÈGE
1	Śadja	Sa
2	Suddha Ri	Ra or Ri_1
3	Chatuśruti Ri	Ri or Ri_2
4	Satśruti Ri	Ru or Ri_3
5	Suddha Ga	Ga or Ga_1
6	Sadharana Ga	Gi or Ga_2
7	Antara Ga	Gu or Ga_3
8	Suddha Ma	Ma or Ma_1
9	Prati Ma	Mi or Ma_2
10	Panchama	Pa
11	Suddha Dha	Dha or Dha_1
12	Chatuśruti Dha	Dhi or Dha_2
13	Satśruti Dha	Dhu or Dha_3
14	Suddha Ni	Na or Ni_1
15	Kaishika Ni	Ni or Ni_2
16	Kākali Ni	Nu or Ni_3

CHART 1. Karnatak Pitches

Although the number of Karnatak pitches appears to be more than the Hindustānī selection of twelve, that is not the case. Karnatak Ri_2 and Ga_1 are the same pitch (they would be termed enharmonic pitches in Western music), as are Ri_3 and Ga_2, Dha_2 and Ni_1, Dha_3 and Ni_2. Each of these pitches has been given two names for reasons of music theory that are discussed in Chapter Three. Chart 2 depicts the pitch correspondences in the

[9]P. Sambamoorthy, *South Indian Music* (Madras: The Indian Music Publishing House, 1958–63), Vol. V, p. 136.

[10]S. Ramanathan, "The Indian Sarigama Notation," *Journal of the Music Academy, Madras*, 32 (1961), 84–85.

Karnatak and Hindustānī traditions, along with a Western pitch sequence that approximates the resulting sequence of intervals. In the chart, Sa is arbitrarily shown as Western pitch "C"; all forms of Re are some form of "D"; all forms of Ga are some form of "E"; and so forth. Enharmonic pitches are bracketed.

Hindustānī:	Sa	Re	Re	Ga	Ga	Ma	Ma̍	Pa	Dha	Dha	Ni	Ni
Karnatak:	Sa	Ri_1	[Ri_2 / Ga_1]	[Ri_3 / Ga_2]	Ga_3	Ma_1	Ma_2	Pa	Dha_1	[Dha_2 / Ni_1]	[Dha_3 / Ni_2]	Ni_3
Western:	C	D♭	[D / E♭♭]	[D♯ / E♭]	E	F	F♯	G	A♭	[A / B♭♭]	[A♯ / B♭]	B

CHART 2. Comparative Pitches

In 1916, the first All-India Music Conference was organized by the Mahārāja of Baroda. One of its chief aims was to provide a uniform system of notation for the entire country. A committee was formed, but it seems to have never made a report. Notation became an issue in South Indian musical circles when teaching institutions began to appear in the 1920's and 1930's. It was discussed at great length at conferences of the Madras Music Academy:

> There was downright condemnation of it by some. They said, "Our music is not intended for notation." Some felt there was no need for it, holding that "even as the Vedas have been preserved without notation, music must be preserved." Still others tolerated it as a necessary evil. Some would have it for students, though not for vidvans. Some welcomed it as a record for posterity, though not an accurate one.[11]

The result of this discussion was the following resolution: "This Conference [16th and 17th sessions of the Conference of the Madras Music Academy, 1940's] recognizes the need for an adequate scheme of notation as a means of preserving our music in some form and appoints a committee consisting of Sri C. S. Iyer, Prof. Sambamurthi and Sri T. L. Venkatarāma Iyer to evolve a scheme of notation on the basis of the symbols adopted in the *Sangita Sampradaya Pradarsini*."[12] The *Saṅgīta Sampradāya Pradārsini* was a work published by Subbrāma Dīkshitar in 1904. It used a system of notation that combined the Indian solfège syllables and some symbols from Western staff notation. It included signs for ornamentation to the extent that it was more or less an accurate record of the music. Since that time, more practical but less conclusive systems have become fairly widespread in South India.

Examples 2-10 and 2-11, 2-12 and 2-13, and 2-14 and 2-15 demonstrate both the consistency and the variety of notation in South India. All these

[11] *Ibid.*, p. 85.
[12] *Ibid.*

examples are variants of a kriti by Tyāgarāja called *Anurāgamu*. The text is in Telugu, the major language of the southern state of Andhra Pradesh and the language spoken by the largest proportion of people in South India. The text is given below. Note the tripartite form of the composition.

Section	*Text*
Pallavi	Anurāgamu lēni menasuna sujñānamu rādu.
Anupallavi	Ghanulaina antara jñānula kerukē gāni.
Caraṇa	Vaga vagagā bhujiyiñcu vāriki trptiyau rīti Saguṇa dhyānamupaini saukhyamu tyāgarāja nuta.

Section	*Translation*
Pallavi	The mind that is bereft of love(devotion) will not be blessed with the divine Jnāna.
Anupallavi	This maxim is well known to enlightened souls.
Caraṇa	Like unto the satisfaction of one who is served with a variety of dishes is the happiness of one who meditates on the lord with attributes.[13]

Example 2-10 is the notation of this kriti by M. Nageswara Rao, who performs it on vīṇā on Nonesuch recording H-72027; Example 2-11 is a transcription made from the recording for purposes of comparison.[14] Example 2-12 is a Telugu notation of the kriti, and Example 2-13 is a transnotation into Nageswara Rao's system of notation. Examples 2-14 and 2-15 are a Tamil variant of the same piece and a transnotation.[15] Tamil is the language of the state of Tamilnadu, whose capital is Madras. Madras is also the music capital of South India. Tamil is spoken by the second largest proportion of people in South India, and is also the major vernacular language of South Indian music.

Each variant of the song *Anurāgamu* in Examples 2-10 through 2-15 would serve a specific purpose for a specific musician—skeletal preservation, an aid to memory, a teaching tool, and so forth. These are not the only notations of this one kriti available, and all the other notations I have seen vary from them.

[13]This translation is by C. Ramanujachari *The Spiritual Heritage of Tyāgarāja* (Madras: Sri Ramakrishna Math), pp. 100–101. A different translation is available on the cover of Nonesuch recording H-72027.

[14]The Karnatak notation is the one given by M. Nageswara Rao in 1973 to a long-time student of his, David Schonfeld. It is printed here by permission of Mr. Schonfeld, who also made the transcription from the recordings as well as the two transnotations to the system of Nageswara Rao, from the Telugu and Tamil variants.

[15]The Telugu notation is from K. V. Srinivasa Ayyangaru (Madras: M. Adi, n.d.), pp. 183–85. The Tamil notation is from P. Sambamoorthy, *Kirtana Sagaram* (Madras: Indian Music Publishing House, 1972), Book V, p. 567.

The reader would be surprised to see the tremendous variation among notation books such as these. Some notation books and South Indian teachers of music outline only skeletal fragments; other teachers notate everything they hear. This variety is confusing, but it also makes it possible for almost everybody to be "correct."

Chart 3 depicts details of the Roman-letter, Telugu, Tamil, and Western notational systems so that the variants in Examples 2-10 through 2-15 can be compared.

ROMAN-LETTER	TELUGU	TAMIL	WESTERN
,		,	varied value: 1 of the smallest unit in the particular count
pitch letter without other symbols	(a) — on top of pitch letters Sa, Ma, Pa, Dha (b) ; (c) c on top of pitch letters Ri and Ni	(a) —— over all pitches included in that count (b) ;	1 count
— under a pitch letter	(a) √ over pitch letters Sa, Ma, Pa, Dha (b) , (c) Ri and Ni without further symbol		½ count
|	|	|	subdivisions of tāla cycle
||	||	||	end of tāla cycle
—	—	—	between first and second half of the tāla subdivision
S R M P D N	సా రి మ పా ధ ని	ஸ ரி ம ப த நி	Sa Ri Ma Pa Dha Ni
• over pitch	• over pitch	• over pitch	high register
• under pitch	• under pitch	• under pitch	low register
		ா	double the duration

CHART 3. Karnatak Notational Systems

EXAMPLE 2-10 Roman-Letter Notation of *Anurāgamu*

PALLAVI

1. || P D | Ṡ , ,ND, || P , | , , DDPM ||
A- nu- rā- gamu lē- ni

2. || P D | Ṡ , , ṘṠ ND, || DPP, , | , , NDPM ||
A- nu- rā- gamu lē- ni

3. || P D | ṠDṘṠ, ND, || PMPD | DṠND—PDPM ||
A- nu- rā- gamu lē- • ni

|| R S | Ṇ Ḍ S , || R M | P D NDPM ||
ma- na- su- na su- jñā- na- mu rā- du

|| P D | Ṡ , , ṘṠ • ND, || DPP, , | , , DDPM ||
A- nu- rā- gamu lē- ni

|| R , | , , ṆḌ Ḍ || S , | , , , , ||
• • •

ANUPALLAVI

1. || P D | Ṡ , Ṙ Ṙ || Ṡ , | , , , , ||
Gha- nu- lai- • na •

2. || P D | Ṡ , Ṙ Ṙ || Ṡ , | , , NDPM ||
Gha- nu- lai- • na •

3. || P D | Ṡ , Ṙ Ṙ || Ṡ , | Ṡ , NDPM ||
Gha- nu- lai- • na •

4. || P D | Ṡ , Ṙ Ṙ || Ṡ,ṘṠ Ṡ | Ṡ,ṘṠ Ṡ NDPM ||
Gha- nu- lai- • na •

5. || P D | Ṡ , Ṙ Ṙ || Ṡ Ṙ | ṖṀ Ṙ Ṙ , ||
Gha- nu- lai- • na an- • ta- • ra

|| Ṡ , | N D PD Ṡ || ṠNND | PDDṠ NDPM ||
jñā- nu- la ke- ru- kē gā- ni (Anu)

CARAṆA

1. || , P P | , P P , P , , M || PD PM | R , S , ||
Va- ga va- ga- gā bhu- ji- yin- cu

2. || , P D | , N D , P , , M || PD PM | R , S , ||
Va- ga va- ga- gā bhu- ji- yin- cu

|| S , | Ṇ Ḍ S , || R M | P D NDPM ||
vā- ri- ki tṛp- ti- yau rī- ti

* || P D | Ṡ , Ṙ Ṙ || Ṡ Ṙ | ṖṀ Ṙ Ṙ , ||
Sa- gu- ṇa dhya- na- mu- pai- ni

|| Ṡ , | N D PD Ṡ || ṠNND | PDDṠ NDPM ||
Sau- khya- mu tyā- ga- rā- • ja nu- ta
(Anu)

*Saṅgatis 1-5, as in Anupallavi

EXAMPLE 2-11 Transcription of *Anuragāmu* from Performance

(Nonesuch H-72027) Vīṇā Performance

EXAMPLE 2-11 (Cont.)

EXAMPLE 2-12 Telugu Notation of *Anurāgamu*

సంగీత సుధాంబుధి] [త్యాగరాజకీర్తనలు

Melody: చ. వగవగగా భుజియించువారికి తృప్తియారీతి

Text: సగుణధ్యానముపైని సౌఖ్యము త్యాగరాజనుత (అను)

ప. పాధా	సా ; నీధా		పమసధ	, ప - పాపమ		
అను	రా ; గము		లే. ..	, . - . ని .		
రీసా	స్రీధ్రాసా ;		రీ ;	మపధపపా , మ		
మన	సు న సు ;		జ్ఞా;	న .ము. రా , దు		
2. పాధా	సనిరిసనీధా		పమపధ	సని - ధాపామా		
అను	రా. . గ. ము		లే. . .	. . - . . . ని		
రీసా	స్రీధ్రాసా ;		రీ ;	మపధపపా , మ		
మన	సున సు ;		జ్ఞా;	న . ము.రా , దు		(అను)
అ. పాధా	సా ; రీరీ		రీసా	రీమారిరీ		
ఘను	లై ; . న		అం	. . తర		

EXAMPLE 2-12 (Cont.)

సాం ; | నీధా - రీసాం || నీధా | పా , మ - ధపామ ||
జ్ఞా ; | నుల - కెరు || కే . | గా , . . - ని . . ||(అను)

చ. పాపా | పాపామా ; || పధపమ | రీ ; సా ; ||
వగ | వగ గా ; || భు.జి . | యిం; చు ; ||

సా ; | నీధా సా ; || రీ రీ | పమపధ - పమపా ||
వా ; | రి కి తృ ; || ప్తియౌ | రీ . . . - తి . . ||

పాధా | సాం ; రీం ; || రీంసాం రీం | రీంమాంరీంరీం ||
సగు | ణ ; ధ్యా ; || న. ము | పై . . ని ||

సాం ; | నీధా - రీ సాం, || నిధ - పా | ; పమ - పధపమ ||
సౌ ; | ఖ్యము - త్యా. , || గ . - రా | ; . జ - ను. త. ||(అను)

EXAMPLE 2-13 Transnotation from Telugu Notation of *Anurāgamu*

PALLAVI

1. || P D | Ṡ , N D || PMPD | , P [,] P PM ||
A- nu- rā- ga- mu lē- ni

|| R S | Ṇ Ḍ S , || R , | MPDP P , , M ||
ma- na- su- na su- || jñā- na- mu rā- du

2. || P D | ṠNṘ-ṠN, D || PMPD | ṠN · D P M ||
A- nu- rā- ga- mu lē- ni

|| R S | Ṇ Ḍ S , || R , | MP DP P , , M ||
ma- na- su- na su- jñā- na- mu rā- du (Anu)

ANUPALLAVI

|| P D | Ṡ , Ṙ Ṙ || Ṙ Ṡ | Ṙ Ṁ Ṙ Ṙ ||
Gha- nu- lai- · na an- · · ta- ra

|| Ṡ , | N D Ṙ Ṡ || N D | P , , M DP , M ||
jñā- nu- la ke- ru- kē gā- ni (Anu)

CARAṆA

| P P | P P M , || PDPM | R , S , ||
Va- ga va- ga- gā bhu- ji- yin- cu

| S , | Ṇ Ḍ S , || R R | PMPD PMP, ||
vā- ri- ki tṛp- ti- yau rī- ti

| P D | Ṡ , Ṙ , || ṘṠ Ṙ | Ṙ Ṁ Ṙ Ṙ ||
Sa- gu- | na dhyā- na- mu · pai- — ni

| Ṡ , | N D · Ṙ Ṡ || ND P | , PM · PDPM ||
sau- khya- mu tyā- ga- rā- | ja nu-ta (Anu)

EXAMPLE 2-14 Tamil Notation of *Anurāgamu*

301. ஸரஸ்வதி. ரூபகம்.

11-வதான ருத்ர (பூ) சக்ரம். 64-வது மேள கர்த்தாவாகிய வாசஸ்பதியின் ஜன்யம். ரிமிதிநி. ஸ ரி ம ப த ஸ்—ஸ் நி த ப ம ரி ஸ. உபாங்க ராகம்.

ப. அனுராகமு லேனி மனஸுன ஸுக்ஞானமு ராது

அ. கனுலேனா அந்தர் க்ஞானுலகே கானி

ச. வக வககா புஜியிஞ்சேவாரிகி த்ருப்தியௌ ரீதி
ஸகுண த்யானமுபைனி ஸௌக்யமு த்யாகராஜனுத

ஆர்வத்துடன் கூடிய உள்ளன்பு இல்லையேல், ஸத்வ அறிவு மனதில் எழாது இவ்வறிவு உள்ளொளி பெற்ற பெரியோர்களுக்கே கைகூடும். வகை வகையாகத் தின்று ருசிப்பதையே வாழ்வின் பயனாகக் கொண்ட மதியீனர்களுக்கு திருப்தி உண்டாகுமா? ஸகுணோபாஸனை மூலம் பெறும் த்ருடமான பக்தி வைராக்யத்தின் வாயிலாகவே, உருவிலியும், கேடிலியும் அழிவிலியுமான பரவஸ்துவை அறியும் இறுதி நிலை வாய்க்கும். இதுவே கைவல்ய ஞான ஸித்தி.

ப. 1.	பா தா	ஸ்ா , ரி -	ஸ் நி நீ ப தா ,	பா , ம	பா ; -	பா , த ப ம
Text:	அ னு	ரா . -	க . . மு .	லே .	. -	. . னி .
2.	பா தா	ப த ஸ்ா , ரி -	ஸ் நி நீ ப தா ,	ப ம பா , நி	நி த பா , த -	பா , த ப ம
	அ னு	ரா . . . -	க . . மு .	லே . . .	. . . . -	. . னி .
3.	பா , நி தா , ரி	ஸ்ா ரி ஸ் -	ஸ் நி நி த	பா தாநித	ஸ்ா ரி ஸ் நி த -	ப த பா ம ப மா
	அ . னு .	ரா . .	க . மு .	லே . . .	. . . . . . -	. . . னி . .
1.	ரி ஸா , ரி	ஸ நி நீ தா -	ப த ஸா	ம ரி ,	ம ப த ப .	ம பா ம
	ம ன .	ஸு . . ன -	ஸு . .	க்ஞா .	ன . மு . -	ரா . து

3. ரீ ஸா , ரி | ஸ நிநீ தா - ஸ ரீ ஸ || ரி மா ரி | ம ப த ரீ ஸா - நி த ப ம ||
ம ன . | ஸ . ன - ஸ . . || க்ஞா . . | ன . மு . . - ரா . . து ||

4. பா , நி தா , ரீ | ஸ் நி தா , ரீ - ஸ்ா , ம் ரீ || ஸ்ா , நி நி த | ப ம பா , த - ஸ்ா ; ||
அ . னு . | ரா . . - க . மு || லே . . . | . . . . - னி ||

அ. 1. ; நி த | , ஸ்ா , - ரீ ரீ || ஸ்ா ; | ஸ்ா , நி நி த ப ம ||
க னு | கெ . - . ன || அந் | . . . த . . . ||

2. பா , த நி த | , ரீ ஸ் நி த - ஸ்ா ரீ || ரீ ஸ் ரீ ம் | , ப் ம் ரீ - ஸ்ா ரீ ஸ் ஸ்ா ||
ர் . க னு | . கெ . . - . ன || அந் . . . | . . . - தர் . . . ||

நி த ப த | , ஸ் நி தா - த ரீ ஸ்ா நி த || பா த நி தா | ப ம ரி ஸ - ரி ம ப ம ||
ச் ஞா . . | . று ல - கே . . . . || கா . . . | . . . . . - னி . . . ||

ச. ; த த | , ப பநிகா - த ப பா ம || ப ம பா , த | நி த ப ம - ரி ஸ ரீ ||
வ க | . வ . க - கா . . . || பு . ஜி . | யி ஞ் . . - சே . . ||

; ம ப | , ம ரீ - ஸ நி தா || ஸா ரி ம | ரீ ப ம - தா பா ||
வா . | ரி கி - த்ரு . . || ப்தி யெள . | . ரீ . - . தி ||

; நி த | , ரீ ஸ் நி த - ஸ்ா ரீ || ரீ ம் ப் ம் | ரீ ஸ் ஸ் நி - த ப தா ||
ரு | . ண . . - த்யா . || ஸா . மு . | பை . . . - . . னி ||

பா த நி தா | த ரீ ஸ்ா நி த - ப நி தா ப ம || ரீ ஸா ரி ஸ | ஸா ரி ம - பா , த ப ம ||
ஸெள . . . | க்ய . . மு . - த்யா . . . . || க ரா . . | . ஜ . - னு . த . ||

EXAMPLE 2-15 Transnotation of Example 2-14

PALLAVI

1. || P D | Ṡ, ,Ṙ — ṠNN, PD,, || P, ,M | P , P, ,D PM ||
A- nu- rā- ga- mu lē- • • ni

2. || P D | PD Ṡ, ,Ṙ—SNN, PD,, || PM P, ,N | ND P, ,D—P, ,D PM ||
A- nu- rā- ga- mu lē- • • • ni

3. || P, ,N D, ,Ṙ | Ṡ ṘṠ—ṠN ND || P D, ND | Ṡ, ṘṠ ND—PDP, MPM, ||
A- nu- rā- ga- mu lē- • • • ni

1. || R S, ,R | SṆṆ, Ḍ—P̣Ḍ S || MR,, | MP DP—MP, M ||
ma- na- su- na su- jñā- na- mu rā- du

2. || R S, ,R | SṆṆ, Ḍ—SR, S || RM, R | MP DṘṠ,—NDPM ||
ma- na- su- na su- jñā- na- mu rā- du

4. || P,,N D,,Ṙ | ṠN D, ,Ṙ—Ṡ,,Ṁ Ṙ || Ṡ,,N ND | PM P, ,D—Ṡ , ||
A- nu- rā- ga- mu lē- • • • ni

ANUPALLAVI

1. || , ND | , Ṡ , , —Ṙ Ṙ || Ṡ , | Ṡ, ,N—NDPM ||
Ghanu- lai- • na an- • tar

2. || P, ,D—ND | , ṘṠND—Ṡ Ṙ || ṘṠṘṀ | , ṖṀṘ—Ṡ, ṘṠ Ṡ ||
Ghanu- lai- • na an- • tar

|| ND PD | , ṠN D—DṘṠ, ND || P DND, | PMRS—RMPM ||
jñā- nu- la- kē gā- ni (anu)

CARANA

|| , DD | , P—PND[,]—DPP, M || PM P, ,D | NDPM—RSR, ||
Vaga va-ga- gā bhu- ji- yiñ- cē

|| , MP | , M R— SṆ Ḍ || S RM | R PM—D P ||
vā- ri- ki tṛp- ti- yau • rī- • ti

|| , N D | , ṘṠND— Ṡ Ṙ || ṘṀṖṀ | ṘṠṠN—DP D ||
Sa- gu- ṇa dhyā- na- mu- pai- • ni

|| P DND, | DṘṠ, ND— PND, PM || R S, RS | S RM—P, ,D PM ||
sau- khya- mu tyā- — ga- rā- • ja nu- ta
(Anu)

THE MELODIC DRONE

An integral part of current musical performance in both North and South India, and one that is vital to any consideration of Hindustānī and Karnatak melodic concepts, is the drone on pitch Sa. The drone is the sounding of a constant melodic pitch or pitch sequence that undergirds elaborate melodic improvisation. It adds a "harmonic" element to the music, as suggested in Example 2-16. (In the example, give each syllable one count and each hyphen one count.)

EXAMPLE 2-16 The Drone Element

Melody:	Sa - $\underline{\text{Re}}$ Sa | Ga Ma - $\underline{\text{Re}}$ | Ga Ma Pa Ga | Ma - ‖
Drone:	Sa———————————————————————

The presence of the drone in contemporany Indian classical music may be one of the prominent differences between today's melodic practice and ancient practice. Shri Chaitanya Deva, who has completed the most fruitful research on the drone, suggests that it became a definite component of chamber ensembles only as late as the seventeenth century.[16] His assertion is based partly on the fact that not until between the fifteenth and the seventeeth centuries did treatises begin to mention drone strings in their descriptions of instruments. Another of his reasons lies more in the realm of melodic practice: In older music, the intervals between successive pitches were very important. Gradually, however, pitch Sa became more and more a point of reference, until the relationship between Sa and the other pitches in a rāga became of prime importance. "With the emergence of the drone in chamber music," Deva asserts, "the musicological system gradually changes towards the description of musical elements in terms of . . . Sa."[17]

In both Hindustānī and Karnatak music, the drone is played primarily on the tāmbūra. A tall instrument, from three and a half to five feet, the tāmbūra is a member of the lute family.[18] The longest part of the tāmbūra is its hollow neck, which ends in a bowl—usually a large gourd (in the North) or a hollowed-out piece of jackfruit (in the South)—that is covered with a slightly convex piece of wood. The different sizes of tāmbūras reflect the particular uses to which they are put. For example, if the instrument is to accompany a man's voice, the bowl is most appropriately a large one, whereas the pitch of a woman's voice may be better matched by an instrument with a smaller bowl. For convenience, small portable tāmbūras are also made. These do not produce the volume and timbre of the full-sized ones, but they fulfill the same musical function (see plates 5, 6, and 7).

The tāmbūra usually has four strings, which extend from tuning pegs at the top end, down the long neck, over the wood sounding board and the bridge placed on it, to the underside of the gourd.[19] Three of the strings are

[16] B. Chaitanya Deva, *The Psychoacoustics of Music and Speech* (Madras: The Music Academy, 1967), p. 71.

[17] *Ibid.*, p. 64.

[18] The tāmbūra might also be classified as a zither. If one accepts as a zither a cordophone whose strings run the entire length of its resonating chamber, then the tāmbūra, with its hollow neck, is a zither.

[19] The number of strings on a tāmbūra is actually rather flexible. In performances of instrumental music in the North, one frequently hears a five-pitch drone, indicating a five-string tāmbūra. Six- and seven-string tāmbūras are also used. This is a matter of personal preference.

Plate 5
North Indian Singer with Tāmbūra

Plate 6
South Indian Processional Group with Portable Tāmbūra

Plate 7
South Indian Processional Group with Full-Sized Tāmbūra

steel; the fourth and lowest-pitched string is brass. The tāmbūra of South India is a somewhat more delicate instrument than its North India counterpart because its long neck is more slender.

The tuning of the tāmbūra is generally Pa Sȧ Sȧ Sa (G c c C). It may also be tuned Ma Sȧ Sȧ Pa, Ni Sȧ Sȧ Pa, or even some other way, depending on the rāga being performed. The most important drone pitch is Sa. The unison and octave interval in the tuning must be precise because the tāmbūra provides the reference pitch for the entire performance. Gross tuning is done with the pegs of the instrument. Extremely fine tuning is accomplished by sliding a small ivory bead up or down each string between the bridge and the point on the gourd where the string is anchored. To make the proper overtones prominent and to prolong the vibrations of each string, one places a thread of wool or silk under each string where it passes over the bridge. To position the thread properly, one slides it under the string until a sudden metallic twang sounds, indicating the spot where the thread should be left.

In performance, the tāmbūra is usually held vertically, with the bowl resting on the floor, or in the lap of the player.[20] The index and middle fingers of the right hand are used to strum the strings: the middle finger plucks Pa, and the index finger slides across Sȧ Sȧ Sa. The sound is produced entirely by open strings, because the strings are not pressed down to the neck at any time. A singer may play the tāmbūra himself or ask a disciple to do it for him. It is an honor to be asked, but it is a role of anonymity, since the name of the tāmbūra player does not appear on the program. (Only in the West do we find the tāmbūra player listed as an artist.)

The soloist, whether vocalist or instrumentalist, decides on the rhythm of the drone pitches—for example,

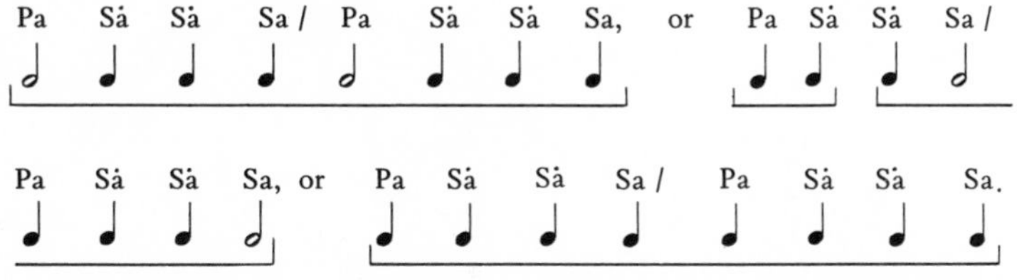

The rhythm of the drone has nothing to do with the rhythm of the selection being performed, because the drone is perceived as constant throughout a performance. The soloist also indicates the speed at which he or she wants the drone sounded.

Another means of producing the drone pitch Sa throughout a performance, and one used rather frequently in the South, is a śruti box. The śruti

[20]The position in which the tāmbūra is held can differ. In the North, some famous vocalists have been known to make their own drone accompaniment, resting the tāmbūra horizontally on the floor in front of them.

box is a small portable organ capable of producing the pitches of the Western chromatic scale.[21] The keeper of the drone adjusts the mechanism so that the pitch chosen for Sa will sound. He then pumps the bellows that are built into the back of the instrument; this keeps the sound constant throughout the performance of a selection. The pitches of the diatonic scale on the śruti box are numbered from 1 to 7, beginning with C. Chromatic pitches are counted as halves. Thus, when a soloist specifies $1\frac{1}{2}$ śrutis as the pitch for Sa, C♯/D♭ is Sa (in this context, the term śruti refers to pitch level rather than to an interval).

The purpose of this chapter has been to introduce some of the elements shared by the Hindustānī and Karnatak traditions. Common to both traditions are the basic components of a performing ensemble—a melody-producing medium and percussion—and the responsibility carried by a soloist. Also shared is the drone, both as a melodic element in performance and as a pitch important in melodic theory. The two traditions share other melodic elements, some notational elements, and certain ideas about notation.

One note of warning must be made at this point: it is risky to make generalizations about anything in Indian classical music. The only generalization that can be made safely is that *no generalization about Indian classical music is possible.* For every assertion, numerous exceptions can be found (as we have already seen in the construction of the tāmbūra, its tuning, and the positions in which it is played). In fact, exceptions are the rule: flexibility is the heart of the Indian traditions of classical music. Readers will note the persistent use of qualifiers in this text—"usually," "generally," "often," "rarely," and the like. If a generalization does slip by without qualification, they should add the appropriate qualifier.

[21]On the harmonium, a similar instrument, a keyboard is provided and the drone keeper presses the key for the pitch desired for Sa. Sometimes the player tapes the key down so that it does not have to be constantly depressed manually. On śruti boxes, a series of sound holes, each coverable with a reed, are drilled into the instrument; in performance the hole that corresponds to the desired pitch is left uncovered to allow air through. Again, the construction of the instruments in general is flexible.

THREE

MELODY

INTRODUCTION

The Indian tradition of writing about music is a very ancient one, beginning, as Indians often say, "in the hoary past." Very early works, especially the *Nāṭya Śāstra*, explained the place of music in drama and offered information on melodic detail and types of compositions. Through the centuries, however, the bulk of writing about music has concerned itself with music theory—in particular, melodic theory. It is possible to trace some of the conceptual history of the melodic system as a whole (called rāga), as well as the histories of particular melodic modes (also generically called rāga).

Indian scholarship has been rich in terminology, much of which remains unexplained because over the centuries different uses have been made of the same terms and different terms have been given to what seem to be the same uses. The earliest treatise from which tentative connections can be made to details of modern theory and practice is the thirteenth-century *Saṅgīta Ratnākara*. Constant effort is being made to draw those connections, to the extent that the "hoary past" seems like only yesterday.

When Westerners read modern scholarly writings in English by Indian musicologists, two things in particular are immediately evident. One is a sense of continuity with the past that reflects the respect held for tradition itself. The other is a love of naming things, which results in an abundance of terminology. Thus, in *The Spiritual Heritage of Tyāgarāja*, a proto-hagiographical tome on the greatest of South India's saint-singers, we read:

> What is there in a name, one may ask. It is name that is everything. Name is fame. . . . When one is highly enraged or highly pleased, one calls names, of abuse or of praise. In the excess of one's hate or love, what comes out of one is mere name. In those short exclamations that break forth, the entire surcharged feeling stands compressed.
>
> The earliest outpourings of man praying to the divine powers are seen in the *Ṛg Vedic* hymns, in the form of praises of the names and qualities of different deities, Agni, Indra. . . .
>
> It is a matter of common experience, as the *Bhāgavata* says . . . that when one keeps on muttering the name of a thing, one's mind develops a love for and a gradual absorption in it.[1]

Lord Vishnu is called by a thousand names, and many of his devotees end each day by reciting in rhythm all those names.[2]

From the reciting of names of the deities, it is but a step to the reciting of chains of names of many things. Writers give chains of names of authoritative sources, as if to reconfirm the existence of a continuous tradition. In a similar vein, one Indian musicologist, discussing degrees of speed in Karnatak music, presents each term for such degrees in three forms:

> This exposition amounts to a reverse anuloma or downward anuloma and may be styled *viloma anuloma*. Likewise, when the speed of singing a Pallavi is kept constant and the speed of counting the tala is progressively made slower and slower, it amounts to a reverse pratiloma or downward pratiloma and may be styled *viloma pratiloma*. Assuming that a musician is capable of performing the Krama Anuloma and Krama Pratiloma and the Viloma

[1] C. Ramanujachari and V. Raghavan, *The Spiritual Heritage of Tyāgarāja* (Madras: Sri Ramakrishna Math, 1966) p. 109.

[2] Hear Odeon recording MOAE 5011, *Smt. M. S. Subbalakshmi* (*Bhaja Govindam; Vishnu Sahasranaman*). (Smt. is the form of polite address to a married Hindu woman.)

> Anuloma and Viloma Pratiloma, it will amount to expounding the Pallavi in all five degrees of speed, i.e. singing the Pallavi in five degrees of speed and reckoning the tala in five degrees of speed.[3]

For an Indian source, this is an extraordinarily clear listing of musical terminology. In many other treatises, the presentation of terms is more confusing.

Confusion in Indian musical terminology is caused by the overlapping use of several languages. In books on Hindustānī music, the older Sanskrit terms are intermingled with Hindi and English. In books on Karnatak music, Sanskrit and Tamil forms and English equivalents are all used, often within a single paragraph. For example: "Rules, if any, relating to the *graha* of the *piece* and the *graha* of its component angas: *Gītas* have to be in sama *graha*; but in a *kriti*, the *eḍuppus* of the pallavi, anupallavi, and charaṇa may be identical or different"[4] (italics mine). Sanskrit *graha* is the Tamil *eḍuppu.* Sanskrit gīta and kriti are types of the English "piece." The remainder of the terms are Sanskrit. Often, terms are left unexplained (even for Indian students) because it is assumed either that the reader knows what is meant or that the written word will be supported by oral explanation. In the sentence quoted above, the author is saying that the rules, if any, about the count on which a piece or a section (*aṅga*) of a piece begins are as follows: in the type of piece called gīta, the sections have to begin on count 1 of a cycle; in the type of piece called kriti, the counts on which the three sections (*pallavi*, *anupallavi*, and *charaṇa*) begin may be identical or different.

Indian musical scholarship offers thousands of discussions of the attributes of individual rāgas, complete with copious terminology. Knowing about one rāga is a complex matter. A comprehensive description most likely will include information on the history of the rāga; on the pitches and any characteristic melodic movement used in it; on its performance time and the mood it evokes; and on its form and its classification in the rāga system as a whole. The complexity of the subject of rāga can be inferred from the fact that this wealth of very specific information applies to any one of hundreds of rāgas.

A cold, wordy description of a rāga bears about the same relationship to a performance of that rāga that an analysis of a composition in Western classical music bears to a performance of that composition. Although the analysis and the performance each derive from the same material, they are two different types of experience. No one either in India or the West would be content to study the analysis and never experience the performance. However, to begin with a theoretical understanding of the details of the rāga is an

[3]P. Sambamoorthy, *South Indian Music*, 3rd ed. (Madras: Indian Music Publishing House, 1958–1963), Vol. IV, p. 42.

[4]*Ibid.*, Vol. III, p. 116.

Indian approach. If the audience did not think in a somewhat analytical manner, how could there be the knowledgeable give and take between audience and artists? Furthermore, as a Karnatak musicologist relates,

> in concerts where printed programmes are not given to the audience beforehand, the listeners have a spicy time in identifying the rāgas sung by musicians. Especially when rare rāgas are sung, the intellectual pleasure that one derives in identifying those rāgas is great and can be compared only to the pleasure that one derives when solving riders in geometry.[5]

Once the rāga has been identified, of course, attention shifts to the music making, to what is being done with the rāga rather than the rāga itself. That will be examined later on in this book. This chapter focuses on what rāga is, and on how the Hindustānī and Karnatak traditions of rāga relate to each other.

HINDUSTĀNĪ MELODIC CONCEPTS

In explaining rāga, one is strongly tempted to make such simplistic conclusive statements as "A rāga is a scale" or "A rāga is a tune." But there is no single Western word equivalent to all of the things "rāga" includes. It is my intention to counter the seemingly inevitable attempt to find similarity between the Indian and Western musical systems by leading the reader to contrast the two. The following five right-hand pages deal with Hindustānī concepts; the following three left-hand pages concern Western concepts, and are coordinated with the discussion of the Hindustānī melodic system. A discussion of Karnatak melodic concepts follows this comparison.

Rāga and Western melodic concepts are explored below through the medium of song. When I refer to a specific Hindustānī rāga, I will give its name in the Hindustānī form—for example, Rāg Mālkosh. Otherwise, the Sanskrit form, rāga, will be used in both the Karnatak and Hindustānī discussions.

The Western song to be examined is "Till the End of Time," and the Hindustānī song is "Sajana āye." Each was chosen for the same three major reasons, in order to assure as common a ground as possible for comparison. First, each had to represent the tradition of classical music in the respective culture. "Till the End of Time" is adapted from Chopin's Polonaise in A♭, and "Sajana āye" is a khyāl chīz (see Chapter Seven). Second, each had to

[5] *Ibid.*, Vol. IV, p. 11.

include the melodic elements considered in this discussion. Third, each had to have the same musical meaning in its notated form. Because a khyāl chīz is seen only in ideal form in notation, and would be performed quite differently, it was necessary to find a song in the Western tradition that would be handled in the same manner. That led me to "Till the End of Time," a popular song in vogue in the 1940's.

Western

EXAMPLE 3-1 "Till the End of Time"

Chorus
Till the end of time, Long as stars are in the blue Long as
there's a spring, a bird to sing I'll go on lov-ing you Till the
end of time, Long as ros-es bloom in May My love for
you will grow deep-er with eve-ry pass-ing day.

An individual who is literate in the Western musical language can tell you quite a bit about the theoretical framework into which this melody fits. For example, it is in a major mode and is notated here in the key of B flat. The B-flat scale may be written as:

B♭ C D E♭ F G A B♭
Do Re Mi Fa Sol La Ti Do

Whenever asked to produce a scale, a Western musician will give the consecutive stepwise order of pitches; in fact, that is the definition of a scale. All major modes have a similar diatonic scale, consisting of seven pitches within one octave, and the following interval arrangement: whole step—whole step—half step—whole step—whole step—whole step—half step (see Example 3-2).

EXAMPLE 3-2 Major Diatonic Scale

W W H W W W H

Hindustānī

EXAMPLE 3-3 "Sajana āye mere dwāre"[6]

An individual who is literate in the Hindustānī musical language can tell you quite a bit about the theoretical framework into which this melody fits. For example, "Sajana āye" is in a particular rāga, Rāg Mālkosh. In scale form, Rāg Mālkosh may be written as:

The idea of "scale" is alien to many Hindustānī rāgas, because melodic shape, rather than an abstract scale, accounts for the differences between one rāga and others. Although I can state that the pitches of Rāg Mālkosh are Sa, Ga, Ma, Dha, and Ni, it would be misleading for me to present them as a scale in Mālkosh, because those pitches in that succession are not characteristic of Mālkosh. (For this reason, the scales of rāgas that are listed in record-liner notes are often difficult to hear in the music.)

It is evident from this example that Rāg Mālkosh is a pentatonic rāga, that is, it has five (*auḍava*) pitches within one saptak. Tradition states that a rāga must have at least five pitches.

Rag Kāmbhojī, the rāga of the second selection on Philips recording 6586003, is very different from Rāg Mālkosh. It can be given meaningfully in

[6]Example 3-2 is my own transcription of the performance of this chīz on Philips recording 6586003, *North India: Vocal Music: Dhrupad and Khyāl.* I have not found this song transcribed in Indian sources. The recording does not begin with this melody; listen for the entry of the drum.

Western

If we extract the pitches heard in the chorus of "Till the End of Time" as they occur for the first time in the song, we obtain the following repertoire:

When those same pitches are arranged in a scale, it is clear that they number more than the basic seven of the B-flat scale:

E, F♯, A♭, and D♭ do not belong in the diatonic scale of the key of B flat. They are chromatic pitches.

The harmonic context of the melody determines the way a particular chromatic pitch will be notated. The G♯ in the phrase "I'll go on loving you," for example, is notated A♭ and not G♯, because it belongs in an F-minor chord: F A♭ C.

In Example 3-1, all the pitches in the key of B-flat major were used, plus four chromatic pitches. Some melodies, however, do not use all the pitches in the key: "Frère Jacques" (Example 3-4), in the key of C, uses only six of seven basic pitches. No pitch B is present, but Western musicians would know that "Frère Jacques," as notated in Example 3-5, is in the key of C. If they heard it sung, they would at least recognize that it is in a major key.

EXAMPLE 3-4 "Frère Jacques"

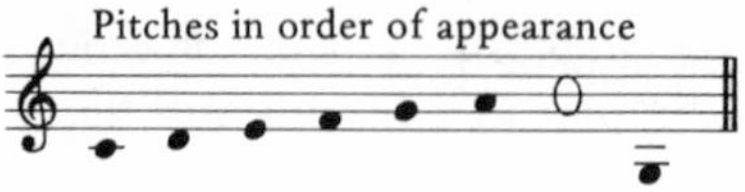

Although characteristic melodic shape plays a part in some Western modes (for example, cadence formulas in the church modes), it is not a part of the major mode.

To produce a pitch that is flat or sharp relative to perfect pitch is an undesirable thing in Western music. The idea of perfect pitch is appropriate to a musical culture whose instruments produce pitches that are fixed accor-

Hindustānī

scale form (see Example 3-5) because contour is not one of its distinguishing characteristics.

EXAMPLE 3-5 Rāg Kāmbhojī in Scale Form

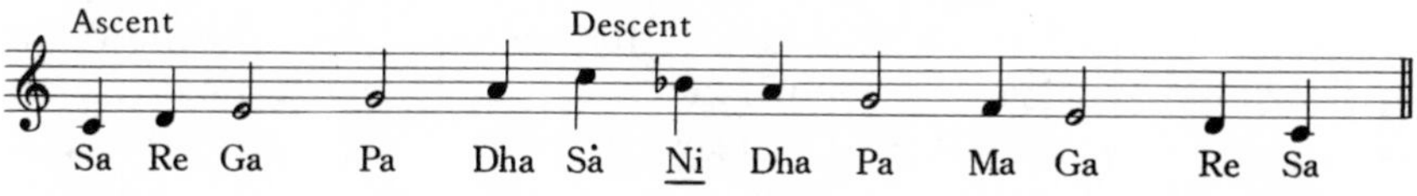

This rāga-reduced-to-scale-form must be presented in both ascent (*ārohana*) and descent (*avārohana*), for the pitches used in ascent are not the same as those in descent: within one octave, Rāg Kāmbhojī has five (*auḍava*) pitches in ascent and seven (*sampūrṇa*) pitches in descent.

Which pitches are used is a crucial factor in distinguishing a particular rāga. *No* pitches other than Sa, Ga, Ma, Dha, and Ni can be used for melody in Rāg Mālkosh. If other pitches are added the rāga will no longer be Rāg Mālkosh. Likewise, the particular pitches given for Rāg Kāmbhojī are the only ones that may be used for melody in Rāg Kāmbhojī.

Before we accept the categorical statement that no other pitches can be added or the rāga becomes a different rāga, a slight retraction is in order. In *some* rāgas, a foreign pitch can *occasionally* be inserted in a *subtle* but *purposeful* fashion by the *best* artists, whose reputation is so impeccable that the use of such a pitch can in no way be interpreted as an error. Also, in some types of melodic figures, "foreign pitches" or an otherwise avoided succession of pitches are considered permissible.

The necessity for this retraction and the inevitable exceptions to tradition emphasize an important fact about Hindustānī classical music: the acceptability of variation by the best of artists is but one example of the flexibility of the melodic system and the important role of the individual musician.

In regard to the omission of pitches, however, the rule appears to be firm. All of the pitches cited above—Sa, Ga, Ma, Dha, and Ni—*must* be used for melody in Rāg Mālkosh. If any is omitted, the rāga will no longer be Rāg Mālkosh. *All of the pitches designated for any particular rāga must be used; if any of them is omitted, the rāga will no longer be that particular rāga.*

The specific pitches that are used in a rāga are only the basis for a more important (and more musically enjoyable) aspect of pitch in Hindustānī rāga: melodic shape. Many Hindustānī rāgas are so "shapely" as to be closer to tune than to scale. The "shapely" nonscalar ascent given for Rāg Mālkosh at the beginning of this discussion is one example of that.

In many tuneful rāgas, the *context* in which pitches occur, not just which pitches occur, "is" the rāga. In Rāg Bihāg (Example 3-7), both forms of

Western

ding to standardized tuning. What constitutes "perfect" has changed even during Western musical history, however.

In the key of B flat—and therefore in the melody "Till the End of Time"—a pitch hierarchy is present. Pitch B♭ is the most important pitch (the tonic) in that melody. It is the base for the most important chord, the B-flat chord for which the key is named. We generally expect, if our ears are accustomed, to hear a melody in that key come to a finish on the B-flat chord, if not on pitch B♭ itself.

Pitch F is the second most important pitch (the dominant), for it is the base for the second most important chord, on which many internal phrases come to rest. And so a hierarchy is taken for granted.

The decision to notate "Till the End of Time" in the key of B flat was probably based on pitch register. Given the range of the song's melody, the key of B flat keeps most of the pitches in the octave just above "middle C," a register that is relatively easy for most people to read. Notated in B flat, then, the melody of the chorus of "Till the End of Time" falls mostly into a "middle" register. Register has nothing to do, however, with determining which mode the song is in.

Grace notes and other forms of additional pitches projected onto basic pitches in a composition are considered "ornamentation" in Western music. But neither the means of articulating pitches (whether connecting them smoothly, or not connecting them, as in staccato) nor the means of ornamenting them with additional pitches affects the tonality of a melody. "Frère Jacques," even as notated in Example 3-6, may be recognized as being in the major key of C.

EXAMPLE 3-6 "Frère Jacques" with Ornamentation

Hindustānī

Ma are used in descending motion, but not in direct succession. The melody turns back at pitch Ga, creating a curve (termed *vakra*): "... the descending scale can be continued stepwise from the high SA (C) via MA *tivra* (F♯) down to ... [E]. After [E] the descent becomes *vakra*; the next note has to be MA(F), from which the descent to the low SA(C) can be continued. The rule is that MA (F) must appear between two GA (E)."[7]

EXAMPLE 3-7 Vakra Melody in Rāg Bihāg

One reason for the development of a number of tuneful rāgas might be that according to tradition, only one form of each of the seven basic pitches can be used in a context. Komal Ga followed by shuddh Ga is against tradition, for example. Although this tradition is not followed to the letter in present-day practice, it has probably contributed to the creation of some lovely melodic movement.

A flagrant exception to this tradition of nonsuccession is Rāg Lālit (Example 3-7), in which shuddh Ma and tivra Ma can occur in immediate juxtaposition.

EXAMPLE 3-8 Pitch Ma in Rāg Lālit

In some rāgas, distinctive melodic shape involves more than merely patterns of ascent or descent or contextual determination. It may involve, for example, other characteristic turns of melody (*pakaḍ*) that make a rāga immediately recognizable to a listener. In performances of Rāg Desī, for example, the phrase or pakaḍ Ga Sa Re Ni Sa occurs frequently. That phrase, combined with other information about the rāga, such as choice of pitches and important pitches, makes the rāga unmistakably Desī.

[7]Walter Kaufmann, *The Ragas of North India* (Bloomington, Ind.: Indiana University Press, 1968), p. 133.

Hindustānī

Example 3-9, a passage from a khyāl in Desī, should clarify the distinction between this pakaḍ and a "rule of descent." If one wishes, one can directly descend G̲a Re Sa in Desī, as the melody does in Example 3-9 just before the barline. However, the phrase G̲a Sa Re N̲i Sa (marked with a bracket in Example 3-8) is another way to descend from G̲a to Sa, and it is a melodic phrase one expects to hear in Desī.

EXAMPLE 3-9 Pakaḍ in Rāg Desī

The intonation of specific pitches "a little lower" is sometimes a distinguishing feature of a particular rāga. In performing Rāg Mālkosh, for example, some musicians sing komal Dha and komal Ni slightly flat; Robin Kumar Chatterji sings komal Ni very flat (relative to the Western half step) in his performance on Philips recording 6586003. In rāgas where intonation is a special feature, the musician draws attention to particular intervals (usually seconds, thirds, sixths, and sevenths) by consciously flatting or sharping a pitch, or more often by using vibrato to produce a pitch that ranges from slightly above to slightly below the "usual" pitch. It is this phenomenon for which the term śruti is used by some practicing musicians.[8]

It is unwise to attempt definitive statements regarding pitch hierarchy in Hindustānī rāga. Pitch hierarchy is, of course, a matter of pitch function: functions that are considered important make the pitches fulfilling them important. Hindustānī musical theory has changed, and the use of terminology shows it. In old melodic theory, the important functions were beginning (*graha*), ending (*nyāsa*), and "predominant" (*aṃśa*). Over time, however, beginning pitches seem to have become relatively unimportant; ending pitches no longer are designated as such, unless one considers *viśrāntisthan* ("notes on which one may stand") as a sort of ending pitch; and even if "predominance" has remained a vital function, its definition is controversial. V. N. Bhaṭkhande designated as "predominant" "that note which, compared

---

[8]See Nazir Jairazbhoy and A. W. Stone, "Intonation in Present-Day North Indian Classical Music," *Bulletin, School of Oriental and African Studies*, 26 (1963), 119–32.

with the other notes in the rāga, is sounded most often with clarity," and he called it *vādī*.[9] The second most predominant note he called *samvādī*. (Both these terms are very old, but through time have been given various meanings.) Nazir Jairazbhoy, who examined even Bhatkhande's own notations, found no statistical evidence to support the view that vādī and samvādī should be defined by frequency.[10]

Attempts to distinguish pitch hierarchy in Hindustānī rāgas are often contradictory and therefore confusing. In his dictionary of North Indian rāgas, Walter Kaufmann states that "strong notes appear frequently, . . . they can become 'recitation notes' or may have 'finalis' functions, . . . The strong notes are the SA, the first note of the scale, and the predominant *vādī* ('speaker') or *aṃsa*."[11] Subsequently, Kaufmann notes that the vādīs of Rāg Mālkosh "are MA (F) and the upper SA (C) . . . . In short, all five notes of the Mālkouns scale have practically equal importance, and melodies may be started or interrupted on any of these notes."[12] Clearly, the definition of "predominance" and the assignment of that function to certain pitches in a rāga are still open to question. Furthermore, whenever performances of the same rāga by different artists are compared, one important difference between them will probably lie in the area of pitch hierarchy. One can read in Kaufmann or on record-liner notes what the vādī is supposed to be, but that pitch may or may not be treated as "predominant" in the performance. "Predominance" would appear to be yet another element of flexibility in Indian musical tradition.

Pitch register is important in distinguishing some rāgas. Rāg Chandrakant melodies, for instance, generally move in the low and middle saptaks. And two closely related rāgas have been distinguished from each other in terms of register—Rāg Maluha-Kedār, the melodies of which usually range within the middle and low saptaks, and Rāg Kedār, the melodies of which rarely range within the low saptak.[13]

The manner of treating specific pitches—whether by connecting them or by ornamenting them with additional pitches—sometimes distinguishes a rāga. In Rāg Kāmbhojī, pitch Ni (komal Ni) is usually sung with a slow undulating vibrato; this can be heard clearly on Philips recording 6586003 (and is transcribed in Example 7-2). In Rāg Komal Re Āsāvarī, komal Dha is approached from above with a slide from komal Ni, as is komal Re from komal Ga. If such elements are missing when the rāga is performed, the artist either is faulted for having performed it incorrectly or is said not to have performed that rāga at all.

[9]Quoted in Nazir Jairazbhoy, "Factors Underlying Important Notes in North Indian Music," *Ethnomusicology*, 16, no. 1 (1972), p. 66.

[10]*Ibid.*

[11]Kaufmann, *Ragas of North India*, p. 5.

[12]*Ibid.*, pp. 535, 537.

[13]*Ibid.*, p. 77.

In concluding this section of the chapter, it must be stressed that all of the possibilities for Hindustānī rāga discussed thus far are not necessarily applicable to every rāga. Some rāgas have the same pitches in both ascent and descent; others do not. Some rāgas use seven pitches within a saptak; some use fewer; still others use more, mostly because of differences of pitch in ascent and descent. Some rāgas are identified by melodic shape, including characteristic melodic turns (pakaḍ), whereas others are not. Some rāgas emphasize one, or two, pitch registers, but in most rāgas the full range is used. Some rāgas are said to have a clear pitch hierarchy, others not. Some rāgas include specific ornamentation; others do not.

Sometimes two rāgas share certain characteristics yet are quite different in others. They may have the same pitches but different melodic shapes, different pitch hierarchies, or different ornamentations. The range of possibilities is great, and it is this very range that makes the subject of rāga so fascinating and so complex.

The next section of this chapter is devoted to Karnatak rāga. The topics are discussed in the order established in the preceding material on Hindustānī rāga.

KARNATAK MELODIC CONCEPTS

In the subsequent discussion of Karnatak rāga, some points will be familiar from the material on Hindustānī rāga, but other points will be new. The Karnatak rāga to which repeated reference will be made is Māyāmālavagaula, the rāga on which students of Karnatak music are taught their first lessons.

As in Hindustānī rāgas, specific pitches are associated with a specific rāga. To refresh the reader's memory of the repertoire of pitches in Karnatak music, the comparative chart of pitches is reproduced here. Enharmonic pitches are bracketed.

Hindustānī:	Sa	$\underline{\text{Re}}$	Re	$\underline{\text{Ga}}$	Ga	Ma	Ma'	Pa	$\underline{\text{Dha}}$	Dha	$\underline{\text{Ni}}$	Ni
Karnatak:	Sa	Ri_1	[Ri_2 Ga_1]	[Ri_3 Ga_2]	Ga_3	Ma_1	Ma_2	Pa	Dha_1	[Dha_2 Ni_1]	[Dha_3 Ni_2]	Ni_3
Karnatak solfège:	Sa	Ra	[Ri Ga]	[Ru Gi]	Gu	Ma	Mi	Pa	Dha	[Dhi Na]	[Dhu Ni]	Nu

CHART 4. Comparative Pitches

The pitches in Rāga Māyāmālavagaula, stated in three ways, all in scale form, are as follows:

1.	Śadja	Suddha Riśabha	Antara Gāṅdhāra	Suddha Madhyama	Panchama	Suddha Dhaivata	Kākali Niśāda	
2.	Sa	Ri_1	Ga_3	Ma_1	Pa	Dha_1	Ni_3	
3.	Sa	Ra	Gu	Ma	Pa	Dha	Nu	Sȧ

The intervals in the lower tetrachord Sa Ra Gu Ma are parallel to the intervals in the upper tetrachord (including the upper octave of Sa) Pa Dha Nu Sȧ, as shown by the brackets above. In Karnatak rāga theory, it is common to think in terms of tetrachord structure. (This is discussed later in this chapter.)

As in Hindustānī rāgas, the selection of pitches in Karnatak rāgas must be enumerated for both ascent (*ārohana*) and descent (*avārohana*), which sometimes differ in pitch content. In Rāga Māyāmālavagaula, however, the same seven pitches are used in both ascent and descent. Such a rāga is designated a sampūrṇa rāga. Tradition requires that a rāga have at least five pitches, but it may have only four in either the ascent or the descent.

The theory is current in Karnatak as well as Hindustānī music that only one form of each of the seven basic pitches can be used in a context. This rule is adhered to more strenuously in Karnatak music but is carried out in a different manner. This is where the enharmonic pitches figure in the pitch structure. In the Hindustānī system, the following ascending sequence would in theory not be permissible, because two forms of Re and two forms of Dha are included:

Sa $\underline{\text{Re}}$ Re Ma Pa $\underline{\text{Dha}}$ Dha Sȧ

But in the Karnatak system, that same ascending sequence is as follows:

Sa Ra Ga Ma Pa Dha Na Sȧ

or

Sa Ri_1 Ga_1 Ma_1 Pa Dha_1 Ni_1 Sȧ

In the Karnatak system, the exploitation of the system of pitch nomenclature to permit adherence to the tradition is preferred to the Hindustānī practice of "deviating" from the theory by means of contextual determination, such as using one form of a pitch in ascent but the other form in descent.

A slight retraction is as much in order here as it was in the discussion of Hindustānī rāga. A respected Karnatak pandit, Subba Rao, composed the rāga shown in Example 3-10. Concerning the presence of two Gas in this rāga, he says, "Both Gandharas are used in a special way."[14] Two Dhas are

[14] B. Subba Rao, *Raganidhi* (Madras: The Music Academy, 1965), Vol. II, pp. 52–53.

used as well, one in ascent and the other in descent, as happens in many Hindustānī rāgas. Subba Rao does not say how his rāga fits into the traditional scheme of things.

EXAMPLE 3-10 Rāga Dvigāṅdhārabushini

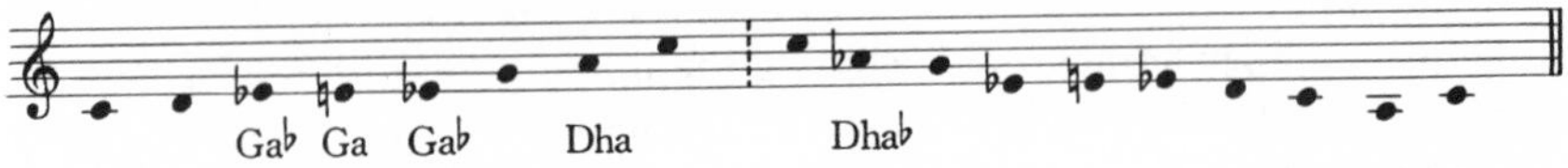

Characteristic melodic shape is prominent in some Karnatak rāgas. If pitches appear in nonscalar order in the acceptable forms of ascent and descent, the rāga is called a *vakra* ("crooked") rāga. Such a rāga can be vakra in ascent, in descent, or in both. The ascent and descent of three vakra rāgas are illustrated in Example 3-11 (the vakra portions are bracketed). Each has a different pitch selection in ascent and descent. Rāga Shrī has five (auḍava) pitches in ascent and seven (sampūrṇa) in descent. Rāga Ānanda-Bhairavī and Rāga Khamās have six (*shadava*) in ascent and seven in descent.

EXAMPLE 3-11 Ascent and Descent of Three Vakra Rāgas

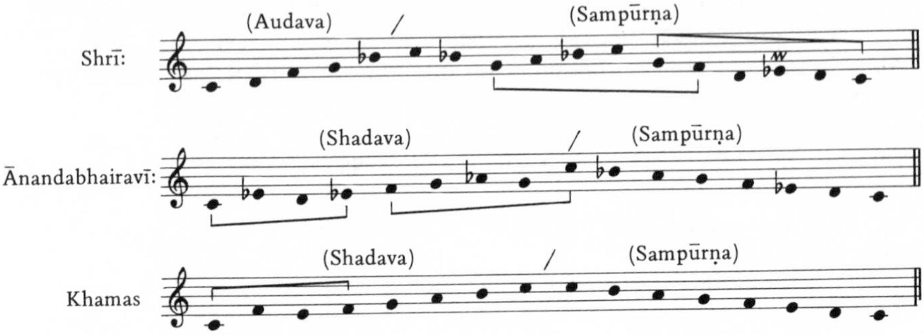

The vakra movement in Rāga Khamās has not been endorsed by everyone. Muttuswāmi Dīkshitar (see Chapter Eight), a nineteenth-century South Indian composer who cultivated variant versions of rāgas, wrote compositions in Rāga Khamās without vakra motion. In addition, the pitches in Rāga Khamās also are found in varying versions. In writing in Khamās, Dīkshitar used seven pitches in both ascent and descent. His contemporary, Tyāgarāja, however, wrote two kritis in Khamās without using the pitch Ni. According to Sambamoorthy, the Kākali Ni pitch "appeared as an interloper with the composers of jāvalis [a "light classical" musical genre] and its use came to be gradually acquiesced in by scholars."[15]

[15]Sambamoorthy, *South Indian Music*, 5th ed. Vol. III, p. 346. A jāvali, "Modi jesevelara" in Rāga Khamās, can be heard on Nonesuch recording H-72040.

Accordingly, Rāga Khamās is classified as a *bhāshāṅga* rāga, one in which a "foreign tone" is admissible. That tone meets the criterion of being consonant with another pitch in the rāga, as Ri_3 is consonant with Ga_3; performers must be careful not to emphasize it if they do use it.

Such allowance for flexibility in Indian musical tradition is one of the most vital aspects of the entire rāga system. It contributes considerably to the feeling of Indian musicians that rāgas are very personal things. Indian musicians talk or write on and on about their favorite rāgas. It is difficult to imagine Western musicians elaborating upon the subtleties of a Western scale or key to this extent. They are usually more concerned with completed compositions.

Some Karnatak rāgas are characterized by melodic patterns (sanchāra) that are not associated particularly with ascent or descent. Rāga Darbār is one such rāga. Its ascent and descent, as well as two *sanchāra*, appear in Example 3-12; "strong pitches" are indicated by white notes.[16]

EXAMPLE 3-12 Rāga Darbār

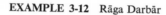

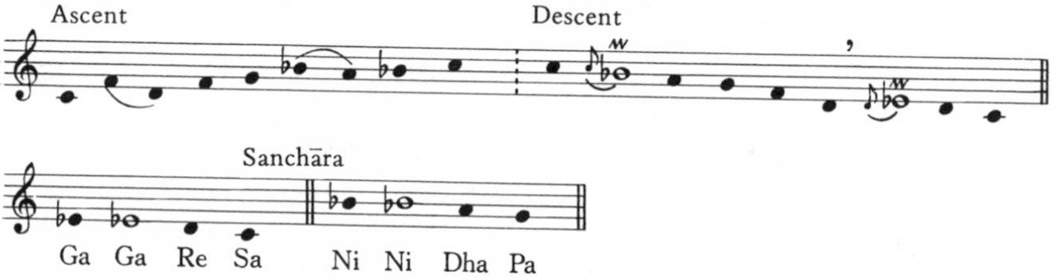

Descriptions of Karnatak rāgas frequently cite *sanchāra*, which are phrases that may occur frequently but do not necessarily play a role in distinguishing one rāga from another, as a Hindustānī pakaḍ would. For instance, the following sanchāra are cited as descriptive of Rāga Māyāmālavagaula. A capital letter indicates a resting point; dots above and below indicate pitch registers.

s r g m p d n Ṡ | g m p d n ṡ ṙ Ṡ

ṡ n d p d n Ṡ | ṡ n d n ṡ ṙ ġ ṙ Ġ

ṁ ġ ṙ Ṡ | ṡ n d P m G | g m p d n ṡ ṙ ṡ n

d P m g r S | s ṇ ḍ ṇ s r S

[16] Subba Rao, *Raganidhi*, Vol. II, p. 46.

In Karnatak rāgas characteristic melodic shapes occur for the most part in the form of patterns of ascent and descent, and are explained in those terms in writings about rāgas:

> The South Indian system on the whole tends to generalize rāgas in the direction of scales while the North Indian system on the whole tends to particularize them in the direction of tunes. . . . While melodic distinctions and relationships among rāgas are often as important psychologically to the South Indian rāga system as they are to the Northern system, they are not systematically controlled in the same way.[17]

The intonation of specific pitches "a little lower" or "a little higher" sometimes distinguishes a particular rāga. In performances of Rāga Sāveri, for example, the svaras Ga and Ni in the passages Sa Ri_2 Ga_3 Ri_2 Sa and Pa Dha_2 Ni_3 Dha_2 Pa are slightly flatted, but not enough so that they would be mistaken for Ga_2 or Ni_2. "In practice it will be found that in many rāgas, the pitch of a particular note is sharped by a śruti during the ascent and flattened by a śruti during the descent."[18]

In the Karnatak tradition, pitch functions are an element in rāga theory but function is not paired with the concept of pitch hierarchy (as in "most important pitch"). The functional pitches that are enumerated are *graha svaras*, pitches on which a composition should begin; *aṃśa svaras*, on which motion can rest or center in improvisation; *nyāsa svaras*, on which a phrase should end; and *jīva svaras* ("life-giving pitches"), which lend individuality to the rāga. For Rāga Māyāmālavagaula, the designations are as follows:

graha svaras:	Sa	Ga		Dha	Ni
aṃśa svaras:		Ga	Pa		
jīva svaras:		Ga			Ni

For Rāga Khamās, they are as follows:

graha svaras:	Sa	Ma	Pa
aṃśa svaras:			Pa

[17]Harold S. Powers, *An Historical and Comparative Approach to the Classification of Rāgas (With an Appendix on Ancient Indian Tunings)*, University of California, Los Angeles, Institute of Ethnomusicology, *Selected Reports*, Vol. I, No. 3 (Los Angeles, 1970), p. 17.

[18]Sambamoorthy, *South Indian Music*, Vol. III, pp. 8–9.

nyāsa svaras: Ma Pa

jīva svaras: Ma Dha Ni

For Rāga Sarasvati, they are as follows:

aṃśa svaras: Pa

nyāsa svaras: Ri Ma

jīva svaras: Ri Ma

In the kriti transcribed in Chapter Two (see Examples 2-10 through 2-15), the pitches listed above for Rāga Sarasvati do indeed seem to fulfill their designated functions. Apparently, it is characteristic of some rāgas to have functions assigned to some pitches, but the inconsistency with which this is done is, again, evidence of variety and individuality within the rāga conception.

Karnatak rāgas, like Hindustānī ones, may stress one pitch register (or saptak) over another, or one tetrachord over another. Rāga Sarasvati is an upāṅga ("upper-portion") rāga, which means that melody is concentrated in the upper tetrachord. The kriti transcribed in Chapter Two offers a clear demonstration of this.

Ornamentation is profuse in Karnatak music, much more so than in Hindustānī rāga. In one Karnatak style of singing and playing—*varika* style—every pitch is rendered with a type of *gamaka* (ornament) called the *kampita*, which consists of a shake of a definite interval, rather than just an indefinite vibrato. In such a style, it is difficult for the uninitiated listener to distinguish the basic melody that is being performed. Performances in varika style vary with the rāga. Rāga Māyāmālavagaula is a "sarva svara gamaka varika rāga," which means that every pitch (sarva svara) can be played or sung with ornamentation (gamaka, which in this case is the kampita). Rāga Shankarābharana is another sarva svara gamaka varika rāga.

In some Karnatak rāgas, specific pitches are subject to specific ornamentation. In Rāga Shrī (see Example 3-11), pitch Ga (in descent only) is sung or played with an undulating vibrato called *andolan*. The composer of the modern Rāga Dvigāṅdhārabushini, Pandit Subba Rao, has suggested that in performing this rāga a "long continued andolan on pitch Ri sounds beautiful"[19].

EXAMPLE 3-13 Ornamentation of Rāga Dvigāṅdhārabushini

[19]Subba Rao, *Raganidhi*, Vol. II, pp. 52–53.

In Rāga Devagāṅdhāri, pitches Ri and Dha are kampita svaras (performed with kampita). In some rāgas, such as Khamās, no particular ornamentation is required.

The Karnatak melodic concepts discussed thus far are in some ways similar to the melodic concepts of the Hindustānī tradition. In both traditions, rāga involves selection of pitches, melodic contour, intonation, pitch functions, and ornamentation. Within each of these analytical categories, however, the details can differ considerably.

ORIGIN OF RĀGAS

The derivation of particular rāgas is a fascinating and puzzling subject. Some rāgas are thought to have developed from tunes that became stylized, their characteristics then being employed for improvisation and the invention of other tunes. This may have occurred especially with rāgas that have distinctive melodic shapes. The names of some rāgas have been helpful to scholars attempting to establish their origins. Malava, Sindhu, Karnātaka, Jaunpurī, and Baṅgāla, for example, are place-names; whether the rāgas of these names were developed from regional melodies or simply evolved in those places, however, is difficult to ascertain. The names of the rāgas Saka, Ahīri, Sāverī (Āsāvarī), and Gujari indicate possible origins in tribal music; those of the rāgas Hejaj, Zila, Imam, and Shahāna are associated with Islamic culture. Some rāgas bear the names of the artists who "composed" them. For example, Miyāṅ kī Toḍī (for Miyan Tansen) and Vilas Khāni Toḍī (for Miyāṅ's son Vilas Khān) are two varieties of Rāga Toḍī. Bhairavī, Kedār, Sarasvati, and Shrī are rāgas named for Hindu deities.

Old and new rāgas intermingle in the contemporary repertoire. The names of the ancient ones have been in currency for a very long time. Most likely, these older rāgas have changed in time while their names remained the same. In his study of the history of Rāga Toḍī, for example, Powers found that it occurs in both Karnatak and Hindustānī music, but in different forms.[20] Concentrating on the *names* of rāgas as his historical clue, Powers explored the possibility that presently different rāgas with the same name may have developed out of a single rāga. By analyzing discussions of both the Karnatak and Hindustānī forms of Toḍī, he found that the two are treated in a more similar fashion than their forms would lead one to expect.

The relationship of other Hindustānī and Karnatak rāgas is less difficult to trace. Nowadays performers in one tradition seem to feel quite free to adopt a rāga from the other tradition and make it their own. Some-

[20]See Powers, "Classification of Rāgas," pp. 1–78.

times this is designated in the name. For instance, Rāga Hindustānī Bihāg, may be featured in a Karnatak concert. Rāga Hansnārāyanī of Hindustānī music derives most likely from the Karnatak Rāga Hansanārāyanī. If such borrowing is current today, it is possible, if not probable, that it has always been the custom.

New rāgas are being created every day. Some will remain in currency, and some will disappear. Hindustānī musicians like to combine two rāgas in order to obtain a different one. This is frequently but not always the explanation for a double rāga name, such as Bhīmpalāsī (Bhīm plus Palāsī). The means of utilizing aspects of two rāgas in one rāga is often to take the lower portion (*poorvāṅga*, amply translated as "lower tetrachord") of one rāga and the upper tetrachord (*uttarāṅga* or *upāṅga*) of another. This occurs in the Hindustānī Rāg Ahīr-Bhairav, for example, in which the pitches and phrases of the lower tetrachord are from Rāg Bhairav and those of the upper from Rāg Kāfī.[21] As shown in Example 3-14, the result is as follows:

Bhairav — Bhairav

Sa Re♭ Ga Ma Pa Dha Ni♭ Ṡa Ṙe♭ Ġa

Kāfī

EXAMPLE 3-14 Rāg Ahīr-Bhairav

In the Hindustānī tradition in particular, rāgas are felt to express specific moods. A rāga should be performed in keeping with its mood in order for it to evoke that mood in those who understand it and hear the rāga that is supposed to express it. Mood and time of day are also felt to be interrelated. Thus performing a rāga in keeping with its mood extends to performing it at the appropriate time of day.

Rāg Mālkosh, it is said, should be performed in a very serious mood. Likewise, Darbārī-Kanaṛā is to be treated in a dignified manner—very

[21] A fine recording of Ahīr-Bhairav is International Music Council's Musicaphon BM 30 SL 2051.

slowly. Both these rāgas should be performed at night. Āsāvarī, a quiet, gentle rāga, is to be sung in the morning. Sāraṅg portrays the tender mood of midday. Yaman, considered a soothing rāga and one that brings luck, is usually performed in the evening at the beginning of a concert.[22]

Some rāgas are also associated with a season—this also for reasons of mood. The Hindustānī Mallar groups of rāgas belong to the monsoon season. During this period, they can be performed at any time of day; in other seasons, they are performed only in the late afternoon or evening.[23] The mood of one of these rāgas, Megh-Mallar, has been depicted in a painting, which in turn is described in this poetic inscription:

> Megh-Mallar is a good, wise king. He dances well and enjoys the pleasures of life with gay abandon. Of a slightly dusky complexion with bright shining eyes, king Megh-Mallar is dressed handsomely, wearing a tiger skin, and adorned with various kinds of bright ornaments. He is in the company of beautiful maidens bedecked with jewels. The king dances with them to the resounding beat of drums and clapping. The dancing and music bring forth clouds of various colors in the sky. The moving clouds thicken to the accompaniment of thunder and lightning, which brings the rain.[24]

The tradition of relating particular rāgas to particular hours of the day or to a particular season of the year, as a way of expressing the moods that rāgas can evoke, has existed for centuries. It may have originated with the practice in early centuries of associating particular music with successive formal stages of the classic Sanskrit drama:

> The idea of assigning melody-types to the successive junctures of the play is easily transferred to the assigning of melody-types to the successive seasons of the year, or the successive hours of the day and night; and the association of a musical entity or musical type with the circumstances and emotional state of a character at a particular moment in a play is not too far from that association of a particular rāga with a particular human or divine personality in a specific physical and emotional state.[25]

The appropriateness of associating a rāga with a specific time of day is partially a matter of the moods that certain combinations of pitches evoke. One writer, for example, associates specific pitches with the psychological significance of the passing of night into day and day into night, saying, "It is the time of mental twilight between the conscious and the non-conscious: a time when one sits for prayer and meditation. The dissonances engendered by

[22] Kaufman, *Ragas of North India*, p. 62.

[23] *Ibid.*, p. 394.

[24] *Ibid.*, p. 396. The painting described here is of the type called *rāgamāla* ("rāga painting"). It is housed at the Art Institute of Chicago.

[25] Powers, "Classification of Rāgas," p. 11.

Ri [komal], Dha [komal], and Ni [shuddh] go well with the 'dreamy' state of mind during these hours."[26] Rāgas associated with the juncture of day and night (which are called *sandhi prakash rāgas*) are also likely to include tivra Ma.

The great Hindustānī musicologist V. N. Bhaṭkhande held that both pitch hierarchy and the tetrachord in which the most important pitch (vādī) appears are also important factors in time-of-day association.[27] Rāgas that stress the upper tetrachord (*uttarāṅga rāgas*), Ma to Sȧ, and include in it their most important pitches are assigned to the later part of the day or night. Rāgas that stress the lower tetrachord (*poorvāṅga rāgas*), Sa to Pa, and include in it their most important pitches are assigned to the time after twilight or dawn.[28] According to Hindustānī musical tradition, the day is divided into eight watches of three hours each, beginning at sunrise (see Chart 5). Chaitanya Deva, an Indian musicologist and scientist, specifies the hours shown in the chart,[29] Walter Kaufmann, though also listing eight three-hour watches, has the first watch begin at 7 A.M. rather than 6 A.M.[30] In the chart, each watch of the day is labeled with a Roman numeral, and the pitches associated with each watch are boxed. Rāgas performed during a certain watch are likely to include the pitches associated with that watch.

It is necessary to stress the flexibility (some would term it disagreement) in applying this general principle of association of rāga with time of day. Kaufmann speaks of this flexibility in regard to Rāg Hindol, a rāga associated with spring (March and April):

> North Indian musicians have differing views about the vadis of this raga. Some hold that the vadi is DHA (A) and the samvadi is GA (E) and that the highly placed vadi serves as an indicator of the performance time, the morning. Others, however, insist that the vadi is GA (E) and the samvadi is DHA (A), which transforms *Hindol* into an evening rāga. Nevertheless, the general view is that *Hindol* is to be performed in the morning. If the raga is correctly performed, its *rasa* represents quiet, dignified joy.[31]

The expression of quiet, dignified joy through Rāg Hindol, seriousness through Rāg Mālkosh, or the gentle quietude of the morning through Rāg Āsāvarī is the musical expression of rasa. Not so much the rasa felt by the robber Kenaram and Bangshi Das, who were "transported to a state of reverie, of aesthetic bliss," as a more general ethos spoken of in such terms as

[26]B. Chaitanya Deva, *Indian Music* (New Delhi: Indian Council for Cultural Relations, 1974), p. 20.

[27]Nazir Jairazbhoy, *The Rāgs of North Indian Music* (Middletown Conn.: Wesleyan University Press, 1971), p. 43.

[28]Deva, *Indian Music*, pp. 19–20.

[29]*Ibid.*, p. 19 (chart modified slightly).

[30]Kaufmann, *Ragas of North India*, p. 15.

[31]*Ibid.*, pp. 114, 116.

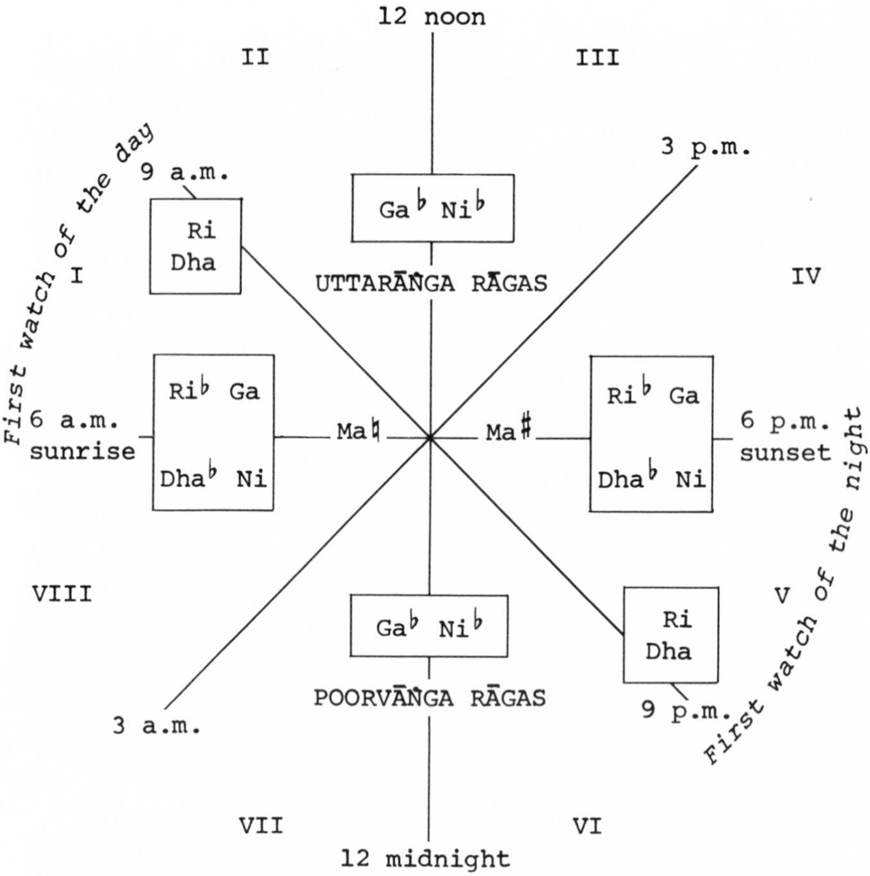

CHART 5. Rāgas and Watches of the Day

steadiness, calm, fatigue, yearning, flirtation, heaviness, lightness, joy, and the like.

Chaitanya Deva tested the psychological effects of the pitches in rāgas and found no causal nexus—with the possible exception of pitch tivra Ma[32]. His desire to conduct such a test is reminiscent of the reactions of Western critics, theorists, and psychologists to the strong emphasis placed upon mood designation and connotation in nineteenth-century Western music, such as the use of descriptive programs by composers of instrumental music. (The designation of a mood for a rāga seems very similar.) Speaking to such mood designation in Western music, Leonard Meyer advanced an analysis that could have been written by an Indian aesthetician:

> . . . all significant responses to music, the affective and aesthetic as well as the designative and connotative, vary with our experience and impressibility. The

[32]See Deva's *Psychoacoustics of Music and Speech* (Madras: The Music Academy, 1967).

> response to style is a learned response, and both the appreciation of style and the ability to learn require intelligence and musical sensitivity. . . there is a causal nexus [between music and referential experience], as is evidenced not only by the practice of composers within a given style but also by the responses of listeners who have learned to understand the style.[33]

Here we have the essentially Indian theory of rasa and *rasika*, as stated for poetry in the eighth to tenth centuries A.D. and espoused for music thereafter.

The associations of mood and time of day with rāgas are still a vital part of Hindustānī tradition. The national radio system schedules performances accordingly, and most artists feel that they should maintain the tradition. However, in Karnatak music today, as musicologist P. Sambamoorthy notes, "there is no questioning the fact that the rāgas sung during their alloted times sound best, but the time-theory of rāgas, generally speaking, may be said to be . . . only advisory and not mandatory."[34] South Indian theory recognizes that all rāgas evoke aesthetic enjoyment. Not all rāgas, however, evoke a particular feeling. Those that do are classified as *rakti rāgas*. This type of rāga is most appropriate for music with words, since the rasa expressed by the text (*sāhitya*) can complement the rasa of the rāga. Rāgas that express a universal emotional feeling are called *ghana rāgas*. The casual attitude toward time-of-day associations and the classification of rāgas into rakti and ghana rasa in South Indian music, in contrast with North Indian practice, are two more examples of how one ancient system has developed into two distinct traditions.

CLASSIFICATION OF RĀGAS

With all the diversity in Karnatak and Hindustānī rāgas, it should not be surprising that scholars have sought to classify them according to some manageable system. Various criteria have been tried through the centuries: musical entities associated with successive formal stages of the classical Sanskrit drama (in the *Nāṭya Śāstra*); style of performance (in the *Bṛihaddeśī*); a system in which main rāgas predominate over female rāgas (*rāginīs*) and sons (*putras*), by some unexplained connection; and general musical characteristics, such as register, pitch hierarchy, melodic shape and mood, and scale type. The most recently adopted means of classifying Hindustānī and Karnatak rāgas is by scale type—called *ṭhāṭ* in the North and *mela* in the South.

[33]Leonard Meyer, *Emotion and Meaning in Music* (Chicago: University of Chicago Press, 1965), pp. 270–71.

[34]Sambamoorthy, *South Indian Music*, Vol. V, p. 245.

Attention to classification has been much greater in the South than in the North. The system in current use there (the *melakarta* rāga system) is found in a recognizably related form as early as the seventeenth century, whereas the Hindustānī ṭhāṭ system is of this century. Furthermore, the melakarta system is endorsed almost universally in South India, whereas the validity of Bhaṭkhande's ṭhāṭ system is still widely disputed in the North.

The classificatory approach to life has been widely applied in the Hindu tradition. Classification as such seems to have been primarily a concern of Hindu rather than Muslim culture in India. Sanskrit poetics, a discipline subject to much theorizing by Hindu pandits from about the eighth century A.D., "grew out of the very practical object of methodically analysing and classifying the decorative devices of expression by themselves, with a view to prescribing definite rules of composition; and this pedagogic outlook undoubtedly received great impetus from the highly developed analytic enquiry into the forms of language made by the normative grammarians."[35] That inquiry into the forms of language laid the groundwork for what has now become the field of linguistics.

After the arrival of the peoples of Islamic faith in India, music making gradually became largely a Muslim sphere in North India. It remained a Hindu sphere in South India. Classification was pursued hotly in South India, but was practically ignored in the North until this century.

The ṭhāṭ system is based on musical practice. That is, it was devised as a means of organizing existing rāgas into groups with basically the same pitch selection. The melakarta rāga system is more theoretical. It was devised as a means of organizing all rāgas that *could* exist, whether or not they already did.

Bhaṭkhande suggested ten ṭhāṭs. These ten ṭhāṭs (see Chart 6) are the basic tunings for a Hindustānī stringed instrument with movable frets, the sitār (see Chapter Four). They are scale types, not rāgas.

1.	Kalyān	Sa	Re	Ga	Ma♯	Pa	Dha	Ni	Ṡa
2.	Bilaval	Sa	Re	Ga	Ma	Pa	Dha	Ni	Ṡa
3.	Khamāj	Sa	Re	Ga	Ma	Pa	Dha	Ni♭	Ṡa
4.	Bhairav	Sa	Re♭	Ga	Ma	Pa	Dha♭	Ni	Ṡa
5.	Pūrvi	Sa	Re♭	Ga	Ma♯	Pa	Dha♭	Ni	Ṡa
6.	Mārvā	Sa	Re♭	Ga	Ma♯	Pa	Dha	Ni	Ṡa
7.	Kāfī	Sa	Re	Ga♭	Ma	Pa	Dha	Ni♭	Ṡa
8.	Āsāvārī	Sa	Re	Ga♭	Ma	Pa	Dha♭	Ni♭	Ṡa
9.	Bhairavī	Sa	Re♭	Ga♭	Ma	Pa	Dha♭	Ni♭	Ṡa
10.	Toḍī	Sa	Re♭	Ga♭	Ma♯	Pa	Dha♭	Ni	Ṡa

CHART 6. Hindustānī Ṭhāṭs

[35]S. K. De, *Sanskrit Poetics as a Study of Aesthetics* (Berkeley and Los Angeles: University of California Press, 1963), pp. 2–3.

For each ṭhāṭ there is also a rāga of the same name. But the rāga also involves a group of characteristics, like those described earlier in this chapter—pitch hierarchy, ascent-descent form, characteristic melodic motion or ornamentation, and the like. Example 3-15 shows Āsāvarī ṭhāṭ and three rāgas that belong in it—Rāg Āsāvarī and two rāgas, Desī and Komal Re Āsāvarī, whose configurations have been discussed in this chapter.

EXAMPLE 3-15 Āsāvarī Ṭhāṭ Rāgas

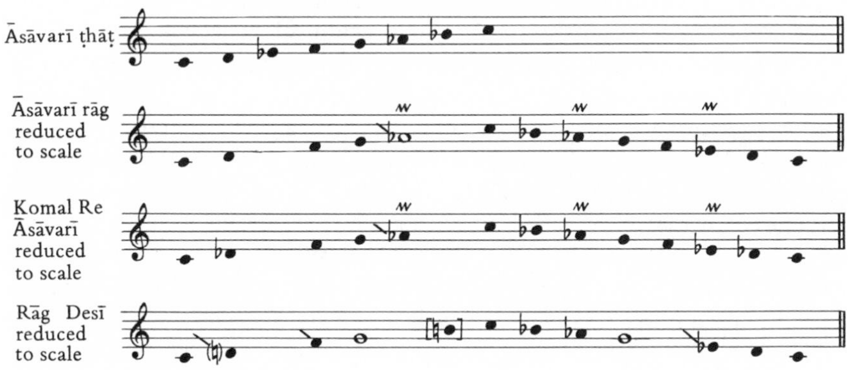

One of the difficulties of Bhaṭkhande's ṭhāṭ system is that he did not explain thoroughly his reasons for classifying certain rāgas together. For example, Rāg Komal Re Āsāvarī, strictly speaking, includes the pitches of Bhairavī ṭhāṭ, but it is not classified as such because of other of its characteristics, which are very close to those of Rāg Āsāvarī.[36] Rāg Mālkosh, on the other hand, has the pitches of both Bhairavī and Āsāvarī ṭhāṭ but by tradition it is classified as belonging to Bhairavī ṭhāṭ (see Example 3-16).

Another difficulty with the Bhaṭkhande ṭhāṭ system is that there are not enough ṭhāṭs to include the variety of scale types that currently appear in

EXAMPLE 3-16 Classification of Rāg Malkosh

[36]In fact, Rāg Komal Re Āsāvarī is sometimes classified in Bhairav ṭhāṭ, which theoretically includes neither Ga nor Ni.

rāgas. To counter this, musicologist Nazir Jairazbhoy has suggested effective extension of the system to 32 ṭhāṭs.[37] But however many scale types there could be, other factors seem as important, if not more so, in Hindustānī rāga. A wholly successful means of classification has not yet been achieved.

The Karnatak system of classification by scale type is worked out far more thoroughly and seems to be more appropriate for the types of rāgas for which it was developed. The significance of a statement made above can be seen more clearly here: ". . . the South Indian [melodic] system on the whole tends to generalize rāgas in the direction of scales while the North Indian system on the whole tends to particularize them in the direction of tunes."[38]

The Karnatak system consists of 72 mela rāgas (scale types), 36 with Ma♮ and 36 with Ma♯. Each of the 72 mela rāgas contains the seven basic pitches (Sa, Ri, Ga, Ma, Pa, Dha, and Ni) in some form. The system is structured so that each variety of each pitch is combined with each variety of each of the other pitches. The idea is to classify all the combinations that *could* occur in a rāga rather than only those combinations that *do* occur in currently used rāgas.

The 72 "parent scales" in the melakarta rāga system appear in Chart 7. The mela rāgas are grouped into twelve subdivisions (*chakras*), each comprising six melas. Chakras I through VI are named Indu, Netra, Agni, Veda, Bana, and Rutu; they are on the left-hand side of the chart. They include melakarta rāgas 1 through 36, each of which includes Sa, Shuddha Ma (Ma♮), Pa, and some form of Ri, Ga, Dha, and Ni. Chakras VII through XII, on the right-hand side of the chart, are named Rishi, Vasu, Brahma, Disi, Rudra, and Aditya. They include melakarta rāgas 37 through 72, each of which includes Sa, Prati Ma (Ma♯), Pa, and some form of Ri, Ga, Dha, and Ni.

Within each chakra, the pitches of the lower tetrachord remain constant; differences appear only in the upper tetrachord. In Chakra I (Indu), the scales of each of the melakarta rāgas differ by one pitch, as follows:

						change	
Kanakāngi	Sa	Ra	Ga	Ma	Pa	Dha	Na
Ratnāngi	Sa	Ra	Ga	Ma	Pa	Dha	Ni
Gānamūrti	Sa	Ra	Ga	Ma	Pa	Dha	Nu
Vanaspati	Sa	Ra	Ga	Ma	Pa	Dhi	Ni
Mānavati	Sa	Ra	Ga	Ma	Pa	Dhi	Nu
Tānarūpi	Sa	Ra	Ga	Ma	Pa	Dhu	Nu

[37]Jairazbhoy, *Rāgs of North Indian Music*, pp. 181–85.
[38]Powers, "Classification of Rāgas," p. 17.

SUDDHA MADHYAMA MELAS (Ma♮)	CHAKRA NO. AND NAME	PURVANGA	MELA NO.	UTTAR-ANGA	MELA NO.	CHAKRA NO. AND NAME	PURVANGA	PRATI MADHYAMA MELAS (Ma♯)
Kanakāngi	I INDU	ra–ga	1	dha–na	37	VII RISHI	ra–ga	Sālagam
Ratnāngi			2	dha–ni	38			Jalārnavam
Gānamūrti			3	dha–nu	39			Jhālavaīāli
Vanaspati			4	dhi–ni	40			Navanītam
Mānavati			5	dhi–nu	41			Pāvani
Tānarūpi			6	dhu–nu	42			Raghupriya
Senāvati	II NETRA	ra–gi	7	dha–na	43	VIII VASU	ra–gi	Gavāmbodhi
Hanumatodi			8	dha–ni	44			Bhavapriya
Dhenuka			9	dha–nu	45			Subhapantuvarāli
Nātakapriya			10	dhi–ni	46			Shadvidhamārgini
Kokilapriya			11	dhi–nu	47			Suvarnāngi
Rūpavati			12	dhu–nu	48			Divyamani
Gāyakapriya	III AGNI	ra–gu	13	dha–na	49	IX BRAHMA	ra–gu	Dhavalāmbari
Vakulābharanam			14	dha–ni	50			Nāmanārayani
Māyāmālavagaula			15	dha–nu	51			Kāmavardhani
Chakravākam			16	dhi–ni	52			Rāmapriya
Sūryakāntam			17	dhi–nu	53			Gamanasrama
Hātakāmbari			18	dhu–nu	54			Visvambhari
Jhankāradhvani	IV VEDA	ri–gi	19	dha–na	55	X DISI	ri–gi	Syāmalāngi
Nathabhairavi			20	dha–ni	56			Shanmukhapriya
Kiravāni			21	dha–nu	57			Simhendramadhyama
Kharaharapriya			22	dhi–ni	58			Hemavati
Gaūrīmanohari			23	dhi–nu	59			Dharmavati
Varunapriya			24	dhu–nu	60			Nitimati
Māraranjani	V BANA	ri–gu	25	dha–na	61	XI RUDRA	ri–gu	Kāntāmani
Chārukesi			26	dha–ni	62			Rishabhapriya
Sarasāngi			27	dha–nu	63			Latāngi
Harikāmbhoji			28	dhi–ni	64			Vāchaspati
Dhīrasankarābharana			29	dhi–nu	65			Mechakalyāni
Nāgānandini			30	dhu–nu	66			Chitrāmbari
Yāgapriya	VI RUTU	ru–gu	31	dha–na	67	XII ADITYA	ru–gu	Sucharitra
Rāgavardhani			32	dha–ni	68			Jyotisvarūpini
Gāngeyabhūshani			33	dha–nu	69			Dhātuvardhani
Vāgadhīsvari			34	dhi–ni	70			Nāsikābhūshani
Sūlini			35	dhi–nu	71			Kosalam
Chalanāta			36	dhu–nu	72			Rasikapriya

CHART 7. Melakarta Rāga System

In another form, those would read:

Kanakāngi	Sa	Ri_1	Ga_1	Ma_1	Pa	Dha_1	Ni_1
Ratnāngi	Sa	Ri_1	Ga_1	Ma_1	Pa	Dha_1	Ni_2
Gānamūrti	Sa	Ri_1	Ga_1	Ma_1	Pa	Dha_1	Ni_3
Vanaspati	Sa	Ri_1	Ga_1	Ma_1	Pa	Dha_2	Ni_2
Mānavati	Sa	Ri_1	Ga_1	Ma_1	Pa	Dha_2	Ni_3
Tānarūpi	Sa	Ri_1	Ga_1	Ma_1	Pa	Dha_3	Ni_3

Dha_2 is not paired with Ni_1, nor Dha_3 with Ni_2, because they are enharmonic spellings of the same pitches. (The numbering and solfège of the Karnatak pitches appears in Chart 4.) Nor is Dha_3 paired with Ni_1, because the pitch of the latter is lower than that of the former, and the melakarta rāgas must be in ascending scale order.

The scales in the melakarta rāga system are not actual rāgas, just as the Hindustānī ṭhāṭs are not rāgas; they are scale types. They are also called *janaka rāgas*, or rāgas that generate other rāgas. There are, however, rāgas with the same name as the names of melas; these are also referred to as melakarta rāgas. Rāga Māyāmālavagaula is one of that sort. It is the fifteenth melakarta rāga, and the third rāga in chakra III (Agni); as such, it is called Agni-go.[39] We can find it accordingly on the chart, and we would know that it includes the pitches Sa, Ra, Gu, Ma, Pa, Dha, and Nu (Sa, Ri_1, Ga_3, Ma_1, Pa, Dha_1, and Ni_3).

Other rāgas, called *janya* (or "generated") *rāgas*, are grouped with the melakarta rāgas. These are rāgas that omit one or more of the seven pitches, feature melodic curves (which makes them vakra rāgas), or have their compass delineated. Example 3-17 presents two janya rāgas (Shrī and Saindhavi) that are grouped with melakarta rāga 22, Kharaharapriya. Rāga Shrī omits Ga and Dha in ascent and is a vakra rāga, and the compass of Rāga Saindhavi goes no higher than madhya Ni. It is difficult to designate which mela a janya rāga belongs with when one or two of its notes are omitted in ascent and descent. Some of the melakarta rāgas have quite a number of janya rāgas associated with them, but others have few.

Constant reference is made to the melakarta scheme, but people do not carry a copy of the chart with them. For this reason, it was deemed necessary to find an efficient way for a person to determine the form of a given melakarta rāga without knowing the names of all the melakarta rāgas and the form of each. Consequently, the method was adopted of numbering the rāgas from 1 to 72 (as shown in Chart 7) and coordinating these numbers with the initial syllables of the melakarta name, as explained below.

[39]The syllables pa, sri, go, bhū, mā, and sha, denote, respectively, the first, second, third, fourth, fifth, and sixth melas in a chakra. (P. Sambamoorthy, *History of Indian Music* [Madras: The Indian Music Publishing House, 1960], p. 48)

EXAMPLE 3-17 Janya Rāgas of Kharaharapriya

If we know the number of the melakarta rāga whose form we wish to determine, we then know immediately whether suddha or prati Ma is used. Then, by knowing which melakarta numbers fall into which chakras, we can pinpoint the chakra to which our rāga belongs. This accomplished, we need know only the characteristics of that chakra and the pattern of change within it in order to determine the form of the rāga.

If, for example, a particular rāga is a "janya of the forty-seventh melakarta rāga" and we wish to know which pitches may be used in that rāga, we would utilize the following process to find out. It is clear from the number 47 that prati Ma (Ma♯) would be included, since melas 37 through 72 use Ma♯. Since Sa and Pa may be used in all melas, three pitches are known: Sa, Ma♯, and Pa. It is also easy to determine that the forty-seventh melakarta will fall in Chakra VIII. Six melas in each chakra divided into 47 melas equals 7, plus a remainder of 5. Thus, the rāga should be the fifth mela in the chakra after the seventh chakra—that is, Chakra VIII. Having learned that melas in the eighth chakra have Ra and Gi in their lower tetrachord, we now know that the following pitches are possible in the janya rāga: Sa, Ra, Gi, Ma♯, and Pa. Only the pitches in the upper tetrachord are missing. Having also learned that the fifth mela within every chakra uses Dhi and Nu, we conclude that the seven possible pitches in this janya rāga are Sa, Ra, Gi, Ma♯, Pa, Dhi, and Nu (Sa, Ri_1, Ga_2, Ma_2, Pa, Dha_2, and Ni_3). The rāga is thus a janya rāga of the melakarta Suvarnāngi.

If, on the other hand, we know that a rāga is a janya of Suvarnāngi but we do not know what its melakarta number is, we must use a different process of deduction to discover which pitches might be used. At this point, we turn to the *Kaṭapayadi formula.* With this formula, the melakarta number can be determined from the first two syllables of the melakarta name—for example, "su" and "va" in the case of Suvarnāngi, and "mā" and "yā" in the case of Māyāmālavagaula. This is possible because the formula has assigned a number to each syllable (actually, to each consonant of the syllable), according to the order in which it appears in the Sanskrit alphabet. The Kaṭapayadi formula is based on the following four subdivisions of the Sanskrit alphabet:[40]

ka di nava—a series of nine (nava) letters beginning with ka (क)

ṭa di nava—a series of nine (nava) letters beginning with ṭa (ट)

pa di pancha—a series of five (pancha) letters beginning with pa (प)

yād yashta—a series of eight (yashta) letters beginning with ya (य)

Chart 8 presents the alphabet and the corresponding numbers assigned by the formula. Note that in the Sanskrit alphabet, each consonant is followed by an aspirated form: k, kh; g, gh, and so forth. Thus, the syllable "su" (सु) is the number 7, and "va" is 4. "Ma" is 5, and "ya" is 1. If we combine the numbers for "suva" and "māyā," we have 74 and 51. However, we must then reverse these numbers in order to obtain the melakarta numbers: 47 instead of 74, 15 instead of 51.

	1	2	3	4	5	6	7	8	9	0
Kadinava	k	kh	g	gh	ng	ch	chh	j	jh	jn
Ṭadinava	ṭ	ṭh	ḍ	ḍh	ṇ	t	th	d	dh	n
Padipancha	p	ph	b	bh	m					
Yādyashta	y	r	l	v	ś	sh	s	h		

CHART 8. Kaṭapayadi Formula

What is the number of melakarta Kanakāngi? Ka is 1 and na is 0; reverse them to get 01, the first mela. Ratnāngi? Ra is 2, but what does one do with two conjunct consonants, such as "tnā" of the second syllable? The rule is that the consonant immediately before the vowel should be taken into consideration. Thus, "nā" yields the number 0; reverse the two numbers to get 02, the second mela. The inevitable exceptions to this rule are melas Chakravākam (16), Divyamani (48), Visvambhari (54), Syāmalāngi (55), Simhendramadhyama (57), Chitrāmbari (66), and Jyotisvarūpini (68), in which the first consonant gives the number.[41] Whereas some of the mela

[40]Adapted from Sambamoorthy, *South Indian Music*, Vol. III, pp. 40–41. Note that the consonants, as written here, include a short "a"—ka, ta, and so on. To indicate a long "a" (ā) or any other vowel, one must add an additional sign. However, it is only the consonants that are important here.

[41]*Ibid.*, pp. 41–42.

names are the original rāga names, others, such as Mālavagaula have had the necessary prefix added to provide a number. The Kaṭapayadi formula does not apply to the names of janya rāgas.

The elaborate systemization involved in rāga classification in the Karnatak tradition would seem to arise at least partially from a love of classifying. This is not an intellectual pleasure shared by many scholars (not to mention performers) of Hindustānī music. However, this classification scheme receives unkind words even from some Karnatak musicians, who feel that it has restricted the whole sphere of melody. Theory does seem to have influenced the practice of music in this case. When the author of this system of 72 melakarta rāgas, Venkatamakhi, first advocated it in his treatise *Caturdandiprakāshika* (1666), he stated that only 19 of the 72 scale types were current at that time. He classified the remaining 53 as "in the process of making" and "to be made hereafter." It took a while for the system to become widespread, but finally it became such a "musical presence" that composers wrote specifically for even the originally theoretical mela rāgas. A few composers—Kotisvara Ayer (1869–1938), for example—even wrote in each of the 72 melas.

This process of basing practice on theory is the opposite of the Hindustānī process, in which theory is based on practice. So little attention is paid to developing theory in the North that no conclusive (or even nearly conclusive) system of classifying rāgas has been devised there. Neither the Hindustānī nor the Karnatak melodic tradition takes the middle path. The South Indian tradition encompasses more possibilities than are current, and the North Indian tradition leaves unclassified many that are current. This is certainly a major distinction between the two traditions

What remains most pertinent in both traditions is not only theory but practice. There is so much evidence that flexibility in practice is the rule, rather than the exception, that performance practice must be given the final word in any discussion. Not enough work has been done on comparative performance practice for us to know if the distinction between the Karnatak and Hindustānī traditions of melodic theory exists in practice as well.

This exposition of rāga, which has only suggested the abundance, the variety, and the complexity of the subject of Indian melody, gives us a glimpse into the mind of the solo artist as he sits on the stage. The glimpse has been only of what he could choose from—rāgas that will suit his mood, the mood and time of the occasion, and the taste of his audience. The drone will be there, giving him Sa (and also Pa or Ma) as a steady base. With so much to recreate in one rāga, it is no wonder that all attention will be focused on only one line—the improvised melody in the rāga or the lines of a song.

We turn now to the melody-making instruments used in the North and South Indian traditions of classical music.

FOUR
MELODY INSTRUMENTS

A profusion of instruments is a part of Indian musical history. In the *Nāṭya Śāstra* (c. 200 B.C.–A.D. 600?), we find an early mention of instruments in India. They were of four types, says the treatise: stringed instruments (*tāta vādya*), wind instruments (*sushira vādya*), instruments struck against each other, such as cymbals (*ghana vādya*), and instruments with membranes (*avanaḍḍha vādya*). This classification, based on elements that vibrate to produce sound, is now the most widely accepted system of classification in the West, where the four categories are called cordophones (stringed instruments), aerophones (wind instruments), idiophones (self-vibrators), and membranophones. The instruments discussed in this chapter are of the stringed and wind categories—tāta vādya and sushira vādya—and also the voice, the most esteemed of all melody instruments in India.

A thirteenth-century treatise, the *Saṅgīta Ratnākara*, offered another system of classification, one that is based on the function of instruments: solo playing (*sushkam*); accompaniment to vocal music (*gītanugam*); accompaniment to dance (*nrittānugam*); and accompaniment to both dance and vocal music (*dvayānugam*).[1] These categories establish one very important point: of the large variety of instruments used in Indian classical music, many have been used for accompaniment as well as, or rather than, for solo performance.

TĀTA VĀDYA: THE STRINGED INSTRUMENTS

In South India, the vīṇā (veena) is the most popular stringed instrument; it is also the oldest type of stringed instrument mentioned in the literature. There has been much discussion and a great deal of disagreement about the instrument called vīṇā in the Vedic writings (1500–500 B.C.). "Vīṇā" has been loosely translated as "lute," and the ancient vīṇā apparently was similar to the instruments used in the ancient Egyptian and Middle Eastern civilizations. The consensus is that it had a hollow belly covered with a board or stretched leather. "The belly is broader towards the back where its end is rounded and tapers toward the front, and it is continued into an upstanding curved arm. The strings are stretched one above the other, from this arm to the belly. These strings vary in their length."[2] This type of vīṇā is found with minor variations in the sculptures of the temples at Sanchi, Bhaja, and Bharhut (second to first century B.C.), at Amaravati (first to second century A.D.), at Nagarjunkonda (second to fourth century A.D.), and at other places.[3] It is pictured placed on the lap and played either with the fingers or with a plectrum.

According to at least one Indian scholar, lute-type vīṇās (with a body and a neck) are found as early as the Amaravati and Nagarjunkonda sculptures of the first or second century A.D. Zither-type vīṇās (with strings stretching the entire length of the body) first appear in the Mahabalipuram reliefs of the sixth and seventh centuries A.D., as well as in the Ajanta (seventh century A.D.) and Ellora (eighth to eleventh century A.D.) cave paintings. All of these types of vīṇās lacked the frets that are now found on the South Indian vīṇā.[4]

One of the zither-type vīṇās consisted of a long pole called a *daṇḍa*, along which the strings were stretched. Resonance seems to have been provided by partial gourds or hollowed-out gourds, or wooden globes, one

[1] P. Sambamoorthy, *The Flute* (Madras: Indian Music Publishing House, 1967), p. 17.

[2] G. H. Tarlekar, "Fretted Vīṇā in Indian Sculpture," *Journal of the Music Academy, Madras*, 36 (1965), 170–71.

[3] See Ananda Coomaraswamy's report in the *Journal of the American Oriental Society*, I.

[4] Tarlekar, "Fretted Vīṇā," p. 171.

toward either end of the daṇḍa and attached to its underside. A twelfth century author, Hemachandra, likened the daṇḍa of a vīṇā to a youthful lover's arms lying over the breasts of his lady—the two gourds of the instrument.[5]

The means of playing the ancient vīṇā have been open to discussion. Bhasa, a dramatist who flourished sometime before the fifth century A.D., mentioned in a play that the vīṇā was played with the fingernails.[6] A modern author interprets a passage in the *Nāṭya Śāstra* as saying that the term "vīṇā" included intruments that could be bowed and instruments that were plucked with the fingernails of one hand.[7] Another modern author cites the *Nāṭya Śāstra* as saying that one type of vīṇā was played with a plectrum and another type with the fingernails.[8]

When such diverse sources as classical literature and Sanskrit treatises mention several different types of vīṇā, we can only conclude that the term "vīṇā" was a generic one. It probably included instruments that had somewhat different shapes and sizes, different numbers of strings, and different ways of being played. Judging from graphic and literary sources, Tarlekar suggests that the vīṇā with frets came into vogue somewhere between the tenth and eleventh centuries A.D.[9] We can be definite only about the forms of the vīṇā that exist now.

The instrument that resembles most closely the zither-type vīṇā described above is the Hindustānī vīṇā or *bīn*, also known as the *rudra vīṇā*, which is found today only in North India (see Plates 8a, 8b).[10] It consists of a stem about three feet long that supports a bamboo fretboard approximately twenty-two inches long and two and a half inches wide. It has twenty-four metal frets, which are set to the half-steps in two octaves. The frets are stationary, fixed in a resinous substance. The two resonating gourds are large, about fourteen inches in diameter. The bīn has four main playing strings, which are tuned to Ma, Sạ, Pạ, and Rẹ. This gives the instrument a total range of over three octaves. (Most of the melody, however, is produced on the first string, which is closest to the player's body.) Three additional strings, which are suspended on the sides and not over the frets, are tuned to Sȧ, Sa, and Sạ. These are drone and rhythm strings. The index and middle fingers of the right hand are

[5]N. B. Divatia, "The Vīṇā in Ancient Times," *Annals of the Bhandarkar Oriental Research Institute*, 12, no. 4 (July 1931), 370. The simile is from Hemachandra's *Triṣaṣṭi-śalākā-puruṣa-carita*, X, viii, 9, a description of the cold season.

[6]Divatia, "The Vīṇā," p. 362. Bhasa's comment is found in his *Pratijñá Yaugandharāyana*, Act II, st. 12.

[7]Divatia, "The Vīṇā," p. 364.

[8]P. S. R. Appa Rao, *A Monograph on bharata's naatya Saastra: Indian Dramatology*, trans. P. S. R. Appa Rao and P. Sri Rama Sastry (Hyderabad: Naatya Maalaa, 1967), p. 110.

[9]Tarlekar, "Fretted Vīṇā," p. 173.

[10]I am grateful to Peter Row, bīnkār (bīn player) and sitārist, for much of this information on the bīn.

Plate 8a
The Hindustānī Vīṇā (Bīn), as held by Asad Ali Khan

Plate 8b
The Hindustānī Bīn, as held by Z. M. Dagar

used for plucking the melody strings; the little finger plays the drone. The index and middle fingers and occasionally the ring finger of the left hand reach around from under the stem to stop the strings. The plectrum used for the bīn is like that of the sitār, but is worn sideways on the finger. Some binkārs use their fingernail rather than a plectrum for plucking. The performer sits cross-legged and holds the instrument at a slant to the left shoulder, the upper gourd resting on the shoulder and the lower gourd on the right knee.[11] A modern version of the bīn is shown in Plate 8b.

The bīn was the primary stringed instrument of Hindustānī classical music into the eighteenth century; it was used to accompany vocal music. As befit their musical role, bīn players (bīnkārs) at the courts of the Mughal emperors had to sit behind the vocalists whom they accompanied.[12] Good bīnkārs were honored musicians, however, and were well patronized. As the type of vocal music that the bīn accompanied gave way in popularity to other types, the use of the instrument declined. On the other hand, it was gradually developed into a concert (i.e., solo) instrument by such musicians as Wazir Khan of Rampur early in the twentieth century. It is seldom played nowadays, but aficionados appreciate its deep and full tone. Among the fine bīnkārs today are Zia Mohiuddin Dagar, Asad Ali Khan, Ahmed Raza, Gopal Krishna, and Peter Row.

The modern vīṇā used in Karnatak music is in some ways drastically different in construction from the northern vīṇā (bīn) (see Plate 9). Most

Plate 9
The Karnatak Vīṇā

[11]The bīn is not to be confused with the vichitra vīṇā, which was developed recently in the North. That instrument has a broader stem, no frets, and sympathetic strings. It is played with wire plectrums worn on the right-hand fingers. The notes are produced by a piece of rounded glass slid over the strings with the left hand. The vichitra vīṇā is somewhat like the gottuvadyam of the South. (S. Krishnaswamy, *Musical Instruments of India* [New Delhi: Government of India, Publications Division, 1965], p. 50.)

[12]O. Gosvami, *The Story of Indian Music* (Bombay: Asia Publishing House, 1957), p. 273.

noticeable is the repositioning of one of its gourds so that the stem runs into it and is thus part of the body of the instrument. This vīṇā is therefore a lute-type instrument rather than a zither, since its stem becomes a neck. Its "gourd" is not actually a gourd any longer; it is a hollowed-out chunk of wood, usually jackfruit, that is closed in by a flat piece of wood. At the opposite end of the stem is attached a "scroll," which is usually carved into the head of a dragon. With the dragon head covered with gold leaf, as it often is, and the rest of the instrument, including the remaining gourd, gaily painted, the modern vīṇā is a gorgeous instrument. The dragon's neck conceals a compartment containing a small amount of sandalwood paste that the player uses to help his fingers slide easily along the wire strings. "The Veena Daṉda represents Shiva, the strings Parvati, the dragon head Vishnu, the bridge Lakshmi, the balancing gourd Brahma, the connecting metal cone Sarasvati. . . . The Veena is thus the abode of divinity and the source of all happiness."[13]

The vīṇā's twenty-four metal frets, which are placed to produce the semitones of two octaves, are fixed in a resinous substance, as they are on the bīn. Also as on the bīn, the vīṇā has four playing strings and three strings (called *tālam* strings) used for drone and rhythm. The vīṇā is tuned as the bīn is. The player (*vainika*) sits cross-legged on the floor. The vīṇā is sometimes played vertically, like the bīn, but is generally played horizontally, with the bowl of the vīṇā on the ground but supported by the right thigh. The small balancing gourd is to the left, touching the left thigh, so the degree of slant is small. The index and middle fingers of the right hand pluck the main strings with wire plectrums or false fingernails while the little finger strokes the drone strings. The left-hand fingers stop the strings and pull them sideways over the frets to produce ornaments and additional pitches. One great vainika, Pithapuram Sangameswara Sastri of Andhra Pradesh (1874–1931), had his vīṇā made with a broader stem (daṇḍa). He is said to have specialized in producing a whole octave on a single fret by deflecting the string across the broad daṇḍa.[14]

"Till about thirty years ago the Veena was an aristocrat among instruments. Professional vainikas could be counted on one's fingers. Very few took to it as a pastime. It was a favourite with amateur lady singers whose fine voice blended with its delicate sound."[15] The vīṇā was and is used to accompany singing, and has also been a solo instrument. Today, many South Indians learn to play it. Some of the more prominent contemporary vīṇā artists are S. Balachander, K. N. Narayanaswami, Nageswara Rao, and D. N. Iyengar. Whether played by professionals or amateurs, as solo or

[13]R. Rangaramanuja Ayyangar, *History of South Indian* (*Carnatic*) *Music from Vedic Times to the Present* (Madras: R. Rangaramanuja Ayyangar, 1972), p. 113. According to B. Chaitanya Deva, *Indian Music* (New Delhi: Indian Council for Cultural Relations, 1974), p. 138, the dragon is the mythical animal *yah*.

[14]Ayyangar, *History of South Indian Music*, p. 273.

[15]*Ibid.*, p. 271.

accompaniment, in the past or in the present, the relationship of vīṇā to voice has been clear: "Between vocal and instrumental music the difference is slight, the vīṇā . . . being considered to be but an imitation or reproduction of the human voice."[16]

Many who have attended a concert of Indian music in the West have seen the sitār, most likely in the exquisite hands of Ravi Shankar. The sitār is the most popular stringed instrument of the plucked-lute variety in North India, and certainly the Indian instrument best known in the West (see Plate 10).

Plate 10
The Sitār (Peter Row, Sitārist)

The introduction of the sitār to India is attributed by legend to the thirteenth-century statesman, poet, and musician Amir Khusrau, who was prominent at the courts of Khilji and Tughlak sultans of Delhi. Khusrau was a descendant of a family who had migrated to India from an area of Central Asia that had been influenced by Persia. He became an accomplished Indian musician and is said to have introduced several Persian elements into Indian classical music, among them the sitār. Some say that the instrument Khusrau adapted and introduced to Indian classical music was the three-

[16]Charles R. Day, *The Music and Musical Instruments of Southern India and the Deccan* (London: Novello, 1891), pp. 60–61.

stringed Persian *sehtar* (*seh* meaning "three" and *tar*, "string"). Ravi Shankar suggests that Amir Khusrau adapted an instrument already known in various forms in India, probably the three-stringed (*trītantri*) vīṇā, to which he gave the Persian name *sehtar*. Khusrau is said to have reversed the order of the strings on this instrument and placed them as they are today—the main playing string on the outside and the bass strings closer to the player's body (the order opposite that of the strings on the bīn).[17]

Documentation of the history of the sitār between the thirteenth and eighteenth centuries is lacking. However, in sixteenth through seventeenth century Mughal paintings, instruments nearly identical with the Persian sehtar are frequently to be found. In the late eighteenth century, one Amrit Sen of Jaipur is said to have introduced three extra strings, thereby increasing the number of strings on the sitār to six, four for melody and two for drone and rhythm (*chikāri* strings). Later, a seventh string (a third chikāri string) was added.[18]

All sitār strings are metal, either copper, brass, bronze, or high-carbon steel. Tunings seem to be only somewhat standardized, as shown in Chart 9. In his discussion of the sitār, Shankar includes the chikāri strings among the playing strings. Unlike the drone strings on a bīn, the sitār chikāri strings extend over the frets.[19]

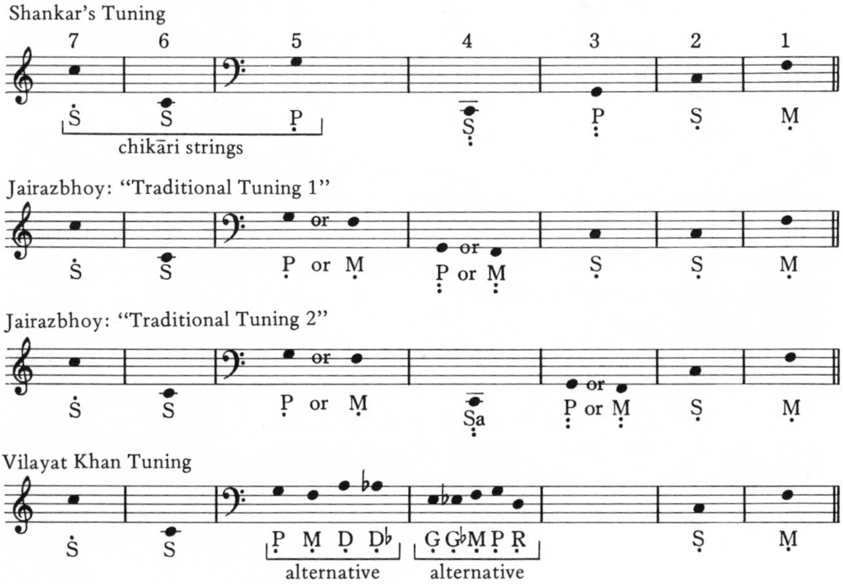

CHART 9. A Selection of Sitār Tunings

[17]Ravi Shankar, *My Music, My Life* (New York: Simon & Schuster, 1968), p. 46.
[18]Gosvami, *Story of Indian Music*, p. 301.
[19]For more specific information on the sitār, see Shankar, *My Music, My Life*, p. 102.

A number of very fine sitarists, not as well known in the West as Shankar, are famous in India. Vilayat Khan is the most outstanding of this group. His grandfather, Imdad Khan, and his father, Enayat Khan, were both preeminent musicians in their time. Vilayat is thus one in a long line of musicians who trace their ancestry back 300 years to North India's most famous musician, Tansen, and the court of the Mughal ruler Akbar. Vilayat Khan has evolved a new method of tuning the playing strings of the sitār, which necessitates the removal of the third string and the replacement of the heavier fourth and fifth strings by a single steel string. The effect of these changes is to eliminate the very low-pitched strings three and four, thereby reducing the range of the instrument. Vilayat Khan's tuning is shown in Chart 9.[20]

There are many other fine sitārists, some known in the West and others known only in India. Among them are Nikhil Banerjee, Debu Chaudhuri, Indernil Bhattacharya, Rais Khan, and Imrat Khan, known also for his artistry on the surbahar. (See the Discography for their recordings.)

The sitār differs in two significant respects from the bīn and the vīṇā. One difference is said to have been a Khusrau innovation: movable frets. Whereas the vīṇā has frets for every semitone in the theory system and fixes them in resin, the sitār has fewer frets (from sixteen to twenty-three on modern instruments, but usually nineteen), and they can be adjusted to the particular tuning (called a ṭhāṭ). The ten basic sitār ṭhāṭs are synonymous with the ten basic scale formations by which Hindustānī rāgas are most frequently classified (see Chart 6).

The other respect in which the sitār differs from the bīn and the vīṇā is that it has sympathetic strings. From twelve to twenty of these strings run parallel to, and below, the main strings. Tuned to the pitches of the rāga being played, they vibrate in sympathy with the playing strings, creating a metallic, shimmering effect. Occasionally, the sitārist will run his finger across them to test their tuning or, it seems, to create a lush sound effect.

The structure of the sitār is basically similar to that of the modern vīṇā. The stem of the sitār forms a neck that runs into a hollowed-out resonating chamber that is a gourd rather than wood. Therefore, it is a lute-type instrument, since its strings run along a neck and across the resonating chamber. A second and smaller gourd, detachable on most sitārs, is located at the top end of the instrument, near the tuning pegs. It functions as much for balance as for resonance. The frets are metal and are attached to the instrument with cords stretched across the underside of the neck.

Sitārists, like bīnkārs and vainikas, sit cross-legged while playing their instrument. The main gourd rests on the sole of the left foot, and the neck

[20]The two traditional tunings and Vilayat Khan's tuning in Chart 9 are from Nazir Jairazbhoy, *The Rāgs of North Indian Music* (Middletown, Conn.: Wesleyan University Press, 1971), pp. 187–88. Several recordings by Vilayat Khan are available on the Odeon label; see the Discography.

slants upward at about a 45-degree angle from the floor.[21] The index and middle fingers of the left hand stop the strings, just to the left of the frets, and the index finger of the right hand plucks the strings with a wire plectrum. Both upward and downward strokes are used—or, as Shankar describes them, inward and outward, referring to the position of the thumb. In sitār playing as well as in vīṇā playing, the strings are often deflected across the frets so as to produce additional pitches or embellishments.

What Ravi Shankar calls "the great sitār explosion" in the West began in early 1966.[22] In his own land, the eastern city of Calcutta and the western metropolis of Bombay have for decades been the centers of sitār music and solo instrumental music in general. Both cities have long harbored private organizations dedicated to sponsoring musical evenings. These music circles, as they are called, are held in small recital halls or in private homes.

If I dwell somewhat on Ravi Shankar and the sitār it is because he and his musical family have been integral to the discovery of Indian music by Westerners. Frequently paired with the sitār and Ravi Shankar in the minds of Western connoisseurs of Indian classical music are his brother-in-law, Ustad Ali Akbar Khan, and the instrument he plays, the sarod (see Plate 11a). Also a stringed instrument that is plucked, the sarod is nevertheless

Plate 11a
Ali Akbar Khan Playing the Sarod
(Tāmbūra in background)

[21]Shankar, *My Music, My Life*, p. 104.
[22]*Ibid.*, p. 92.

Plate 11b
Charles Capwell, Sarodist

very different from the bīn, the vīṇā, and the sitār. Its ancestry is certainly different, in that it is most likely non-Indian. Even the details of its development in India are difficult to trace precisely.

The sarod probably originated from the rebāb, an instrument from the Middle East.[23] The use of the sarod in Indian classical music is to be traced from the influence of another of the master musicians in India's musical history, Tansen (c. 1520–1590 A.D.), a fabulous singer and bīnkār in the court of the great Mughal Akbar (1556–1605). To Tansen is attributed the invention of a stringed instrument called the rebāb, somewhat different from the Persian or Afghan instrument of the same name.

From the time of Akbar and Tansen, the making of music in Mughal courts began to be associated with particular families. Two branches of Tansen's family specialized in different instruments. From his daughter Saraswati, who married a noted bīn player, Misri Singh, came the bīnkar branch. The descendants of his son, Bilas Khan (who converted from Hinduism to Islam),[24] specialized in playing the rebāb developed by Tansen and became known as the rabābiyā gharānā (*ghar* meaning "house" and *gharānā* meaning "family" or "household"). Today, the rebāb has been

[23]The rebāb became the rebec of Persia and Arabia, to which the parentage of the violin family is ascribed. (Krishnaswamy, *Musical Instruments of India*, p. 52.)

[24]Under Muslim patronage, many Hindu musicians converted. The name "Khan" signifies a Muslim. Misri Singh converted to Islam and was renamed Nabat Khan. Master musicians of the Islamic faith are referred to as *Ustad*, meaning "teacher." The Hindu equivalent is *Pandit*. Thus, Pandit Ravi Shankar but Ustad Ali Akbar Khan.

replaced by the sarod in performances of classical music, but most sarod players trace their lineage back to the rabābiyā and even back to Afghan rebāb traditions.

"It is said that Khan Saheb Asadullah Khan introduced this instrument [the sarod] in Bengal more than a century ago and since then Bengal has become noted for the manufacture and the popularisation of this instrument."[25] In Bengal, Ustad Ali Akbar Khan's father, Ustad Allauddin Khan, developed a style that differs in some ways from the older sarod styles. Part of the difference lies in the construction of the instrument itself.

The sarod is constructed on the principle of the rebāb, in that it has a hollow circular belly to which is attached a tapering neck whose slim top portion holds the tuning pegs. Therefore, it is a lute-type instrument. The shape of the belly of both instruments is distinctive in that it is pinched just below the place where the neck is attached. The shallow, pinched belly of the rebāb was apparently designed to facilitate bowing, but its successor, the sarod, is plucked.

The use of wood for the belly of the sarod and the use of parchment to cover the belly were retained from rebāb construction. The sarod is usually three to three and a half feet long and has a body of teakwood overlaid with a fingerboard of polished metal, which facilitates sliding the finger along the strings. Unlike all the other stringed instruments discussed thus far, it has no frets. The left hand is used for stopping the strings along the smooth fingerboard. The sarod is played with a plectrum held in the right hand. The plectrum is like a rounded-off triangle about one and a half to two inches across the base and from apex to base. The apex hits the strings. The plectrum is made either of coconut shell or of wire. Its base is embedded in beeswax so that it is easier to hold between thumb and index finger.

The stringing on the sarod is a departure from that on the rebāb. The six gut playing strings on the latter are replaced by four or five metal strings on the former (five strings on the old style but four on the Allauddin Khan instrument). These are tuned P̤a Sạ Pạ Sa Ma and Sạ Pạ Sa Ma, respectively. The lowest string is brass and the rest are steel. The lowest-pitched string, Kharaj Sa (or Pa), is closest to the player's face. In addition, there are three to five chikāri (drone and rhythm) strings and anywhere from eleven to sixteen sympathetic strings (see Plate 12).

The sarod has four bridges, the main one that sits on the parchment over the belly, a secondary bridge (called a jawari bridge) at the neck of the instrument,[26] and two smaller bridges attached to the pegged side of the instrument (see Plate 12). The jawari bridge is wide, and is constructed so

[25]Krishnaswamy, *Musical Instruments of India*, p. 48. Further discussion of the musical situation in Bengal in the late nineteenth and early twentieth centuries can be found in Dhurjati Mukerji, "Indian Culture and Music," *The Cultural Heritage of India* (Calcutta: The Ramakrishna Mission, 1962), Vol. II, pp. 601–13.

[26]I am much indebted to Charles Capwell for his contribution to this discussion of the construction of the sarod.

Plate 12
The Sarod

that it will add a buzz to the sounds produced by the four strings it supports (one drone string and three sympathetic strings, all of which are called jawari strings because they cross that bridge).[27] The main bridge holds strings at three levels. Over the top go the playing strings, one jawari string (a drone string tuned to Sa), and the other two drone strings (tuned to Sȧ and Sȧ). One level down, the remaining three jawari strings (the sympathetic strings) go through small holes in the bridge. The lowest level of holes is for the remainder of the sympathetic strings. The sympathetic strings, called *tarab*, are all made of steel.

Two sarod players who have concertized widely in India and whose recordings are available in this country are Sharan Rani (a female) and

[27]This special buzzing effect is also obtained on two Japanese lutes, the *biwa* and the *shamisen*. In Japanese, this effect is called *sawari*.

Amjad Ali Khan. Although a number of women and girls study stringed instruments in North India, it is unusual for a female to pursue a career in public performance. (It is far more usual for females to be vocalists.) Sharan Rani thus stands out among contemporary instrumental soloists. Amjad Ali Khan of Delhi has toured in England and is beginning to attract serious attention in the United States.

India has long contributed its instruments to the musical tradition of the West, and vice versa. The sitār and sarod are a twentieth-century contribution from India to the West. In the opposite direction, the violin long ago found its way from the West into the instrumental repertoire of the subcontinent. It is the first bowed lute-type instrument to be discussed here.

One account of the introduction of the violin into Indian music tells us that the instrument was adopted for string accompaniment in South India at the end of the eighteenth century, when a Tanjore court minister, Varahappaiar, who was also an accomplished musician, visited the British Governor's compound in Madras on business. There he saw, tried, and carried back to Tanjore a violin (and also a piano) presented to him by the governor. The violin filled the need for an accompanying instrument (besides the sāraṅgī) that could duplicate, by bowing, the long breath of vocal style. Its elegant shape and artistic construction were appreciated, as was its sonorous tone.[28]

A more widely accepted account credits Balaswami Dikshitar (1786–1858) as being the first South Indian musician to adapt the violin to Karnatak music. Balaswami came from a family of musicians and was the younger brother of the great composer Muttuswami Dikshitar (see Chapter Eight). Because of his family ties and his own skill from the time he was a young boy, he was well placed to attract the attention of patrons. Chinnayya Mudaliyar arranged for him to study Western violin with the bandmaster at Fort St. George in Madras.[29] Believing that the instrument could be made suitable for his own musical tradition, Balaswami retuned it from G D A E to Sạ Pạ Sa Pa and began to experiment. He concertized successfully for the rest of his life on the violin, as well as on other instruments.

Another artist whom many Indian music historians dub a pioneer in the introduction of the violin to India is Vaḍivelu (1810–1845). He was the youngest of four brothers who achieved such musical fame that they were known as the Tanjore Quartet (the others were Ponnayya [1804–?], Chinnaya [1806–1856], and Sivanandam [1808–?]). They were the sons of Subbaraya Oduvar, a musician and dance master at the court of Tanjore. Vaḍivelu grew up learning Bhārata Nāṭyam (dance), music (particularly singing), and literature. He had the ability to repeat anything after one hearing. He performed often with his father and older brothers, and was so impressive that

[28] T. K. Jayarama Aiyar, "The Violin in Karnatic Music," *Indian Music Journal*, 4 (October-November 1955), 27–28.

[29] L. Shankar, *The Art of Violin Accompaniment in South Indian Classical Vocal Music* (Ann Arbor, Mich.: University Microfilms, 1974), pp. 130–31.

at fourteen he became a court musician—the youngest.[30] Western music was encouraged at the artistically active Tanjore court, and a Catholic priest (a foreigner) who was a violinist taught Vaḍivelu to play some Western tunes on the violin. For two years Vaḍivelu practiced the instrument playing Indian rather than Western music, and he began to play solos on it at court as well as to accompany his brọthers' vocal concerts.[31] Mahārāja Svāti Tirunāl, the ruler of Travancore and a legẹndary Indian patron of the arts, brought the four brothers to his court in 1830 and even built them a spacious dwelling.

> Vaḍivelu, as a singer-violinist, so delighted the court with his art that in 1834 Swāti Tirunāl Mahārāja honored him with the gift of a solid ivory violin. Vaḍivelu sang during the dance performance and accompanied himself on the fiddle as only he could do. Verily, it was a feast fit for the Gods and brought down to the dark dull earth the faint echoes of the glories of Indra Sabhai where flitted past in mazy dance Rambha, Urvasi, Menaka, Thilottama, casting upon the audience "the charm of woven paces and waving hands" while from the dim background swells the witching music of the golden throated Gandharvas, Tumburus, Viswawasu and their like.[32]

Karnatak musicians sit crosslegged to play the violin, holding the instrument vertically and balancing it between the chest and the right foot. The left hand is then free to move up and down the fingerboard. This posture and the fingering technique in Karnatak violin playing reduces the volume of the sound.[33] One violinist, Mysore Chowdiah (1895–1967), designed a violin with seven strings, "which produced noticeably more sound than the [four-stringed] other."[34] Customarily, the violin is pitched an octave higher than the voice of the singer it is accompanying.[35]

Although the violin is played as a solo instrument by a few Karnatak musicians (it is also played as a solo instrument in Hindustānī music), its primary role in the South is to participate in vocal performances.[36] Well-known violinists in the South are T. N. Krishnan, L. Vaidyanathan, L. Subramanian, L. Shankar, and V. Thyagarajan. Their counterparts in the North include V. G. Jog, Gajanarao Joshi, and Damodhar Hari Joglekar.

[30] *Ibid.*, p. 132.

[31] *Ibid.*, p. 133. According to Ayyangar, *History of South Indian Music*, p. 321, the violin was brought to India by an Italian.

[32] T. Shankaran, *The Hindu* (1970); quoted in Shankar, *Violin Accompaniment*, pp. 133–34.

[33] Ayyangar, *History of South Indian Music*, p. 323. See also Plate 7, which shows the position in which the violin is played in procession.

[34] Shankar, *Violin Accompaniment*, p. 172.

[35] Hindustānī violinist Damodhar Hari Joglekar asserts that Indian musicians should tune the instrument as Westerners do. See Joglekar's *Violin athvā Belā Shāstra* (Munbai: Sangit Vidyamandir, 1963).

[36] Recordings are available of violin-sitār duets performed by V. G. Jog and Ravi Shankar. Further comments on violin music appear in Chapter Eight.

Plate 13
The Violin, in Karnatak Playing Position
(L. Subramanian, Violinist)

One variety of bowed lute reigns in each of the two traditions of classical music in India—the violin in South India and the sāraṅgī in the North. The sāraṅgī used to predominate in both areas, but is now at home only in the North. It was said in 1891, "The use of the sāraṅgī in Southern India—except in conjunction with Nautches [dancers]—is rapidly being discontinued, and an English fiddle tuned as a vīṇa or sāraṅgī is often substituted for it. Farther North the instrument appears likely to hold its place for a long time to come."[37] In the South, the sāraṅgī is seldom played.

The sāraṅgī captured the imagination of nineteenth-century Britishers in India. Remarked one Captain Taylor, "The sāraṅgī is used by Mahomedan musicians more than by Hindu; and I imagine it may have been introduced into India by the Mahomedans, possibly from Persia. It forms an excellent accompaniment to the voice; and an old friend of mine, an excellent musician and violin player, the late Captain Giberne, Bombay Army, used to prefer

[37]Day, *Music and Musical Instruments of Southern India*, p. 93.

one of these instruments to his own violin for concerted pieces in which the violin took a soprano part."[38] Captain Charles Day wrote in 1891, "Curiously enough, as was the case with the violin in England at one time, the instrument is considered to be rather vulgar, and hence, musicians, though they admire and like it much, will usually employ either a low caste Hindu or a Musselman to play it."[39] It has been suggested that one main reason why the sāraṅgī was played by Muslims and lower-caste Hindus was that the strings were made of animal gut.[40]

The reason for such attention by Britishers may have been the sāraṅgī's association with dancing girls, who are mentioned in numerous sources. Although dancing in temples was accorded respect in early Hindu thought, girls who danced in public were likely to be prostitutes. They—and their accompanists—were not considered respectable people. How is it, then, that the sāraṅgī figures so largely in contemporary North Indian classical music?

In the splendid Mughal courts, performers were lavishly patronized. Among troupes of subsidized performers were male and female dancers attached to the royal household. Among the musicians at court, the drummers and sāraṅgī players who accompanied the dancers were of lower status than those who played for darbār (formal court) sessions. Nevertheless, they were the vehicle for the relocation of the sāraṅgī from folk to classical use. This was a slow process. It resulted not from the quality of the musicians or from any major changes in the instrument itself, but because the type of music the sāraṅgī accompanied gradually became more favored.

Dhrupad, the type of song preferred in the sixteenth and seventeenth centuries, was accompanied on bīn and a drum called a pakhāvaj. Dhrupad gradually gave way to khyāl in the eighteenth century and to ṭhumṛī in the nineteenth century. Bīn and pakhāvaj were considered unsuitable as accompaniment instruments for khyāl and ṭhumṛī, and the sāraṅgī and tablā took their places. Efforts are now being made to elevate the sāraṅgī one more step, to a solo role. The leading sāraṅgī soloist nowadays is Ram Narain.

The sāraṅgī is a rather small instrument, usually about two feet high. It is made of a single hollowed-out block of wood. Like the sarod, it has a pinched belly, which facilitates bowing, and a tapered neck. But the belly, which is covered with parchment, is square at the end, and the neck is not nearly as long or as graceful as that of the sarod.

The sāraṅgī's three main playing strings are gut. There may be a fourth, brass string, which is used as a drone. Thirty-five to forty sympathetic wire strings (Captain Day mentioned only fifteen), tuned chromatically, are attached to pegs along the side of the fingerboard. The instrument is held vertically, the belly resting on the lap and the pegbox end resting on the left

[38]Meadows Taylor, "Catalogue of Indian Musical Instruments, Presented by P. T. French," *Proceedings of the Royal Irish Academy*, 9 (1864–1866), 115.

[39]Day, *Music and Musical Instruments of Southern India*, p. 126.

[40]Personal correspondence with Dr. Robert Brown, 1975.

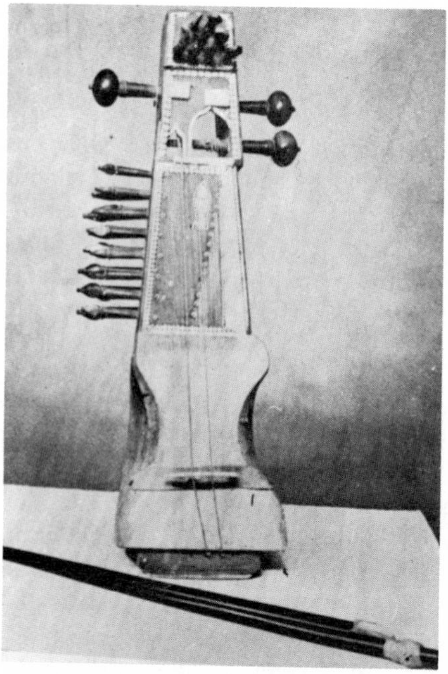

Plate 14
The Sāraṅgī

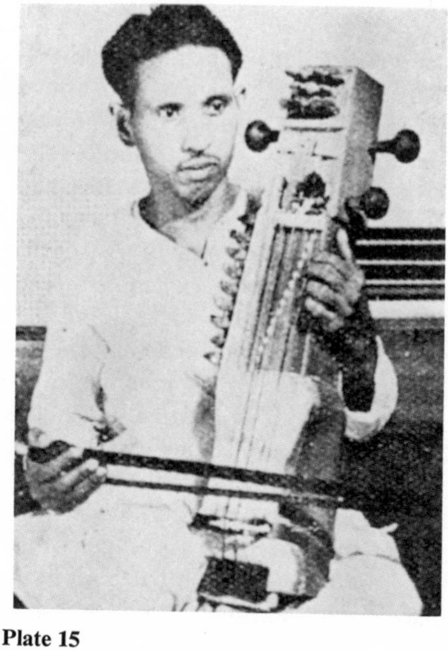

Plate 15
The Sāraṅgī (Munir Khan, Sāraṅgīyā)

shoulder. The horsehair bow is worked with the right hand, and the strings are stopped with the left hand.

There are no frets on a sāraṅgī. The method of stopping the strings is to press against the side of the string with the finger at the base of the nail, not with the fingertip. For these reasons and others the instrument is very difficult to master. But since the sāraṅgī is capable of producing a very close approximation of the human voice, and because it is used primarily to accompany the voice, it has continued in currency. Considered good accompanists are Sabri Khan and Inder Lal.

SUSHIRA VĀDYA: THE WIND INSTRUMENTS

In India, the playing of the flute is at least as old as the Vedas. The *Yajurveda* includes in the list of occupations the playing of vīṇā, venu (flute), and mṛdañga (drum), and the blowing of conches for signals and ceremonies.

A fascinating evolutionary history of the Indian flute was postulated by the Western organologist F. W. Galpin.[41] In its earliest form, the instrument was a long reed, open at both ends and played vertically. This was the type of flute popular among various Asiatic peoples of ancient times, including the early Egyptian dynasties. In eastern Asia, a different type of flute was known. It was also played vertically, but it had a closed resonating chamber with five or six finger holes. In China, it was known as the *hsüan* and was used in temple music.

From the hsüan, the Chinese developed a variant called the *ch'ih*. This flute had a tubular resonating chamber, and both of its ends were plugged. Midway along the tube was a mouth hole, to each side of which three finger holes were placed. The instrument thus became a transverse flute. When Buddhism reached China from India in the first century B.C. and was approved as one of the state religions, the ch'ih became associated with it and was eventually transported to India. The transverse position of the instrument was accepted there, but the mouth hole was moved to the left, the right end was unblocked, and the finger holes were placed between the mouth hole and the open end. The tube no longer was a resonator, and the result was a vertical flute blown transversely.

The flute is depicted in Buddhist art of the first century B.C. in India (at Sanchi). It is also pictured in murals in the Buddhist caves at Ajanta and Ellora (which date from the second century B.C. to about the eighth century A.D.). In these murals, the flute is played by human and celestial beings, both as accompaniment to vocal music and as a part of instrumental ensembles. For several centuries, it has been recognized as the instrument by which the playful deity Krishna entices his devotees to him.

[41] F. W. Galpin, "Additional Note on the Harp and Flute," pp. 330–31, in G. T. Garrett, ed., *The Legacy of India* (Oxford: Clarendon Press, 1937), pp. 327–34.

Plate 16a
The Hindustānī Flute (G. S. Sachdev, Flutist)

Plate 16b
The Karnatak Flute (T. Viswanathan, Flutist;
Accompanied on Mṛdaṅga by T. Ranganathan)

Galpin traces the same flute to the West: "On its return to China in due course it became the 'foreign' *ti-tzu*, while westward it travelled in the early Middle Ages through Byzantium and, later still, through North Africa to become the beautiful instrument of the modern orchestra."[42] Krishnaswamy, one of India's foremost experts on musical instruments, makes the same assertion: "The flute is one of the many Indian musical instruments which went West and became domiciled there."[43] Neither source documents the alleged transmission of the instrument to the West.

The next chapter in the history of the flute allegedly began when a flute was made with seven holes, on which it was possible to play the seven *svaras* easily. The flutist played the seven pitches in ascending order by closing all the holes and opening them in succession from right to left toward the mouth hole. During one period in the history of the Indian flute, a different instrument was needed for each different scale. It later became the practice to produce semitones by partially closing and opening the finger holes. Thus, any scale could be obtained on a single instrument. Later, with the addition of an eighth hole to the flute in South India, an additional lower-octave pitch was made available. All subsequent Karnatak flutes have had eight finger holes. The usual range of such flutes is two and a half octaves, the range of most human voices.[44]

In its latest form, then, the Indian flute is a cylindrical tube of uniform bore, closed at one end. It is made of straight, clean, smooth bamboo that is free from notches or other flaws. Some of the flutes used in the North, especially those used in eastern Bengal, are longer than those of the South. In most parts of the country, flutes are played at a slight declination from the horizontal.

The seventeenth-century Mughal emperor Jehangir recalls in his memoirs that he honored a flutist, Ustad Muhammad, by weighing him and then giving him, in rupees, the equivalent of pounds of flesh to pounds of silver. The musician was also given an elephant on which he and his money could ride.

Among concert instruments today, the flute enjoys the same solo status as the vīṇā in the South and the various stringed instruments in the North.[45] The most prominent South Indian flutists are T. R. Mahalingam, N. Ramani, and T. Viswanathan. The most famous North Indian flutists are the late Pannalal Ghosh, H. Himangshu Biswas, Hari Prasad Chaurasia, and Vijay Raghav Rao. G. S. Sachdev, a disciple of Vijay Raghav Rao, is teaching flute in the United States, as is T. Viswanathan.

[42] *Ibid.*, p. 331.

[43] Krishnaswamy, *Musical Instruments of India*, p. 63.

[44] Sambamoorthy, *The Flute*, pp. 38–39.

[45] In the South, the musician who is said to have elevated the flute to its status of primary instrument in recent times is Sarabha Sastri (1872–1904).

The reed instruments important to contemporary Indian classical music are of the double-reed type. In this respect, they are similar to the Western oboe. In the South, the predominant double reed is the *nagasvaram*, which has traditionally been associated with performance in Hindu temples. Only recently has it been played in more secular concert situations. It is most appropriately played outdoors, because its sound, and the sound of the *tavil* (drum) that traditionally accompanies it, carry very well. Nagasvaram and tavil frequently figure in temple processions.

> The procession of the temple deity started at 8 P.M. Pazhanivel . . . set the pace with his thrilling strokes on the Tavil. What an arresting backdrop for the flow of melody to come! The opening phrases of Rajaratnam's [the player's] Todi [rāga] soared like a rocket in the placid, night sky. Would that we had a clue to the name "Nagaswaram!" The torrential flow of sound, chunks of melody gyrating in terrific speed, the expansive Rāga spreading out like a magic carpet, and the crowd of listeners thrown into hysteria by the swelling cascade of transcendental music that tingled in the ear and made every hair stand on end! It was 2 A.M. when the music was wound up and the deity lodged in the Sanctum. It was Todi all the time.[46]

Until about the second quarter of this century, nagasvaram players kept most strictly such traditions as the allotment of different parts of the day to different rāgas and the preference for sustained and elaborate improvisation rather than songs.[47]

The nagasvaram is two to two and a half feet long (see p. 22). Usually made of wood, it has a conical bore flaring out toward the lower end, and a separate, detachable bell. Ordinarily, it has twelve holes—eight in front and two on each side. Only the upper seven, however, are used for playing. The remaining ones can be filled with wax to adjust the pitch register at the player's discretion. The double reed is fixed on a metal staple at the top end of the instrument and therefore does not extend down into the instrument. Spare reeds and an ivory needle with which the reeds are cleaned and adjusted are attached to the mouthpiece and trail down decoratively when the nagasvaram is played.

In playing the instrument, performers exploit to the fullest the technique of covering the finger holes only partially. In addition, they vary their tongue and lip contact with the reed. Oustanding players include Sheikh Chinna Maulana, T. N. Rajarathnam Pillai, and K. Pichiappa.

The drone instrument used with the nagasvaram is frequently not the tāmbūra, whose delicate sound would be lost, but the *ottu*, another double-reed instrument. The ottu is larger than the nagasvaram but has only five or six holes, which are placed toward its lower end. Performers close the holes

[46]Ayyangar, *History of South Indian Music*, App. I, p. xii.
[47]Ayyangar, *History of South Indian Music*, App. I, pp. xii–xvii.

wholly or partially in order to obtain the desired drone pitch.[48] The technique of circular breathing, which uses the cheek cavity as an air chamber, keeps the source of air (and therefore the drone) constant.

The *shehnai*, the predominant double-reed instrument of the North, is smaller than the nagasvaram: it is from one to one and a half feet long. The shehnai is made of wood, except for the metal bell at its enlarged lower end; the bore is conical. It has seven playing holes and one or two more for adjusting the pitch. The double reed is attached to a narrow stem that rises out of the top of the instrument (see Plate 17).

Plate 17
The Shehnai (A. Kādir Durvesh)

Like the nagasvaram, one plays the shehnai by controlling the flow of air through the column (though with a different technique), and obtains desired pitches by partially or completely covering the holes. The accompanying drone (*śruti* or *sur*) is provided by a fellow reed instrument, which looks like the shehnai but has only two or three holes. These are stopped wholly or partially with wax so that the player can tune the drone to the desired pitch.

The shehnai (or *surnai*) may have been introduced into India by the Muslims. Certainly, one of its most prominent uses was in the ensemble called the *naubat* (or *nahabet*), which played at Mughal courts. The naubat consisted of a varying number of specific instruments: kettledrums of various

[48]The descriptions of the nagasvaram and the ottu are derived from Krishnaswamy, *Musical Instruments of India*, pp. 66–68.

sizes, other types of drums, trumpets, horns, cymbals, and shehnais with their accompanying drones. In his classic book, Captain Day describes the activities of this ensemble at the court of Akbar:

> The general practice then was that the Nahabet played first at midnight and the second time at dawn. An hour before sunrise the musicians commenced to play the Surnais, an hour later there was a short prelude which in turn was followed by pieces introducing the . . . other wind instruments, with the occasional use of the largest drum of all (Damama or Nahabet), but which did not introduce the Nakkera (or smaller drum). After this the Surnais and Nafirs (small trumpets) were played alone; an hour later there was a general crescendo, and then followed seven distinct performances, brought to a conclusion by the chanting of various prayers for blessings upon the Emperor, and then the day's service was finished by the Surnais players playing softly to a pianissimo of the drums.[49]

Plate 18
The Naubat Ensemble Performing at Court
(18th Century Painting)

[49]Day, *Music and Musical Instruments of Southern India*, p. 96.

To this day, the shehnai has also been associated with Hindu festivals. It conjures visions of folk music in the minds of the Northerners. However, one musician in particular, Ustad Bismillah Khan, has been trying for several decades to establish the shehnai on the concert stage as well. He performs very beautiful classical music (some of his recordings are listed in the Discography), and he is frequently invited to initiate weekend-long festivals of classical music, thereby beginning them auspiciously.

Indian instruments differ from those in the West in one striking way: their specifications are not standardized. Nagasvaram are from two to two and a half feet long; one vainika had his vīṇā built with an exceptionally broad stem; the number of holes in a flute, playing strings on a sāraṅgī, and sympathetic strings on a sitār are variable. Such flexibility seems very sensible for a musical tradition that puts such emphasis on the individual, giving him full responsibility for conveying the musical tradition in improvisation. In a sense, he is able to improvise his instruments as well, in order to make them most appropriate for his own music.

The most striking contrast between Hindustānī and Karnatak instruments is to be found in the category of plucked stringed instruments. On the Karnatak vīṇā, the frets, and therefore the pitches, are fixed in resin. The Hindustānī bīn, whose frets are fixed, has fallen out of favor. Among the other Hindustānī plucked stringed instruments, sitārs are built with movable frets and the sarod has no frets. The only Hindustānī instrument with inflexible pitch is the harmonium (to be discussed in Chapter Seven), and the use of it is a constant source of dispute.

This difference in instrument construction is appropriate to the difference between the two traditions in their approach to rāga, particularly as manifested in rāga classification. The Karnatak system of rāga classification, which seeks to encompass every rāga that might be created, operates as a relatively closed system when Karnatak musicians agree to create within it, as it would appear most of them do. Thus, it is unnecessary to build into the melody instruments an allowance for something that might develop outside that system. The vīṇā is built in accordance with that system: it has frets, for any semitones that might be desired. Thus, the fixed frets of the vīṇā present no problem. In Hindustānī music, on the other hand, the range of possibilities is limited neither by the classification system nor by the instrument-tuning mechanisms.

When the instruments discussed here are arranged according to purpose—either solo or accompanying (see Chart 10)—it would seem that instrumental solo performance has been increasing in importance in North India. Indeed, that has been the case for at least the last two hundred years. The recent popularity of the sitār and the sarod are strong evidence of this trend, since neither instrument has ever been used primarily for vocal accompaniment.

	TRADITIONALLY ACCOMPANIMENT FOR VOICE	RELATIVELY RECENTLY SOLO	TRADITIONALLY SOLO
Stringed	Vīṇā (Karnatak) Bīn (Hindustānī)	Vīṇā Bīn	Sitār (H) Sarod (H)
Wind	Violin (K) Sāraṅgī (H) Flute (H and K)	Violin (H and K) Sāraṅgī (H)	Flute (H and K) Shehnai (H) Nagasvaram (K)

CHART 10. Instruments Arranged According to Purpose

Many Westerners seem to be under the impression that Indian classical music is primarily instrumental. This is probably because Ravi Shankar and other instrumentalists have been the leading Indian artists to tour in the West. But in fact the voice has been considered the solo instrument par excellence in India for many centuries. The preeminence of the voice may be due in part to its status as the only instrument that can render text. And the intonation of texts in sacred rituals—at least as we know it in Aryan-Sanskritic tradition—is one of the oldest Indo-European ideal practices. Indeed, it is generally said that Indian classical music evolved from the chanting of the *Sāma Veda*, which was a more tuneful rendering of the hymns of the *Ṛg Veda*. Vocal music has thus been linked with reverence and worship in the the Indian mind for many millenia. This respect for the voice and vocal music could probably be traced through time. Certainly it remains strong in South India, to the point that instrumental music is recognized as idiomatic rendering of vocal music.

It is probably significant that solo instrumental music began to come to the fore under Muslim rule in North India. The use of music for worship is not part of the Islamic tradition, and tuneful rendering of the call to prayer is not considered music. Thus, there would have been less reason for the North Indian Muslims to elevate vocal music over instrumental music. But this is a complex historical question, one that has not yet been thoroughly investigated.

One finds less emphasis on achieving a certain "beautiful tonal quality" among Indian vocalists than among Western vocalists. "Having a beautiful voice" has not necessarily been a criterion for becoming a vocalist in India. The emphasis is placed instead on musicality, the ability to handle musical materials with superb control and, ultimately, with artistic sensitivity. A singer can do that with a less than resonant, or even slightly raspy, voice.

A singer is expected to cultivate a two-and-one-half-octave range. A three-octave range is the ideal, for it encompasses several different vocal qualities in one voice. Breath control is important, for it determines how well an artist can sing sustained, slow passages as well as highly ornamental vocalises.

The value and prominence of the voice in the instrumental index is best appreciated, perhaps, in the following dialogue:

A King once approached a Sage and asked to be taught the craft of image-making. The following dialogue ensued:

KING: O Sinless One! Be good enough to teach me the methods of image-making.

SAGE: One who does not know the laws of painting can never understand the laws of image-making.

KING: Be then good enough, O Sage, to teach me the laws of painting.

SAGE: But it is difficult to understand the laws of painting without any knowledge of the technique of dancing.

KING: Kindly instruct me then in the art of dancing.

SAGE: This is difficult to understand without a thorough knowledge of instrumental music.

KING: Teach me then, O Sage, the laws of instrumental music.

SAGE: But the laws of instrumental music cannot be learned without a deep knowledge of the art of vocal music.

KING: If vocal music be the source of all arts, reveal to me, then O Sage, the laws of vocal music.[50]

[50]Gosvami, *Story of Indian Music*, p. xv (unnumbered).

FIVE
METER

The second basic element of Indian classical music to be discussed is meter. The Sanskrit word for meter is *tāla* (called *tāl* in North India and *tāla* or *tālam* in South India). The word refers both to the metric system as a whole and to individual meters.

HINDUSTĀNĪ METRIC CONCEPTS

On the next pages we will contrast Western and Hindustānī concepts in parallel fashion, using "Till the End of Time" as the Western example and the Hindustānī *chhotā khyāl* (a vocal genre discussed in Chapter Seven) *chīz* "Pāyaliyā jhankār." Following this discussion we will examine Karnatak metric concepts.

Western

EXAMPLE 5-1 "Till the End of Time"

Chorus
Till the end of time, Long as stars are in the blue ___ Long as
there's a spring, a bird to sing I'll go on lov - ing you ___ Till the
end of time, ___ Long as ros - es bloom in May ___ My love for
you will grow deep - er with eve - ry pass - ing day.

"Till the End of Time" is in a certain meter. "Frère Jacques" happens to be in the same meter. That meter, signified by the time signature 4/4, is defined by the events in a single unit—a measure. A measure in 4/4 contains four beats, each having the value of a quarter note (♩). In standard Western notation, barlines mark off the measures. Since "Till the End of Time" does not begin on the first count of the meter, the measure preceding the first barline is incomplete.

Meters also imply a pattern of stress. In 4/4, the first beat is the strongest, the third beat is the next strongest, and the second and fourth beats are "offbeats":

>♩ ♩ >♩ ♩

Other examples of meter are 3/4, which implies a stress pattern of >♩ ♩ ♩ or >♩ ♩ >♩ . A 6/8 grouping of six eighth notes (♪ , half the value of a quarter note ♩), is subdivided 3 + 3: >♪ ♪ ♪ >♪ ♪ ♪ . Different meters are used for different types of music, particularly varieties of dance: 3/4 for a waltz, 4/4 for a march, and so forth.

Hindustānī

EXAMPLE 5-2 "Pāyaliyā jhankār"[1]

Rāg Pūriyā Dhanashrī, Tīntāl

Sthāī
Pā - ya - lī - yā jha - n - kā - - r mo - ri
jha - na - na jha - na - na bā - je jha - n - kā - rī /
Aṅtarā
Pi - yā sa - m - jhā - uṅ sa - m - jha - t na - hīṅ
sā - s na - na - d mo - rī de - gi gā - ri. /

"Pāyaliyā jhankār" is in a certain tāla. That tāla, signified by the name *tīntāl*, is defined by the events in a single unit—a cycle. A cycle in tīntāl contains a total of sixteen counts (here notated as 16 ♩ s), I have chosen to put a barline at the end of each cycle in the notation above. The double bar in line two of the song indicates the beginning of the second section (*aṅtarā*) of the song, not the beginning of a new tāla cycle. Since the song does not begin on the first count of the meter, the measure preceding the first barline is incomplete.

Tāla structures also include an internal pattern of durations. In tīntāl, there are four sections (four *vibhāg*) with four counts (four *mātrās*) in each section: 4 + 4 + 4 + 4 counts. The counts that begin each segment delineate the pattern of durations and thus are important structural counts. In tīntāl, those counts are 1, 5, 9, and 13:

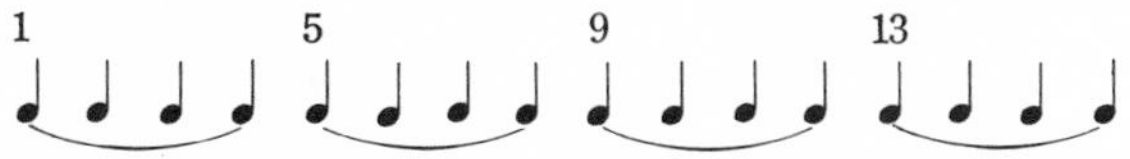
1
5
9
13

[1]This song appears in Indian notation in V. N. Bhaṭkande, comp., and L. N. Garg, ed., *Krāmik Pustak Mālikā*, 2nd ed. (Hathras: Saṅgīt Karyalaya, 1963), Vol. IV, p. 348. B. D. Yadav has translated the text of the song as follows (see Bonnie C. Wade, *Khyāl: A Study in Hindustānī Classical Vocal Music* [Ann Arbor, Mich.: University Microfilms, 1971], Vol. I, p. 496):

Sthāī: My anklets jingle jhanana jhanana.

Aṅtarā: I cannot make my beloved understand and my mother- and sister-in-law abuse me.

Western

A single measure is usually too short a unit in which to complete a musical idea, so several measures are combined into a phrase. Phrase structure in a song is flexible. The structure of "Till the End of Time" provides a good demonstration of this:

8 beats plus 8 beats plus 16 beats

8 beats plus 8 beats plus 16 beats, etc.

(In the notation of the song, each phrase is marked by a slur.) In this song, the phrases all begin on beat 3 of a measure and end on a later beat 2.

Hindustānī

In order to keep the place in the cycle, and to emphasize the conceptualized subdivisions while the melodic and rhythmic phrases seem to obscure them, audiences in India may count out the tāla cycle with hand motions. In tīntāl, they would clap softly on counts 1, 5, and 13; those counts are referred to as *tālī* ("clap"). On count 9, they would wave their hand to the side silently; this is called *khālī* ("empty"). The tīntāl structure thus has three (*tīn*) tālī and one khālī. It is notated as follows:

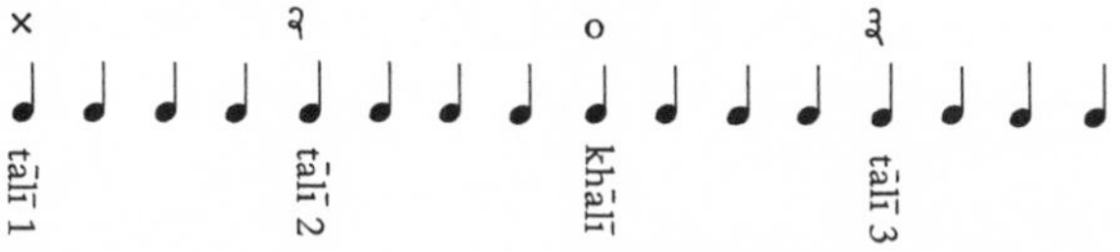

Count 1 is marked by an × or a plus because it is the most important structural pitch in any tāla. It is also given a special name—*sam*. It is referred to as sam whether it is tālī or khālī in the count of the particular tāla. In rūpak tāl, for instance, sam is khālī:

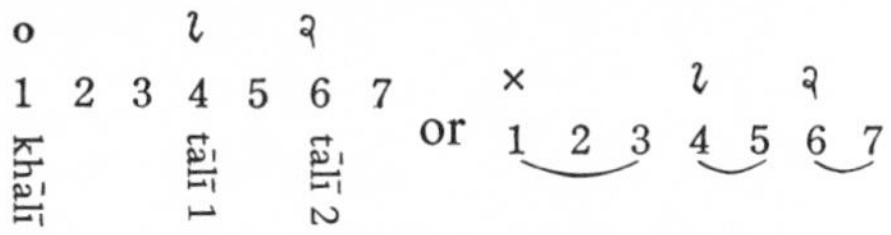

(१ is the Arabic form of the number 1. Here, it indicates the first tālī.)

Other examples of Hindustānī tālas are kaharavā (8 counts 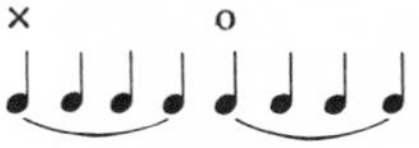), ektāl (12 counts: ), and dhamār (14 counts: ). (४ is the Arabic form of the number 4.) A variety of tālas are used in North India. Some are used only for instrumental performances, some only for vocal performances, and some for both. The most widely used tāla at present is tīntāl.

A single cycle may be a sufficiently long unit to accommodate a complete musical idea. However, two or more cycles are often combined into a phrase. In "Pāyaliyā jhankār," the first section of the song (*sthāī*) has two phrases of 16 counts each. (In the notation, each phrase is marked by a slur.) The phrases begin on khālī (count 9) and end on the next count 8. In the second section of the song (aṅtarā), the phrase structure is the same. The phrase structure may, however, be quite different from this; it is flexible.

Although in Indian melodies two or more tāla cycles can be combined into a musical phrase, the metric base remains the same in the recurring cycles.

Western

If a Western melody begins on any beat other than the first beat (the downbeat) of a measure, we feel it is necessary, at least in notation, to complete that first incomplete measure. We do this by lessening the number of beats in the last measure. "Till the End of Time" begins on a beat 3, so we notate the final measure with only two beats. If one sings this melody casually, however, the final pitch would probably not end precisely at the end of the second beat. So which is the beat of finality? Do we Westerners in fact concern ourselves with the beat of finality? Certainly it is not stressed in our music theory as much as the final pitch and final chord.

Speed

In Western classical music, the speed at which a composition is to be performed is specified in relative terms or in specific terms—or both. Terms such as "largo," "allegro", and "vivace" are relative, whereas metronome markings are specific. The relative speeds are numerous—largo, adagio, moderato, allegro, vivace, presto, and so on.

Variations of the established speed are achieved by slowing it (ritardando), gradually quickening it (accelerando), or varying it at will (rubato). These devices are either indicated in the notated score or are employed by the performer or conductor in his or her interpretation of the piece.

Hindustānī

If a section of a Hindustānī melody begins on any count other than the first count of a cycle, it is necessary to complete that first incomplete cycle. The sthāī of "Pāyaliyā jhankār" begins on count 9 and ends on count 8, as does the aṅtarā.

In Hindustānī music, that final count 8 could not be a cadence point for the melody as a whole, however. Count 1 of the next cycle of the tāla must be the count of finality. One accomplishes this by repeating the portion of the initial line of the melody that leads up to and includes count 1. In "Pāyaliyā jhankār," counts 9 to 1 (the counts corresponding to the words "Pāyaliyā jhankār") are repeated. The performer can go beyond count 1 to finish a text phrase, but that count 1 marks the "official" end of the melodic-rhythmic phrase. Thus, the beginning of the song is used as an ending; the first count of a tāla cycle serves both as a beginning and as an ending. This is an important characteristic of musical structure in Hindustānī classical music.

Speed

In Indian classical music, the speed at which a composition is performed is specified in relative terms. Formerly, it was measured in terms of the heartbeat, but even that was relative. The relative speeds in the Hindustānī system are conceptualized as in levels: slow, medium, and fast.

Variation of the established speed is achieved in Hindustānī music by two principal methods. One is to accelerate the tāla counts. At the beginning of a "slow performance," for example, a cycle of 16 counts may take 32 seconds to complete. As the performance progresses and the speed increases, that cycle may take only 20 seconds. The means of achieving this acceleration vary. It has been found that in some performances of khyāl (a vocal genre), the acceleration takes place very subtly and gradually throughout the melodic phrases sung by the soloist.[2] In other performances, the vocalist increases the speed only at the beginning of a tāla cycle; other vocalists apparently direct the accompanying drummer to increase the rate of his beats while the soloist pauses for a cycle or two to rest.

The second method of varying the established speed does not actually change the speed of the counts. Rather, it changes the rhythmic density. For example, 𝅗𝅥 𝅗𝅥 𝅗𝅥 𝅗𝅥 (at MM 𝅗𝅥 = 48) becomes twice as dense when each count is subdivided as follows: ♩♩ ♩♩ ♩♩ ♩♩. The basic speed has not changed.

[2]Wade, *Khyāl: A Study in Hindustānī Classical Vocal Music*, Vol. I, p. 273.

KARNATAK METRIC CONCEPTS

A Karnatak tāla also consists of a cycle, but the principles of organization of the cycles are somewhat different in Karnatak tālas than they are in Hindustānī tālas. In Karnatak music, some tālas consist of one single unit without subdivision; most are subdivided, however.

The Karnatak idea about subdivisions (a subdivision is called an *āṅga*) is different from the Hindustānī notion. In Hindustānī tāla, the terms tālī and khālī refer to the single beats that mark the subdivisions of a tāla cycle: "In tīntāl, count 9 is khālī." One could also say, "There are three tālī counts in tīntāl," but the term "tālī" does not refer specifically to a subdivision of 4 counts of duration. No indication is given by the terms tālī and khālī themselves of how many counts the subdivision includes. In Karnatak practice, the terms used in speaking about subdivisions of a tāla cycle refer not only to the initial count of a subdivision but also to the duration of the subdivision as a whole.

In the major Karnatak tālas, there are three types of subdivision. Their count values and symbols in notation are as follows:

Anudrutam	1 count	U
Drutam	2 counts	0
Laghu	Variable number of counts	$|^n$

In order to specify the number of counts in a *laghu*, one needs another term. The terms used are simply numbers: 3 (*tiśra*), 4 (*chaturaśra*), and so on. The *jāti* (types of laghu) permitted in the system are these:[3]

Laghu of 3 counts	tiśra jāti	$|^3$
Laghu of 4 counts	chaturaśra jāti	$|^4$
Laghu of 5 counts	khaṇḍa jāti	$|^5$
Laghu of 7 counts	miśra jāti	$|^7$
Laghu of 9 counts	sankīrṇa jāti	$|^9$

Tāla cycles consist of varying combinations of anudrutam, drutam, and laghu. The basic form of *tripuṭa tāla*, for example, is laghu plus drutam plus drutam, notated $|^n$ 0 0. This is only a skeletal outline of tripuṭa tāla;

[3] Āṅgas of 8, 12, and 16 *akṣaras* (counts, like the Hindustānī mātrās) occur in the medieval tālas as they are interpreted in the South. Lengths of 6, 10, 13, 14, and 15 are included in the theory but almost never used. (Robert Brown, *The Mṛdaṅga: A Study of Drumming in South India* (Ann Arbor, Mich.: University Microfilms, 1965), Vol. I, p. 7.

five types of this tāla are available in the system because of the variable values of the laghu:

Triputa tāla tiśra jāti	$\begin{vmatrix} ^3 & 0 & 0 \\ 3 + 2 + 2 \end{vmatrix}$	7 counts
Triputa tāla caturaśra jāti	$\begin{vmatrix} ^4 & 0 & 0 \\ 4 + 2 + 2 \end{vmatrix}$	8 counts
Triputa tāla khaṇḍa jāti	$\begin{vmatrix} ^5 & 0 & 0 \\ 5 + 2 + 2 \end{vmatrix}$	9 counts
Triputa tāla miśra jāti	$\begin{vmatrix} ^7 & 0 & 0 \\ 7 + 2 + 2 \end{vmatrix}$	11 counts
Triputa tāla sankīrṇa jāti	$\begin{vmatrix} ^9 & 0 & 0 \\ 9 + 2 + 2 \end{vmatrix}$	13 counts

The Hindustānī system presents a remarkable contrast: it has only one type of tīntāl, one type of ektāl, one type of rūpak tāl, one type of any tāla. Each Hindustānī tāla is a discrete entity, not organized into any system.

As with Hindustānī tāla, however, the subdivisions in a Karnatak tāla structure, however they are conceived, do not imply stress. The whole emphasis is on counts falling at regular and theoretically exact intervals.[4]

In Chart 11, the traditional Karnatak tāla system can be seen in one clear sweep. Seven tāla structures (including triputa) form a core repertoire; there are five types of each of these structures.[5] The seven tālas are listed vertically in the far left column; the types of laghu are listed across the top. Note that when a tāla includes more than one laghu, all the laghu have the same number of counts. Wavy lines inside the appropriate boxes indicate the tālas that are actually used today. (Karnatak theoretical tāla classification, like Karnatak rāga classification, includes what *could* be used as well as what is used.

The most widely used tāla at present is triputa tāla caturaśra jāti, otherwise known as Ādi tāla. It has a cycle of 8 counts (or akṣaras), and an even rather than an odd number of counts in the laghu: $|^4 \, 0 \, 0 \, (4 + 2 + 2)$. Many references to Ādi tāla, however, speak of 4 counts—2 + 1 + 1—and then calculate half counts (called *mātrā*).[6]

[4]Brown, *The Mṛdaṅga*, Vol. I, p. 129.
[5]The tālas are used for kriti and the other prominent musical forms, such as *pāḍam*, *tillānā*, and *varṇam*, that make up the majority of compositions on a concert program. See Chapter Eight for a discussion of these forms. Numerous tālas other than those in this system exist. They are used widely for other forms.
[6]There is considerable confusion regarding the value of a mātrā. According to P. Sambamoorthy, for example, one mātrā equals four akshāras (*South Indian Music*, 5th ed. [Madras: Indian Music Publishing House, 1958], III, 110.) A recent doctoral dissertation on Hindustānī tālas explains that the Karnatak mātrā is of varying length—either one or two akṣaras (Rebecca Stewart, *The Tablā in Perspective* [Ann Arbor, Mich.: University Microfilms, 1974], p. 78). In any case, the mātrā value seems to depend on whether it is considered a component in the drutam, anudrutam, or laghu.

TĀLAS ↓	JĀTIS→ 4 CATU-RAŚRA	3 TIŚRA	7 MIŚRA	5 KHAṆḌA	9 SANKĪRṆA
Dhruva	$\vert^{4}$ 0 $\vert^{4}$ $\vert^{4}$	$\vert^{3}$ 0 $\vert^{3}$ $\vert^{3}$	$\vert^{7}$ 0 $\vert^{7}$ $\vert^{7}$	$\vert^{5}$ 0 $\vert^{5}$ $\vert^{5}$	$\vert^{9}$ 0 $\vert^{9}$ $\vert^{9}$
Naṭya	$\vert^{4}$ 0 $\vert^{4}$	$\vert^{3}$ 0 $\vert^{3}$	$\vert^{7}$ 0 $\vert^{7}$	$\vert^{5}$ 0 $\vert^{5}$	$\vert^{9}$ 0 $\vert^{9}$
Rūpaka	0 $\vert^{4}$	0 $\vert^{3}$	0 $\vert^{7}$	0 $\vert^{5}$	0 $\vert^{9}$
Tripuṭa	$\vert^{4}$ 0 0	$\vert^{3}$ 0 0	$\vert^{7}$ 0 0	$\vert^{5}$ 0 0	$\vert^{9}$ 0 0
Jhampa	$\vert^{4}$ U 0	$\vert^{3}$ U 0	$\vert^{7}$ U 0	$\vert^{5}$ U 0	$\vert^{9}$ U 0
Aṭa	$\vert^{4}$ $\vert^{4}$ 0 0	$\vert^{3}$ $\vert^{3}$ 0 0	$\vert^{7}$ $\vert^{7}$ 0 0	$\vert^{5}$ $\vert^{5}$ 0 0	$\vert^{9}$ $\vert^{9}$ 0 0
Eka	$\vert^{4}$	$\vert^{3}$	$\vert^{7}$	$\vert^{5}$	$\vert^{9}$

CHART 11. The Karnatak Tāla System

A smaller but nevertheless important group of tālas are also used frequently in South Indian music—the *cāpu tālas*, particularly *miśra cāpu* (7 counts) and *khaṇḍa cāpu* (sometimes called Jhampa: 5 counts). "They are of characteristically quick movement and are said to derive from folk music. Each consists of two āṅgas, a shorter one plus a longer one in asymmetrical relationship, Miśra Cāpu being 3 + 4 and Khaṇḍa Cāpu 2 + 3."[7] These tālas are not thought of as being structured by anudrutam, drutam, or laghu.

Even more noticeably than audiences in the North, South Indian audiences keep the tāla during performances. The means of keeping it (*krīya*) is by claps and waves, which are applied to the tāla in the following manner:

Āṅga	*Symbol*	*Krīya*	*Krīya Notation Symbols*
Anudrutam	U	clap	+
Drutam	0	clap and wave	+ o
Laghu	$\vert^{n}$	clap plus finger counts	+ plus finger counts

To indicate the finger counts of the laghu, one touches the thumb to the little finger and progresses toward the index finger. Thus, Ādi tāla would be kept as follows:

[7]Brown, *The Mṛdaṅga*, Vol. I, p. 12.

	1	2	3	4	5	6	7	8
Counts:	1	2	3	4	5	6	7	8
Tāla:	$\|^4$				o		o	
Krīya:	+				+	o	+	o
	clap	little finger	ring finger	middle finger	clap	wave	clap	wave

Laghus with 7 or 9 counts are indicated in the following manner:

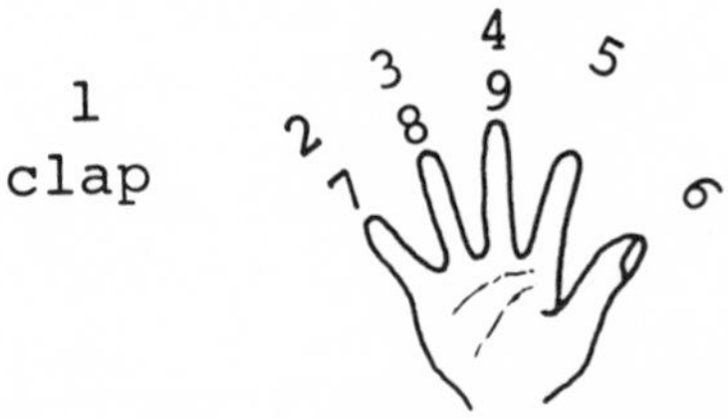

When a singer keeps tāla, he usually hits his right hand on his right thigh for a handclap (which is convenient because he is seated cross-legged), and either waves or hits his thigh with palm turned upward for a wave.

For comparative purposes, the terminology for Hindustānī and Karnatak tāla is given in Chart 12.

	KARNATAK	HINDUSTĀNĪ
One cycle of the tāla	āvarta	āvarta
A subdivision of the āvarta	āṅga	vibhāg
Types of āṅga:		
One count	anudrutam	
Two counts	drutam	
Variable finger counts	laghu	
Type of laghu	jāti	
Counts marking off the beginning of vibhāg:		
Clapped		tālī
Shown by silent wave		khālī
Count 1 of a tāla cycle	sama	sam
A single count	akṣara	mātrā
A half count	mātrā	
Subdivisions of a single count:		
Duple	dvikāla	dugun
Quadruple	chatuskāla	chaugun
Hand motions to "keep tāla"	krīya	krīya*
Speed	kāla/laya	laya
Slow	vilambita/cauka	vilambit
Medium	madhya	madhya
Fast	druta	drut

*Most practicing musicians call this "tālī."

CHART 12. Hindustānī and Karnatak Tāla Terminology

In Karnatak music, as in Hindustānī music, a single cycle can be sufficiently long to accommodate a complete musical idea. However, two or more cycles are often combined into a longer phrase. The completion of a phrase is usually signaled by a recurring melodic phrase, as in Hindustānī music. That phrase always appears at the same place in the tāla cycle and thus marks an important structural point in the tāla.

In Karnatak music, this important structural point is one of two such points in the tāla cycle. This point—the count in the tāla cycle on which a piece, a new section of a piece, or a main phrase of a piece begins—is named *eḍuppu* (a Tamil word) or *graha* (a Sanskrit word). The tāla count on which eḍuppu falls depends on the composition. In the kriti in Examples 8-2 and 8-3, for instance, eḍuppu is a half count past count 1. Completion of melodic phrases, even in improvisation that is based on a composition, is marked by the repetition of a particular melodic phrase, beginning at eḍuppu. Thus, eḍuppu is an important place for rhythmic cadences.[8]

The second important structural point in the tāla cycle is inherent in the tāla itself: it is count 1, called sam or sama. In Karnatak music, count 1 does not consistently receive special emphasis as an ending point of melodic phrases (due to the importance of eḍuppu), but the ultimate cadence realized by the drummer is almost always on sama.

Cadences at count 1 in Hindustānī performances indicate the beginning of a new tāla cycle. In Karnatak pieces, however, since cadences can come on any beat, it is more difficult (particularly in even tālas like Ādi tāla) to find your place unless you know the composition. The widespread custom of audience participation through keeping the tāla is testimony to the high level of musical education on the part of the audience.

As in North India, relative speeds in Karnatak music are conceptualized as in levels: slow, medium, and fast. The terms for these are practically the same in both cases: *vilambita* (Hindustānī *vilambit*) or *cauka*, *madhya*, and *druta* (Hindustānī *drut*), respectively.

One basic difference between Karnatak and Hindustānī performance practice is in regard to speed (called *kāla* or *laya* in Karnatak practice, *laya* in Hindustānī practice). In Karnatak music, once the basic speed is established, acceleration of the tāla counts *is not permissible.* Since the audience is keeping tāla, any acceleration will be noticeable immediately. Slight fluctuations in speed do occur in practice, of course, but theory demands that they be slight. An increase in speed is achieved instead by an increase in the rhythmic density:

> A favorite procedure in South India is to present a melodic or rhythmic pattern (sometimes a very long one, an entire composition or major section thereof) and then double it in speed while the *tāla* continues in constant pace.

[8] *Ibid.*, p. 336.

The same procedure can be followed with speeds four times as fast, or sometimes three times as fast, half as fast, etcetera. In all cases the interest derives from the interplay between the pattern of melody and rhythm and the pattern of the *tāla* as they change in relationship. The two most common doublings are a speed twice as fast (*dvikāla*) and a speed four times as fast (*catuskāla*). A *trikāla* pattern goes through the three stages of presentation: in first speed, then in *dvikāla* and *catuskāla* relationships.[9]

Meter and rhythm in Indian classical music are best discussed in connection with the instruments and performance practices that utilize them. Chapter Six continues the discussion of tāla by focusing on percussion instruments and drumming practice in light of the metric concepts presented in this chapter.

SIX

RHYTHM INSTRUMENTS AND DRUMMING

GHANA AND AVANḌḌHA VĀDYA: IDIOPHONES AND MEMBRANOPHONES

The two categories in the ancient classification system for musical instruments that pertain here are *ghana* and *avanaḍḍha*. *Ghana vādya* (ghana: "to beat or strike"; "a strike or blow") are idiophones, instruments that are struck against each other, or, more widely defined, instruments whose sound is created by the vibrating body itself.[1] *Avanḍḍha vādya* are instruments to

[1]S. Krishnaswamy, *Musical Instruments of India* (Delhi: Government of India Press, 1965), p. 21. B. C. Deva, in *Indian Music* (New Delhi: Indian Council for Cultural Relations, 1974), p. 99, explains ghana vādya as the "solid" instruments, from the Hindi घन : "solid," "bell," "gong." Claudie Marcel-DuBois, in *Les Instruments de musique de l'Inde ancienne* (Paris: Presses Universitaires de France, 1941), p. 25, translates ghana as "metal" and comments that the difference between the ancient Indian system and our modern one is that ghana vādya idiophones included only metal types. It would appear that her interpretation is incorrect.

which a skin is attached—in modern terminology, membranophones. Both categories comprise primarily percussion instruments. Percussion instruments seem to have always been varied and numerous in Indian musical history. Drums, cymbals, gongs, and bells constitute the catalogue of rhythm instruments, with drums the most prominent. With one exception, the drums used in North and South Indian classical music today are very different. The exception is the *mṛdaṅga* of the South and the similar *pakhāvaj* of the North.

Mṛdaṅga, the dominant drum in Karnatak music, is one of the most ancient of the Indian drums. It is said to have been invented by Brahma to accompany the dancing of Lord Shiva, and to have first been played by Ganesha, the elephant-headed son of Shiva.[2] Since the word "mṛdaṅga" means "made of clay," the instrument must originally have been a pottery drum, but for many centuries now it has been made of wood. Carved from a jackfruit log, it is barrel-shaped on the outside. On the inside, the bore toward the two ends is slightly conical. The mṛdaṅga is made in two main sizes, one approximately twenty-five inches long and sounding within the approximate pitch area of Ṣa to Re (C to D below middle C) and the other approximately twenty-three inches long and sounding in the pitch area of Ma to Pa (F to G below Middle C). The former is for accompanying male voices, the latter for accompanying female voices, a vīṇā, or a bamboo flute.[3]

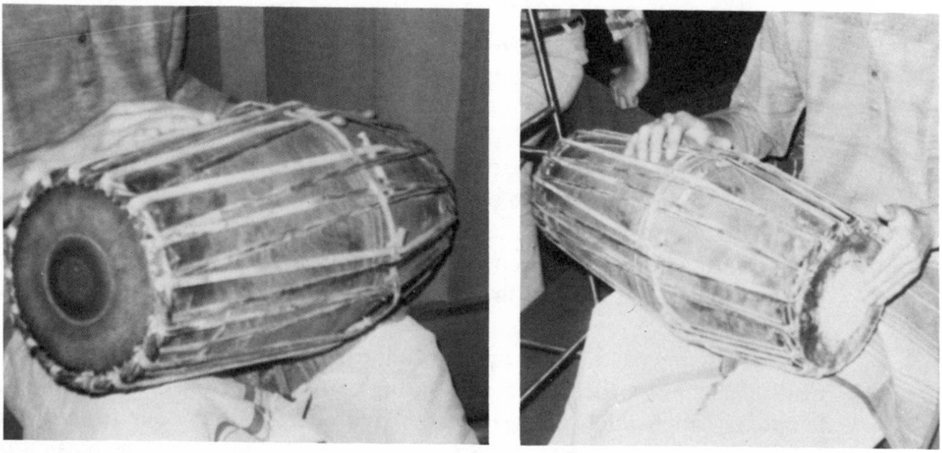

Plate 19
The Mṛdaṅga

[2]H. A. Popley, *The Music of India*, 3rd ed. (New Delhi: Y.M.C.A. Publishing House, 1966), p. 123. "Mṛdaṅga" is the Sanskrit word. Often, it appears in Dravidianized form as "mṛdaṅgam" or "mridangam."

[3]Robert Brown, *The Mṛdaṅga: A Study of Drumming in South India* (Ann Arbor, Mich.: University Microfilms, 1974), Vol. I, p. 19. For more information on the construction of the mṛdaṅga, see Chapter Two of this source. According to Brown, p. 20, a lowering in the standard pitch area has taken place since 1925 or 1935, perhaps because of the popularity of a male singer, Ariyakudi Ramanuja Ayyangar, who was a bass.

The mṛdaṅga has a playing head at each end. Each head is composite; that is, each is made of several layers of skin. The design of the heads, which is extremely complex, is meant to provide maximum clarity, variety, and controllability of tone. The several layers are of cowhide and goatskin. A rim of buffalo thong is braided around the edge of each head. This rim provides an anchor for extremely high tension: buffalo-hide lacing is pulled through it at sixteen points and stretched in a V pattern over the body from head to head.[4]

The preparation of the right-hand head once it is lashed to the drum demands great skill on the part of the maker.

> First, the center hole of the outer skin... must be enlarged to fit the required basic pitch of the instrument. This is done by inserting a metal plate between the skins and cutting the top one with a knife.... After the hole has been properly cut, the surface of the second skin, which shows through the hole, is again scraped. A thin layer of plain well-boiled rice is applied as adhesive and allowed to dry in the sun. It must be used soon after it is prepared, and it provides the base for the application of the black tuning mixture. This tuning mixture is now applied to the second skin through the hole, giving the head a clear and pleasant musical pitch, and putting the tonic and first partial of the drum into perfect octave relationship to one another.[5]

The paste on the right head may last for weeks or even months if the drum is not used constantly. Most professional drummers, however, must change instruments at least once during a performance because the paste begins to chip, affecting the tone. The skin must be scraped completely clean before new paste is applied.[6]

The final stage in preparing the right head is the insertion of thin pieces of straw between the first and second heads. These form radii from the center to the sixteen points where the thong is lashed to the edge of the head. The two vibrating heads are thereby kept from touching each other, and the tone is noticeably improved. The straws are broken off so as not to extend into the playing area.

A tuning paste is also applied to the left head, but it is not a "permanent" paste, as on the right head. During performance, the drummer uses a temporary application of paste made from coarse wheat flour to alter the quality and pitch of the tone.[7] A further means of controlling the tension of the heads, and therefore the basic pitch, is to wedge blocks of wood between the thong braces and the walls of the instrument.

Several distinctly different sounds are possible on the mṛdaṅga. The heads may be hit on the ring of the top skin, on the tuning-paste spot of the

[4] *Ibid.*, p. 33.
[5] *Ibid.*, p. 36.
[6] *Ibid.*, p. 41.
[7] *Ibid.*, p. 26.

second skin, or on both places at once. One, two, or three fingers and even the palm may be used in these different places. Damped or undamped sounds are possible. A very clear musical pitch, its octave, or a pitch a half step above the basic pitch can be produced.[8]

The mṛdaṅga occupies a peculiar position in South Indian culture:

> The repair and manufacture of *mṛdaṅgas* is a highly skilled craft requiring long training and experience, but because it involves the handling of dead animal material it is pursued only by persons of low caste. It is indicative of the supreme cultural prestige and antiquity of the instrument that a large number of the famous performers of the past and present are Brahmans. Its use requires not only constant manual contact with animal hide, but with the skin of a butchered cow. Drummers know how to make only minor repairs on their instruments and most frequently bring them to the professional specialist for care. . . . Although his social position is an inferior and servile one, he has the innate dignity of the skilled and indispensable craftsman.[9]

Mṛdaṅga artists of note include T. Ranganathan and Trichy S. Shankaran. Especially notable is Palghat Mani Iyer.

The northern Pakhāvaj is the same type of instrument as the mṛdaṅga, and is very similar to it. Indeed, it is sometimes called *mṛdaṅg* in the North. The pakhāvaj is a modified barrel-shaped drum, constructed in various sizes: "Its dimensions fluctuate from approximately 66 to 76 cm in length, and from 20 to 30 cm in diameter at its greatest girth, an asymetrically placed point which is between $2\frac{1}{2}$ and 5 cm closer to the *bāyāṅ* [left] end than the *dāhinā* [right]. The presence of this point places the pakhāvaj somewhere between a double cone and a barrel, . . ."[10]

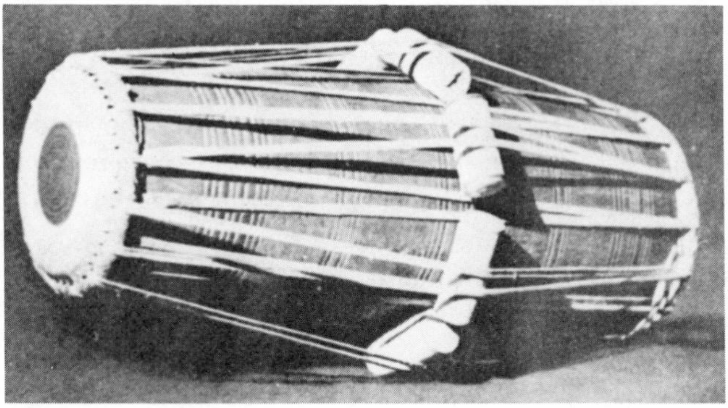

Plate 20
The Pakhāvaj

[8] *Ibid.*, p. 45.

[9] *Ibid.*, pp. 22–23.

[10] Rebecca Stewart, *The Tablā in Perspective*. (Ann Arbor, Mich.: University Microfilms, 1974) p. 11.

The design of the heads on the pakhāvaj is slightly different: the outer layer of skin is cut away more than on the mṛdaṅga. This leaves more of the surface of the second layer exposed and makes the playing area wider. This difference apparently lowers the degree to which the higher partials are damped on the pakhāvaj, and its pitch is therefore not as clear as that of the mṛdaṅga.[11] The *dāhinā* (right) head is from 16½ to 19 centimeters in diameter, the *bāyāṅ* (left) head from 25½ to 28 centimeters. A wheat-flour paste (*āṭā*) is placed on the pakhāvaj bāyāṅ head prior to each performance.[12]

The quality of the leather on the heads of the pakhāvaj and mṛdaṅga is also different, as is the tensions on their surfaces. The cylindrical blocks of wood between the leather braces and the body of the pakhāvaj are bigger than those on the Karnatak instrument. Some of the playing techniques differ as well.

The name "pakhāvaj" may have been derived from the *āvaj*, a drum used in Mughal courts. In the memoirs of the emperor Akbar, the āvaj is described as "two kettle drums joined together at the reverse ends, their heads covered with skins and braced with thongs."[13] The pakhāvaj was the predominant drum in Mughal times: it was used to accompany vocal music, such instruments as the bīn and rebāb, and dancing. The relatively rare bīn performances today are still accompanied by pakhāvaj, as are the more frequent occasions of dhrupad singing. Gopal Dass, Madhavrao Alkutkar, and Lakshmi Narayan Pawar have been among the few notable pakhāvaj players in recent times.

In Karnatak classical music, the mṛdaṅga is sometimes supplemented by another membranophone, the *kanjīra* (similar to the Western tambourine). In the West, this type of instrument is not usually associated with classical music, as it is in India. Experts on the kanjīra are said to be able to produce, with one hand only, all the variations and patterns that are played on the mṛdaṅga.[14]

The great percussionist Pudukkotai Mamundiya Pillai, who lived in the late nineteenth and early twentieth centuries, is said to have been responsible for the development of the kanjīra as a concert instrument.[15] Usually, it is one of the instruments found in the *tāla vādya kacceri*, an ensemble of drums and other percussion instruments that take turns performing rhythmic variations in a given tāla. The brilliant technique used on the kanjīra "must

[11]Brown, *The Mṛdaṅga*, Vol. I, p. 46. It is not clear whether this pertains to both heads. Krishnaswamy says that the left side is about the same on both drums, but the right sides differ "in the distribution of the prepared parts" (*Musical Instruments of India*, p. 73).

[12]Stewart, *The Tablā*, p. 11.

[13]Quoted in Krishnaswamy, *Musical Instruments of India*, p. 75.

[14]Krishnaswamy, *Musical Instruments of India*, p. 77. The kanjīra is widely used in folk songs and devotional music as well.

[15]L. Shankar, *The Art of Violin Accompaniment in South Indian Classical Music* (Ann Arbor Mich.: University Microfilms, 1974), p. 162.

be influenced by the fact that it is frequently used in conjunction with mṛdaṅga. The tāla vādya kacceri in fact, often becomes a kind of contest in rhythmic dexterity, with each of the several performers on the different instruments trying to outdo the others in imaginative play."[16] Kanjīra specialists include C. K. Shyam and S. Sunder.

The kanjīra is a simple circular wooden frame about ten inches in diameter and two and a half inches deep. Some kind of skin (preferably wild lizard) is stretched across one side. Since the other side is left open, the instrument is a single-headed frame drum. Desired pitches may be obtained by applying a little water to the kanjīra skin. This reduces the tension of the skin. Variations in sound are produced by pressing the skin near the rim with all four playing fingers (index to little). Three or four slits are made in the frame on the open side of the kanjīra. One or more pieces of metal or coin are then inserted in a crossbar inside the slits. These produce a jingling sound when the instrument is shaken.[17]

For at least the last one hundred years, yet another percussion instrument has been used in Karnatak classical performance—the *ghaṭam*. Like the kanjīra, the ghaṭam supplements the mṛdaṅga. Unlike the kanjīra, it is not a membranophone but rather a spherical clay pot without any skin head. Accordingly, it is an idiophone. The specially made pot has a big belly and thus a large playing area. Usually, the playing area is about a foot and a half in diameter, but this depends on the pitch desired, which must be in tune with the drone pitch.[18] The player hits the neck, the center, and the bottom of the pot to produce different sounds. For further variety of sound, he uses both hands, both wrists, all ten fingers, and even his fingernails. "The general effect [is] a fast and scintillating crackling."[19] The player also can move the narrow open mouth of the pot alternately away from and against his bare stomach. This produces a rising pitch similar to the one sounded by the mṛdaṅga.

Ayyangar relates an anecdote about the bare stomach of the ghaṭam player.[20] Salem Subbier, a player of *jaltarang*, made disparaging remarks about the most outstanding ghaṭam player of recent memory, Pazhani

[16]Brown, *The Mṛdaṅga*, Vol. I, p. 50.

[17]Krishnaswamy, *Musical Instruments of India*, p. 77. However, Brown states that the instrument has a single jingle in its rim (*The Mṛdaṅga*, Vol. I, p. 50), and, indeed, the picture on p. 77 of Krishnaswamy appears to bear this out.

[18]Brown, *The Mṛdaṅga*, Vol. I, p. 51.

[19]*Ibid.*

[20]This anecdote appears in Ayyangar's *History of South Indian Music*, p. 315. It is a curious anecdote, since it is a perfectly acceptable Karnatak custom to perform in traditional style—wearing the white *dhoti* (a long, white cloth that the individual wraps around himself—in effect, a man's sari) tied high, just above the waist. Perhaps this custom was less acceptable in British colonial times than it is at present.

Jaltarang, the unfortunate Subbier's instrument, is a set of eighteen (or so) porcelain cups of different sizes, which are filled with water and tuned to different pitches. The cups are arranged in a semicircle and are played with two slender sticks. The performer must therefore turn continually in order to hit the various cups. Both Hindustānī and Karnatak music are performed on the jaltarang.

Krishna Iyer: "O the reputation of a half naked man fisting an earthen pot! Once he comes to my house, I can expose his poor rhythm." Krishna Iyer heard about this remark and determined to get back at Subbier. Soon he had an opportunity: he was to provide ghaṭam accompaniment for Subbier in a wedding concert. Early the day of the wedding, he sent word to Subbier that he would be well advised to leave his coat at home. The message irritated Subbier, and he did not heed it. When it was Krishna Iyer's turn to play solo, during the concert, Subbier kept time with his melody, as was the custom. Iyer kept on playing, challenging Subbier with a rapid flow of more and more intricate rhythms. The jaltarang player sweated profusely in his coat. Finally, when the ghaṭam solo ended, Subbier removed his dripping coat with relief. That was the moment Krishna Iyer had been waiting for. "Wooly headed noodle," he shouted to the boy who had delivered the message to Subbier, "so you did not warn Subbier this morning to leave his coat behind! What a shame for a half naked dandy to face an audience!"

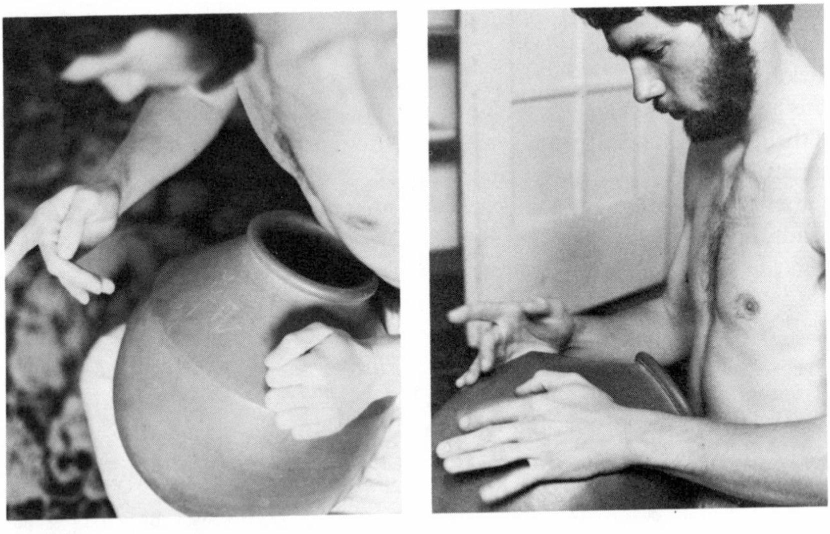

Plate 21
The Ghaṭam (Being Played by G. Gillette)

The ghaṭam player sometimes throws his instrument into the air, interrupting but not disrupting the continuity of either his rhythm patterns or the tāla. Formerly, the player accentuated the final climax by throwing the instrument high in the air, timing its fall perfectly so that it would break with a crash exactly on the last beat of the last rhythmic pattern. This practice was inexpensive because the clay pot was an ordinary one. Nowadays, however, the clay used for the ghaṭam is mixed with iron filings and then baked.

The pot is no longer allowed to break because of the expense of replacing a good one.[21] Ghaṭam specialists include R. Gurumurthy, Vellore T. G. Ramabhadran, and Sundarmier Palghat.

The other prominent idiophones used in Karnatak classical music are *tālam*, the cymbals used prominently in the accompaniment to *Bhārata Nāṭyam*, a classical dance style. Tālam are small, concave, made of bronze, and usually connected by cord. Generally, only the edges are struck. Tālam are used by a dance master (*naṭṭuvanar*) to beat the tāla and also sometimes the rhythms of the dance patterns. In *Bhārata Nāṭyam*, tālam are part of an accompaniment ensemble that includes the mṛdaṅga, a tāmbūra, and perhaps a flute and vīṇā, in addition to the vocalist(s). Many varieties of small paired cymbals are found in India, most of which provide rhythmic accompaniment for devotional music, drama, and religious discourse.

As we noted in Chapter Four, a drum called the tavil has traditionally been used to accompany the nagasvaram. The tavil is generally classed as a barrel-shaped drum, although one might better call it a cylindrical drum with a slight bulge in the middle. This bulge seems to be of no particular importance.[22] The instrument is carved from a single block of wood, and has rather short sides and two large heads. The skins of the heads are stretched over thick hoops made of hemp and six or seven bamboo sticks bundled and bound together with hemp. Interlaced leather thongs fasten the hoops to the shell of the drum. The instrument is tuned to the desired pitch area by a band of leather around the laced thongs at about the middle of the drum. The design of the heads is not as complex as that of the mṛdaṅga heads. Neither of the two heads of the tavil is tuned to a specific pitch. The right head is played with the wrist and fingers, and the left head is struck with a stick.

The primary percussion instrument in North India since the eighteenth century has been the tablā. A tablā is in fact two separate drums, one played by each hand, but it is considered one drum with two heads. "Tablā" is the name by which the right drum is usually called. More precisely, it is called "dāhinā" or "dāyāṅ," meaning "right." "*Bāyāṅ*," which means "left," indicates the left drum. The two drums are totally unalike, but complement each other beautifully.

The history of the tablā is not clear, but various theories have been offered. A fanciful one, dubbed a "fairy tale" by Chaitanya Deva, concerns two professional pakhāvaj players during Emperor Akbar's time (1556–1605) who were bitter and constant rivals. One of them (Sudhar Khan) happened to lose in a drumming competition. Unable to bear the defeat, he dashed his drum onto the floor. The pakhāvaj broke in two, and the parts were made into tablā and bāyāṅ.[23] Another theory is that the tablā, like the sitār and

[21]Brown, *The Mṛdaṅga*, Vol. I, p. 52.
[22]*Ibid.*, pp. 54–55.
[23]Deva, *Indian Music*, p. 114.

Plate 22
The Tablā

other instruments, was introduced into Indian classical music by Amir Khusrau in the thirteenth century; this theory assumes that the tablā was imported from farther west.

The term "tablā" is traceable directly to the Arabic "*ṭabl*," a generic term meaning drum. This term was borrowed from the Aramaic term "*tabla*," which itself was adapted from the Akkadian word "tabalu" or "tapalu."[24] Rebecca Stewart, who has done copious research on the history of the tablā, reports that the many variants of the term "tablā" may be found from northern Africa to southern Russia, and from northern China to South America and the Caribbean. The term has not always been attached to the same physical types of drum, however. By the second quarter of the seventeenth century, the names "atables" and "tabales" had appeared in accounts of travels through the Punjab, the region in Northwest India through which peoples migrated into the subcontinent from the West. The first iconographic depiction of an instrument that closely resembles the present-day Indian tablā was found in 1808.[25]

[24]Stewart, *The Tablā*, p. 6. Stewart cites H. E. Hause, "Terms for Musical Instruments in the Sudanic Languages," *Supplement to the Journal of the American Oriental Society*, No. 7 (Jan.-Mar. 1948), p. 8, and adds in a footnote (p. 20), "It should be noted that the long accepted etymological derivation of *tabl* from the Latin *tabula* (Curt Sachs, *History of Musical Instruments*, p. 249) is incorrect."

[25]Stewart, *The Tablā*, p. 6.

> For a period of approximately fifty years before this date, however, a veritable flood of Mughal-style miniatures show pairs of instruments which attest to the presence of two types of hand-played drum pairs in contiguous areas of northwestern India: the Punjab (wooden cylindrical pairs) and the Delhi-Rajasthan-Oudh area (metal or clay hemispherical pairs). . . . It appears that sometime during the middle or latter half of the 18th century these two drum types were combined: for the right hand, the fixed-pitch cylindrical Punjabi "tabla" was chosen; for the left hand, the variable-pitch hemispherical Delhi "dūggī."[26]

Basing her opinion on both pictorial and literary descriptions, Stewart asserts that this instrument underwent several major and minor alterations between 1750 and 1850, and that the tablā used today is probably no more than seventy to one hundred years old. Like the sāraṅgī, the tablā rose to popularity as the types of music it accompanied rose in popularity—vocal khyāl and ṭhumṛī and the developing instrumental solo forms.

The dāhinā (right drum) is the higher and more precisely pitched of the pair. Its shape is rather like a pot fashioned on a potter's wheel, wider at the bottom and tapering upward. Its widest point is about five to six and a half centimeters above its base. It is made of oak or rosewood. The bāyaṅ is tuned to a general pitch area approximately an octave lower.[27] Nowadays, bāyāṅ are made of German silver, a silver-white alloy formed of copper, zinc, and nickel. Formerly, bāyāṅ were made of pottery (and even now the less expensive ones are), but professional performers would not use a pottery instrument in performance. The sizes of tablā and bāyāṅ vary greatly, partly to suit the player's aesthetic taste, partly to fit the size of his hand, and partly according to the instrument they are likely to be used with, whether for accompanying or other purposes.

The tablā and bāyāṅ heads are both of the composite type, with the top layer of skin cut to a narrow band around the outer edge. Both heads are of goatskin. A circle of black tuning paste applied to the surface of the second layer controls the vibrations of the head. This circle, which is applied in the center of the tablā, is close to an edge on the bāyāṅ, presumably to allow room for the use of the wrist and heel of the left hand. On both drums the paste is permanent; to change it, one must replace the head.

A small goat-hide hoop is placed at the bottom of each drum. A larger, interlaced goat-hide hoop holds the skin in position on the top of each drum, and goat-hide lacing lashed between the two hoops holds the skin tense. Small cylinder-shaped blocks of wood are wedged between the lacing and the body of the drum on the dāhinā. It is extremely difficult to insert these blocks,

[26] *Ibid.*, pp. 7, 10.

[27] The tuning of the bāyaṅ is certainly not standardized. Some teachers assert that the instrument is not tuned at all. Others give various intervals, mostly an octave below the dāhinā.

and drummers prefer not to do it themselves because they might injure their hands. Once the blocks are in place, one may adjust the tension of the head by hammering them up or down.

Precise tuning of the tablā is done with a small hammer made of German silver. The hammer is held in the left hand, and the right hand does the testing. For general tuning, the wedged blocks are hit; for fine tuning, the hoop around the head is tapped. The tension must be equal all the way around the head, and the same clear sound, at the same precise pitch, must be achieved. If the tuning begins to slip during a performance, the drummer stops to fix it—without interrupting the continuity of the tāla (unless the soloist he is accompanying also stops to tune, and usually not even then). The drum is tuned to Sa (or perhaps Pa) of the soloist's voice or of the solo instrument. Tuning the bāyāṅ is less complicated than tuning the dāhinā because the former is tuned to a general pitch area rather than to a precise pitch. Tapping the hoop around the head with the hammer usually suffices. The thongs on the bāyāṅ are sometimes threaded through metal rings two and a half centimeters in diameter, which can be pushed up or down to tighten or loosen the tension on the head.

Plate 23
Sharda Sahai Playing the Tablā

The sounds produced on the tablā and bāyāṅ are either open or closed (damped or undamped). There is a repertoire of strokes for each hand separately and for the hands together. The index, third, and fourth fingers of the right hand are used, and one stroke calls for the hand to be almost flattened and the fingers to be straight and rocked sideways on the head. On the bāyāṅ, the index and middle fingers of the left hand are used, as well as the heel of the hand (for pressure). A range of pitch can be produced on the bāyāṅ either by exerting pressure with the heel of the hand or by sliding the hand lightly across the head toward the paste. Exploitation of the range by a drummer is greatly admired.[28] Drummers usually keep a supply of powder nearby to sprinkle on the drumheads. The powder makes it easier to move the fingers and hands quickly. There are many fine tablā artists, although few have been soloists. Among those of note are the late Chatur Lal, Alla Rakha, Jnan Prakash Ghosh, Lateef Ahmed Khan, Zakir Hussein Khan, Fais Khan, Anand Gopal Bandyopadhya (also called Gopal Banerjee), Shamta Prasad, Krishan Maharaj, and Sharda Sahai.

Plate 24
Close-up of Player's Hands on the Tablā

The *naghāṛa* is the drum that was used in the naubat ensemble in Mughal courts (see p. 110) to accompany the shehnai, and it is still frequently used with shehnai on the concert stage. It is a single-headed conical drum,

[28]Stewart's *The Tablā* is a fine study of the relationship of tablā technique to the technique used in playing other North Indian drums.

or, as Stewart describes it, "the more pointed half of an egg in shape"[29] with a shell of riveted copper, brass, or sheet iron. The size of the naghāṛa varies extremely, but often a concert instrument will have a diameter of two and a half to three feet.

Two naghāṛas, one much smaller than that described above, are used to accompany shehnai players. The pair is played by one drummer. The larger drum (*dhama*) is made of metal, and its height and diameter are of equal proportions. The smaller drum (*jhil*) is made of clay or metal. Usually, it is shallower—from twenty-three to twenty-five centimeters high—and the diameter of its head is twenty-eight to thirty centimeters.

> Though the relative sophistication of the method for binding the head to the drum is less, this method is basically similar to that used on the tablā, pakhāvaj, and dholak [a drum used in folk music]: the binding laces are not drawn directly through the skin of the head, but in both cases are secured to other cords which form part of a band which encircles the upper rim of the drum. This method of binding ensures a more even distribution of tension and hoops to secure the head to the drum. The lacings form an X-type grid. Though neither drum lends itself readily to precise tuning, the tension of both heads may be altered: that of the dhama by an application of water; that of the jhil by heat. The dhama often has a glutinous tuning paste placed under the center of its head.[30]

The traditional means of playing the naghāṛa is with sticks. The instruments produce a sharp, resonant sound that can carry quite far. Plate 25 illustrates a pair of naghāṛa of greatly contrasting sizes.

Plate 25
A Pair of Naghāṛa

[29] *Ibid.*, p. 13.
[30] *Ibid.*

Drumming is more of a requisite for musical performance in India than in the West. In the West, a solo melody instrument would most likely be complemented by a piano or small instrumental ensemble. In India (North or South), a solo melody instrument is complemented by a drone instrument (as already discussed) and a drum. A vocal solo is accompanied by an ensemble that includes drum, drone, and a stringed melody instrument.

> Commencement of formal training in [mṛdañgam] is usually marked by a pūjā ceremony to Gaṇeṣa, the god of auspicious beginnings. The teacher may pass the instrument to the student in a special way signifying the acceptance of their relationship and all that it implies. In the case of *mṛdañgam*, the drum is held vertically with the outstretched fingers under the braiding of the *valandalai* [right-hand head], and the student accepts it in the same manner. The first lesson is also a special one, likewise dedicated to the elephant deity.
>
> Piḷḷayār Pādam ("lesson dedicated to Piḷḷayār, or Gaṇeṣa") . . . contains every stroke used later except . . . NAM. Although obviously beyond the capabilities of the raw beginner, it is important that the first thing learned should be this ceremonial offering of the sounds of the drum to the deity of beginnings. As in all the lessons, the student imitates as well as he can the teacher's hand position and tone. . . . One important attitude is at once clarified: the student should attempt to perform things beyond his present ability, to exceed himself in technique.[31]

As we noted earlier, the sounds produced on the mṛdañga are of two basic types: damped and undamped. Given the complex construction of the drum, which makes it capable of precise pitch, it is more accurate to say that the two types of sound produced approximate either noise or pitch. Fourteen main strokes are used in mṛdañga playing as performed by T. Ranganathan. Three have individual names, and the rest are referred to by seven syllables (generically called *solkattu*).[32] The fourteen strokes are as follows:

Named strokes (3): gumiki, cāppu, araicāppu
Strokes indicated by syllable (11):

Tom (2)	Di (1)	Ki (1)
Nam (2)	Dim (1)	Ta (1)
Ta (3)		

Presumably, such syllables were originally meant to imitate the sounds of the strokes to which they referred, but with time the use of syllables became more complex.

[31] Brown, *The Mṛdañga*, Vol. I, pp. 116–17.
[32] *Ibid.*, p. 92.

Single strokes are combined into stroking patterns, and, thus, single syllables are combined into euphonious, easily recited syllable patterns that indicate such stroking patterns. A distinction must be made here between a syllable that is being used to refer to one of those main strokes and that syllable when it is used in a syllable/stroking pattern. In a pattern context, for instance, the syllable Ta is used for eleven different strokes. On the other hand, one stroke can be referred to by a variety of syllables. One damped right-hand stroke, for example, may be called Di, Ḍa, Ḍu, Ka, Ki, Ku, Mi, Gi, or Ta.[33] The choice of which syllable to use depends on the context—the syllable pattern. "In addition to their purely rhythmic configuration as duration structures in time, the patterns have qualities of pitch, timbre, intensity, a kinesthetic feeling related to their physical production and a vocal form in the shape of spoken syllables."[34] These patterns are usually not heard in concert, but they are always in a drummer's head.

The basic idea behind rhythmic development in Karnatak drumming is to take a set of primary materials—a wealth of forms and a wealth of patterns—and constantly rearrange, change, and extend them. In this respect, development in rhythm is like development in melody. For example, a germinal stroking pattern can act as a motive for seemingly inexhaustible possibilities. To begin with, one germinal pattern can be used as the basis for compositions in several tālas. Examples 6-1 and 6-2 illustrate the pattern TANATA JONUTA JOṆU in compositions in two tālas: Example 6-1 is in Ādi tāla, whose structure is 4 + 2 + 2, and Example 6-2 is in Khaṇḍa Cāpu tāla, whose structure is 2 + 3. To fit into the latter, JOṆU is repeated, so that pattern becomes TANATA JONUTA JOṆU JOṆU.[35]

In these examples as I have notated them, no indication of the stroking technique is given; therefore, left-hand and right-hand movements are not specified. Each count of the tāla is shown by an arabic numeral. Subdivisions within the tāla cycle are marked with a single slash, and the end of a cycle is marked with a double slash—for example, Ādi tāla: 1 2 3 4/5 6/7 8//; Khaṇḍa Cāpu tāla: 1 2/3 4 5//. All strokes shown within a count are of equal duration unless otherwise indicated. A segment of time of that duration that is not filled by a stroke is indicated by a dot: the duration of • • • equals the duration of TANATA. (A dot beneath a letter is part of the transliteration of the letter; it has no rhythmic significance.)

[33] *Ibid.*, p. 96. For a good discussion of the structure of this drum language, see Chapter Five of this source.

[34] *Ibid.*, p. 60.

[35] Examples 6-1 and 6-2 are from Brown, *The Mṛdaṅga*, Vol. II, pp. 139–40 and 227–30, respectively. Brown indicates stroking techniques as well. In Example 6-1, the repetition of TANATA JONUTA JOṆU (count 2) is played without the left hand. Therefore, although the syllables repeat, the sound of the pattern when drummed is slightly different.

EXAMPLE 6-1 Stroking Pattern in Ādi Tāla

1								2							
TA	NA	TA	JO	NU	TA	JO	ṆU	TA	NA	TA	JO	NU	TA	JO	ṆU
3								4							
TA	NA	TA	JO	NU	TA	JO	ṆU	TA	NA	TA	TAN	·	TAN	·	TA/
5								6							
TA	NA	TA	JO	NU	TA	JO	ṆU	TA	NA	TA	JO	NU	TA	JO	ṆU/
7								8							
TA	NA	TA	JO	NU	TA	JO	ṆU	TA	NA	TA	TAN	·	TAN	·	TA//
1								2							
TA	NA	TA	TAM	·	TAM	·	TA	NA	TA	TA	TAM	·	TAM	·	TA
3								4							
TA	NA	TA	TAN	·	TAN	·	TA	TON	·	DA	·	TAM	·	·	· /
5								6							
·	·	TA	NA	TA	TAN	·	TAN	·	TA	TON	·	DA	·	TAM	· /
7								8							
·	·	·	·	TA	NA	TA	TAN	·	TAN	·	TA	TON	·	DA	· //
1															
TAM															

EXAMPLE 6-2 Stroking Pattern in Khaṇḍa Cāpu Tāla

1 2 /3 4 5 //1 2 /3 4 5 //

TA NA TA JO NU TA JO ṆU JO ṆU//TA NA TA JO NU TA JO ṆU JO ṆU//

TA NA TA JO NU TA JO ṆU JO ṆU//TA NA TA TAM · TAM · TAM · TA//

Repeat the preceding four cycles.

TA NA TA JO NU TA JO ṆU JO ṆU//TA NA TA JO NU TA JO NU JO ṆU//

TA NA TA TAM · TAM · TAM · TA//

Repeat the preceding three cycles.

TA NA TA JO NU TA JO ṆU JO ṆU//TA NA TA TAM · TAM · TAM · TA//

TA NA TA JO NU TA JO ṆU JO ṆU//TA NA TA TAM · TAM · TAM · TA//

TA NA TA TAM · TAM · TAM · TA// Repeat the preceding cycle.

TA NA TA TAM · TAM · TA NA NA//TA TAM · TAM · TA TA NA TA TAM//

· TA NA NA TA TAM · TA

(Mōrā begins here:) TA NA//TA TAM · TAM · TA TAM · · · //

//TA NA TA TAM · TAM · TA TAM · //

// · · TA NA TA TAM · TAM · TA //

//TAM

In Example 6-1, each tāla count is subdivided into eight strokes, or eight equal durations. In Example 6-2, each tāla count is subdivided into two strokes or two equal durations. In each example, the strokes TA, TAM, and TAN are drummed the same way. The spoken nasals "m" and "n" in TAM and TAN indicate a prolongation that is matched on the drum by the absence of a new stroke in the succeeding unit of time.

Examples 6-1 and 6-2 both end in a *mōrā*. A mōrā is a cadential phrase that is played three times and ends on an important count of the tāla—either sama (count 1) or eḍuppu, the count on which a composition begins. Cross-rhythms are created purposely in a mōrā because each repetition begins at a different moment in the tāla cycle. The mōrā pattern in Example 6-1 is TA NA TA TAN • TAN • TA TON • DA • TAM. The beginning of each of the three occurrences of this pattern in the example is marked by a box around the initial stroke TA. There is an equal amount of time between appearance one and appearance two of the pattern, and between appearance two and appearance three. This mōrā ends on sama.

The mōrā pattern in Example 6-2 is shorter: TA NA TA TAM • TAM • TA TAM; it, too ends on sama. Mōrās can be less symmetrical and quite a bit more complex than this. The phrases can even be of different lengths, as long as the essence of mōrā is kept—the pull of cross-rhythm and its resolution at the appointed place.[36]

Students beginning to study mṛdaṅga learn to produce the basic strokes, then basic patterns. From the earliest lessons, they learn the principle and technique of playing in levels of speed (the only means of acceleration allowed in Karnatak music). The principle is demonstrated here with a basic stroke pattern, TA DI TOM NAM. In Example 6-3, the pattern is in four levels of speed. In Example 6-4, each stroke of the pattern is played three times so that the student becomes accustomed to triplets. When the pattern is played in duple levels of speed, cross-rhythms are created. The purpose of the exercise is to teach the student to control exact units of time. The student should also attempt to execute each stroke at the same dynamic level.[37]

So that students may learn the principle of gradual growth from a germinal idea, lessons are given in which patterns are inserted between the TA, DI, TOM, and NAM strokes. These insertions are fundamental combinations of strokes that increase gradually from a length of two syllables to one of twenty-two syllables. These are not taught as in a tāla. Example 6-5 shows such insertions.[38] The main strokes are in italics. The insertions made between those syllables are: (1) • KITA (which is two drumming strokes in

[36] *Ibid.*, Vol. I, p. 165.

[37] These exercises are described fully in Brown, *The Mṛdaṅga*, Vol. I, Chapter Seven.

[38] Example 6-5 is adapted from Brown, *The Mṛdaṅga*, Vol. II, pp. 4–7, 12.

EXAMPLE 6-3 Stroking Pattern in Four Levels of Speed

```
TA                                                 DI
TA                       DI                        TOM                       NAM                    /
TA          DI           TOM          NAM          /TA          DI           TOM          NAM       /
TA     DI   TOM    NAM/TA        DI   TOM    NAM/TA        DI   TOM    NAM/TA        DI   TOM    NAM/

TOM                                                NAM                                              /
TA                       DI                        TOM                       NAM                    /
TA          DI           TOM          NAM          /TA          DI           TOM          NAM       /
TA     DI   TOM    NAM/TA        DI   TOM    NAM/TA        DI   TOM    NAM/TA        DI   TOM    NAM/
```

EXAMPLE 6-4 Stroking Pattern of Triplets in Levels of Speed

```
TA          TA         TA         DI            DI            DI
TA     TA   TA     DI  DI     DI  TOM    TOM    TOM    NAM    NAM    NAM/

NOM         NOM        NOM        TAM           TAM           TAM       /
TA     TA   TA     DI  DI     DI  TOM    TOM    TOM    NAM    NAM    NAM/
```

one count, as in (♩ ♫ · ♫ ki ta); (2) KITA TAKA (♫ ♫); (3) • KITA TAKA (♩ ♫ ♫); (4) repeat of preceding main stroke plus KITA; (5) repeat of preceding main stroke plus KITA TAKA; and (6) • KITA TAKA TAKA.

EXAMPLE 6-5 Principle of Gradual Growth from a Germinal Idea

TA	·	KITA	*DI*	·	KITA	*TOM*	·	KITA	*NAM*	·
KITA	*TA*	KITA	TAKA	*DI*	KITA	TAKA	*TOM*	KITA	TAKA	*NAM*
KITA	TAKA	*TA*	·	KITA	TAKA	*DI*	·	KITA	TAKA	*TOM*
·	KITA	TAKA	*NAM*	·	KITA	TAKA	*TA*	TA	KITA	*DI*
DI	KITA	*TOM*	TOM	KITA	*NAM*	NAM	KITA	*TA*	TA	KITA
TAKA	*DI*	DI	KITA	TAKA	*TOM*	TOM	KITA	TAKA	*NAM*	
NAM	KITA	TAKA	*TA*	·	KITA	TAKA	TAKA	*DI*	·	KITA
TAKA	TAKA	*TOM*	·	KITA	TAKA	TAKA	*NAM*	·	KITA	TAKA
TAKA	*TA*	[etc.]								

A number of other fundamental combinations of strokes are inserted as this learning exercise proceeds. With the insertion pattern TARIGIḌU—for instance, in the line TA • KITA KIṬATAKA DIKUTAKA TARIGIḌU—the point made earlier about euphonic syllable choice comes into play. The pattern TARIGIḌU is played just like KIṬATAKA. It would be awkward to say TA • KITA KIṬATAKA DIKUTAKA KITATAKA.

> There seems to be only one logical explanation for this phenomenon. . . . That is, that the practice of forming solkattus has now advanced far beyond the point where it represents a simple suggestion of the drum sound, much less an exact vocal parallel. The drum syllables lead a life of their own, so to speak. . . . The stringing together of longer patterns depends on aesthetic and euphonic conditions . . . the practice of representing rhythmic pattern by spoken syllables is more than a science, it is an art, and it is entirely concerned with the beauty of sound.[39]

At a later stage of training, the student of mṛdaṅga begins to put the ideas of germinal motive and gradual elaboration into the framework of a tāla. He also learns how to create other shapes. For example, he may start with a long pattern and gradually reduce it. This is called *gopuccha*, the shape of a cow's tail—thick at the beginning and tapering to thin. These shapes can be used in the mōrā. This is demonstrated in Example 6-6, a composition in Ādi tāla in which each count is divided into four equal

[39] *Ibid.*, Vol. I, pp. 135–36.

EXAMPLE 6-6 Gopuccha Shape

Ādi tāla

1				2				3				4			
TA	DIN	TA	DIN	TAKA	DIN	TA	DIN	TA	DIN	TA	DIN	NA	TAM	TAM	·/
A				A′								B			
5				6				7				8			
TA	DIN	TA	DIN	TAKA	DIN	TA	DIN	/TA	DIN	TA	DIN	NA	TAM	TAM	·//
1				2				3				4			
TA	DIN	TA	DIN	NA	TAM	TAM	·	TA	DIN	TA	DIN	NA	TAM	TAM	·/
5				6				7				8			
[NA]	TAM	TAM	·	TAM	·	[NA]	TAM	/TAM	·	TAM	·	[NA]	TAM	TAM	·//
B′															
1															
TAM															

durations.[40] The structure, including the morā with a letter assigned to each count, is as follows:

AA′AB	://
AB	://
B^1	three times (mōrā)

In Example 6-6, the first occurrences of A, A′, and B, and B^1 are bracketed. Each initial stroke of the mōrā pattern is boxed. The pattern TAKA is drummed in one unit of time, which is shown by a slur.

Example 6-6 can be changed gradually by infix, the procedure of substituting new strokes for the basic strokes, usually in double time. This is illustrated in Example 6-7 with just two counts.

EXAMPLE 6-7 Principle of Gradual Change Through Infix

1				2			
TA	DIN	TA	DIN	TAKA	DIN	TA	DIN
TA	DIN	TA	DIN	TAKA	DINA	TA	DIN
TA	DIN	TA	DIN	TAKA	DINA	TA	DINNA
TA	DIN	TA	DINA	TAKA	DINA	TA	DINNA
TA	DINA	TA	DINA	TAKA	DINA	TA	DINNA

Another shape (*yati*) and one which can come into mōrā as well as in compositions, is *damaru yati*: >< . A damaru yati pattern, divorced from the tāla, is shown in Example 6-8. Example 6-9 illustrates the same pattern, but in the way a drummer would think of it—in terms of DARIKIḌA with various prefixes. The pattern DARIKIḌA fills only one unit of time.

EXAMPLE 6-8 Damaru Yati

TAN DA KA TAN DA TAN DARIKIḌA
TA KA TAN DA TAN DARIKIḌA
TAN DA TAN DARIKIḌA
TAN DARIKIḌA
TAN TAN DARIKIḌA
TAN DA TAN DARIKIḌA TAM

EXAMPLE 6-9 Principle of Prefix

TAN DA	KA	TAN DA	TAN DARIKIḌA	
TA	KA	TAN DA	TAN DARIKIḌA	
		TAN DA	TAN DARIKIḌA	
			TAN DARIKIḌA	
		TAN	TAN DARIKIḌA	
		TAN DA	TAN DARIKIḌA	TAM

[40]Brown, *The Mṛdaṅga*, Vol. II, Lesson 61, pp. 110–11.

This brief introduction to Karnatak drumming, specifically mṛdañga drumming, gives only a glimpse at a most complex subject. No attempt has been made to discuss such matters as timbre combinations and relationships of sounds produced by the left and right hands. Rather, we have considered some of the principles by which a drummer can improvise and create, either in an accompanying role or in solo performance.

HINDUSTĀNĪ DRUMMING

In North India too, drumming is a highly cultivated art. A serious student begins lessons with a pūjā to Lord Gaṇeṣa, much as he would in South India, and must work diligently for many years in order to become an accomplished drummer.

The principal drumming tradition in North India today is the tablā tradition. The tradition includes some elements that will be familiar from our discussion of Karnatak drumming. Tablā strokes, like mṛdañga strokes, are spoken in syllables, generically called *bols*. As with mṛdañga solkattu, there can be a variety of bols for one stroke, or varying strokes for one bol. The choice of syllable depends on the context.

The subject of tablā strokes themselves, not to mention patterns of strokes, is a fascinating one historically, because many of them may have been derived from other Hindustānī drum traditions—specifically, those of the pakhāvaj and folk dholak, and the naghāṛa.[41] This is not surprising, since the tablā itself is a composite of two drum types and is of recent origin. "The tablā's function, more than that of any other drum today, is to bring together and re-combine heretofore almost entirely separate techniques and principles of construction."[42]

Another aspect of the subject of tablā bols is, in part, a geographical one. The use of the instrument developed in several different court centers (Lucknow, Benares, and Delhi, in particular), and traditions of playing (termed *bāj*) differed somewhat. Accordingly, the bol may change according to the tradition and/or the geographical area, but the stroke type will remain the same. Conversely, the stroke type may change, but the bol will remain the same.[43] The lack of interest among Hindustānī musicians in the business of classification (which we noted in the case of rāga) shows up again with

[41] Stewart, *The Tablā*, is an important study of the Hindustānī drumming traditions. However, Pandit Sharda Sahai, of the Benares tradition of drumming, has pointed out difficulties with drumming information. For example, it may be more difficult than one realizes to document naghāṛa and dholak patterns, because so many naghāṛa and dholak players study with tablā players.

[42] *Ibid.*, p. 18.

[43] *Ibid.*, p. 22.

tāla: little effort has been made to standardize and classify the various tablā strokes and bols. The bols that appear in this section are of the Benares bāj.[44]

In our description of Karnatak drumming, we spoke of the *process* by which a stroking pattern is expanded, reduced, structured into a mōrā, and so forth, within the framework of tāla. In Hindustānī drumming, the germinal stroking patterns are there, and tāla is certainly there, but structural types such as the Karnatak mōrā are more numerous and contribute an additional prominent framework within which such a process takes place. These structures may be spoken of as "compositions," as long as it is understood that certain of them can either be previously composed or composed "on the spot." Some of these "compositions" are *uthān*, *moharā*, *mukhṛā*, *theka*, and *kāyadā*.

One characteristic that distinguishes these types from each other is the presence or absence of a cadential *tihāī*. A tihāī is a stroking pattern that is played exactly three times in succession, and is so timed that the last stroke falls on count 1 of a following cycle, on a cadential sam.[45] A very short tihāī, for example, might be built on the stroking pattern taka dha. If each repetition is given a duration of two counts, the tihāī would be taka dha taka dha

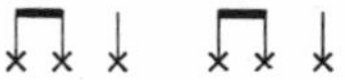

taka dha. Played in tīntāl, it would start on count 12 in order to end on the

next count 1:

×				२				
1	2	3	4	5	6	7	8	
o				३				×
9	10	11	12	13	14	15	16	/1
			taka	dha	taka	dha	taka	/dha

A longer and more complex tihāī in tīntāl is given in Example 6-10. The pattern on which it is based is 5 counts long: ka tirakita dhe te te dha S ra dha gi na dha. Each count but the last is in triplet rhythm. (Therefore, if we assigned the Western notational symbol ♩ to each count, the rhythm would be

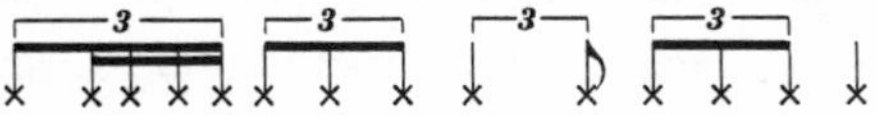

; if we assign the Western notational symbol 𝅗𝅥 to each count, the rhythm would be

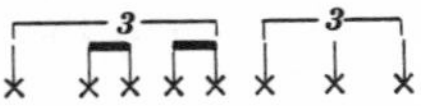

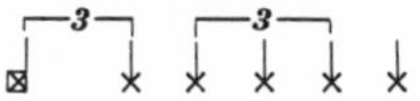

.) In this tihāī, there is a gap between repetitions of the pattern. This gap must be the same length every time it occurs. In Example

[44]These bols were taught to me by Pandit Sharda Sahai.

[45]Tihāīs are frequent in vocal music and in melody-instrumental solo music as well, but the repetitions in these cases do not have to be exact.

6-10, the gap is one count long and falls on counts 6 and 12 of the 16-count cycle (shown by S). Within the triplet pattern Dha S ra the symbol S indicates that no new stroke fills the subdivision of the count. All strokes within one count are underlined.

EXAMPLE 6-10 Hindustānī Tihāī

×			
(*)Ka tirakita	dhe te te	dha S ra	dha gi na
२			
Dha	S	ka tirakita	dhe te te
o			
Dha S ra	dha gi na	dha	S
३			
Ka tirakita	dhe te te	dha S ra	dha gi na/
×			
Dha			

Drummers become skilled at fashioning tihāīs on the spur of the moment when they sense from the melody that the soloist is about to create a cadence, or when they are playing solo performances themselves. The tablā player is always aware of precisely where he is in the tāla cycle and therefore how many counts are left in which to play a tihāī. It becomes second nature to him to do the calculations in a flash and to design a tihāī that will end on count 1.[46] However short or long a tihāī is, it must create a drive to the cadence.

Among the tablā composition-types that include a tihāī in their structure are uthān and moharā. Uthān is the composition-type with which a player of the Benares bāj begins a concert. It consists of a brief introduction that is entirely of closed (damped) strokes, followed by a section that introduces open (nondamped) strokes and increases the rhythmic density, then ends in a tihāī. Uthāns of the Benares bāj always begin with the same introduction (but it can be extended at will). The remainder either is a traditional composition or is composed "in process" according to the concept of the structural type. Example 6-11 illustrates a uthān in tīntāl (without the introduction) that ends in the tīhāī shown out of context in Example 6-10.

A moharā is a mini-structure that occurs at cadences. It is a brief composition that ends in a tihāī. Played at a very fast speed, a moharā usually consumes only the last 4 counts (or 8) of tīntāl. Because it occurs very quickly, it is frequently inserted at cadences when the drummer is accompanying a melody-making soloist. In Example 6-12, the moharā begins at count 9 in

[46]Sometimes a drummer—or a melody-making soloist—will purposely make the listener (or his accompanist) think a cadence is coming by producing what seems to be a tihāī. But he ends it just before or just after sam, and the musicians proceed with further improvisation. The idea is to throw the listener (and accompanists) off the track (and keep all on their toes).

EXAMPLE 6-11 Tīntāl Uthān with Tihāī

×			
Dha S ra	dha gi na	dha gi na	ti gi na
२			
Dha ge na	dhe te te	dhe te te	ta ki na
o			
Ta ka dhin	S ta S	gi gi te	te gi gi
३			
Dhin S dhin	S dhin S	ka ta ka	ta ka ta
×			
Ka tirakita	dhe te te	dha S ra	dha gi na
२			
Dha	S	ka tirakita	dhe te te
o			
Dha S ra	dha gi na	dha	S
३			
Ka tirakita	dhe te te	dha S ra	dha gi na/
×			
Dha			

EXAMPLE 6-12 Moharā

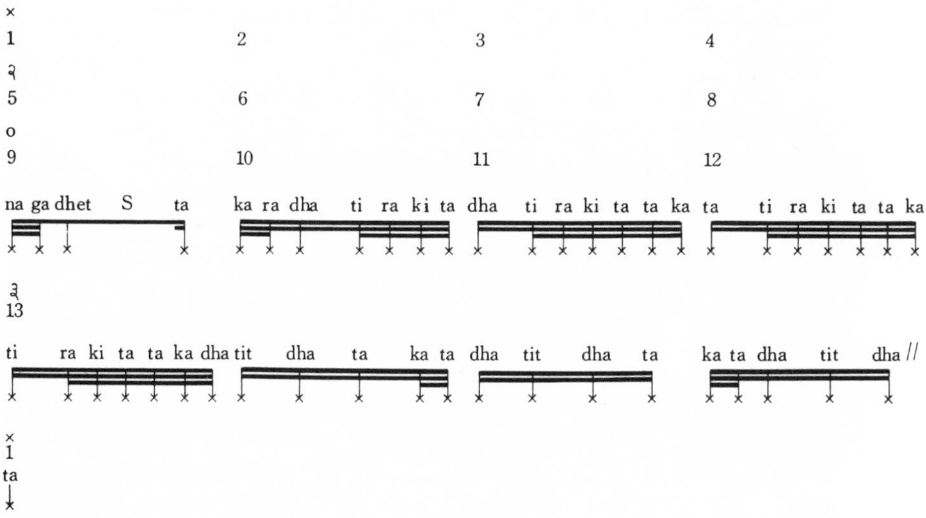

tīntāl (though it would most likely be played twice as fast and, therefore, begin at count 13). The tihāī pattern is DHA TIT DHA TA. A gap of one-fourth count is left between the repetitions of that pattern, but here the gap is filled by the strokes KATA (which are not part of the tihāī itself). This is a common practice.[47] In Example 6-12, one count is shown as one Western quarter note.

A tablā structure that is similar to the mohaṛā but does not end in a tihāī is the mukhṛā. A mukhṛā is 4 (or 8) counts long (when it is in tīntāl). It creates a drive to the cadence, but it does not do this with a tihāī. Both mohaṛā and mukhrā can be traditional compositions, or they can be composed in process.

Two other types of structure that do not include tihāī are theka and kāyadā. A theka is a one-cycle-long traditional composition that is associated with a particular tāla.[48] Thekas are used in learning to play a tāla and are also the basic material used in accompanying certain types of performances. A theka for tīntāl—the most common one—is given in Example 6-13. In accompanying solo melody, a drummer would, for instance, punctuate a cadence by playing the first eight counts of this theka and then launching into the mohaṛā in Example 6-12 or a mukhṛā to complete the cycle.

EXAMPLE 6-13 Tīntāl Theka

×				२				
1	2	3	4	5	6	7	8	
DHA	DHIN	DHIN	DHA	DHA	DHIN	DHIN	DHA	
o				३				×
9	10	11	12	13	14	15	16	/ 1
DHA	TIN	TIN	TA	TA	DHIN	DHIN	DHA	/ DHA

As a demonstration of how bols for different drums in North India are different, the thekas for the one tāla that is shared by the pakhāvaj and the tablā are given in Examples 6-14 and 6-15. Pakhāvaj chautāl was adapted to the tablā and called ektāl. It has a cycle of twelve counts:

× o २ o ३ ४
2 + 2 + 2 + 2 + 2 + 2 or 4 + 4 + 2 + 2

A kāyadā is a composition that presents a theme that is then varied. The variations are called *palta*. Each successive palta is more a variation of the preceding palta than of the original theme, and by the time thirty or forty variations have been created, the theme (in Western thinking) is no longer there. In Indian thinking, the theme is still there because the continuity is there.[49] A very simple tīntāl kāyadā, followed by four paltas, is given in

[47]If this entire mohaṛā were repeated exactly three times and ended on sam, it would itself constitute a tihāī.

[48]Theka is apparently of very recent origin: such a composition was not really a part of pakhāvaj tradition until recently. In Hindustānī drumming, another type of composition called theka occurs in solo tablā sequences, but it is not discussed here.

[49]As in the case of tracing ancient music theory to the present, the one-to-one relationships are difficult to see; the continuity is the reality.

EXAMPLE 6-14 Chautāl (Pakhāvaj Bols)

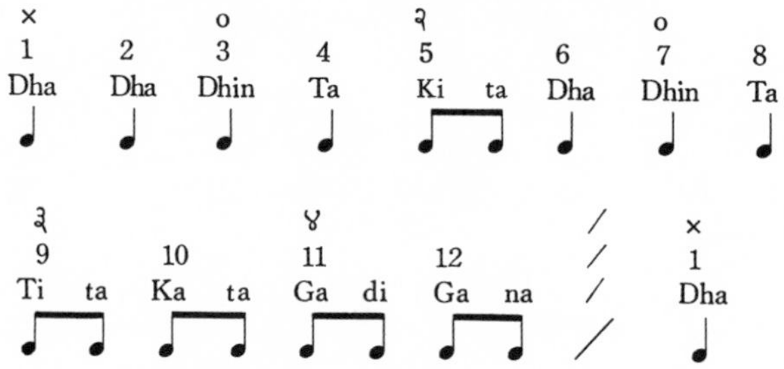

EXAMPLE 6-15 Ektāl (Tablā Bols)

Example 6-16. The kāyadā is one cycle long. The four counts in the vibhāg that begins with khāli (counts 9, 10, 11, and 12) use the right hand only, and the tīntāl structure is thereby stated very clearly. DHA is played by the left and right hand together, but TA is played by the right hand only.

The first palta takes line 1 of the kāyadā, repeats it three times, and follows with line 2 of the kāyadā. That fills one cycle of tīntāl. The second half of the variation does the same thing, but the proportion of khālī must be retained, so two of the repetitions are with the right hand only:

Kāyadā		Two-Cycle-Long Palta	
×		×	
tālī	4 counts	tālī	8 counts
२		o	
tālī	4 counts	tālī	8 counts
o		×	
khālī	4 counts	khālī	8 counts
३		o	
tālī	4 counts	tālī	8 counts

Many of the paltas that are two cycles long maintain those proportions. The subtle changes in each variation continue as the drummer shows his skill

EXAMPLE 6-16 Tīntāl Kāyadā with Paltas

Tīntāl Kāyadā

×			
DHA	DHA	TI	TE
२			
DHA	DHA	TI	NA
o			
TA	TA	TI	TE
३			
DHA	DHA	TI	NA/

Palta 1

×				२				
DHA	DHA	TI	TE	DHA	DHA	TI	TE	8 counts
o				३				
DHA	DHA	TI	TE	DHA	DHA	TI	NA/	8 counts
×				२				
TA	TA	TI	TE	TA	TA	TI	TE	8 counts
o				३				
DHA	DHA	TI	TE	DHA	DHA	TI	NA/	8 counts

Palta 2

×				२			
DHA	DHA	TI	TE	DHA	TI	TE	DHA
o				३			
DHA	DHA	TI	TE	DHA	DHA	TI	NA/
×				२			
TA	TA	TI	TE	TA	TI	TE	DHA
o				३			
DHA	DHA	TI	TE	DHA	DHA	TI	NA/

Palta 3

×				२			
DHA	TI	TE	DHA	DHA	TI	TE	DHA
o				३			
DHA	DHA	TI	TE	DHA	DHA	TI	NA/
×				२			
TA	TI	TE	TA	TA	TI	TE	DHA
o				३			
DHA	DHA	TI	TE	DHA	DHA	TI	NA/

Palta 4

×				२			
DHA	DHA	DHA	TI	TE	DHA	DHA	TI
o				३			
TE	DHA	TI	TE	DHA	DHA	TI	NA/
×				२			
TA	TA	TA	TI	TE	TA	TA	TI
o				३			
TE	TA	TI	TE	DHA	DHA	TI	NA/

in bol manipulation. If the piece were continued, the complexity of the variations would be increased gradually and imaginatively.

These are but a few of the tablā composition-types. These types are distinguished by functions, as, for example, those used at cadences. Other types, such as tukṛa, chakradar tukṛa, rela, paran, and peshkar (which are not discussed here), are used when the tablā is played solo, whether at designated moments during an instrumental performance, or in a tablā solo performance. They are distinguished by types of bols used, type of variation involved, and even whether or not variation techniques are used at all.

Hindustani tablā drumming is a complicated topic, one that has only been glimpsed here. In fact, it is so complicated that for the most part only other drummers can really tell what a drummer is doing in a solo performance. This is undoubtedly why lengthy solos by drummers are relatively rare in concerts of Hindustānī music.

SEVEN

PERFORMANCE GENRES OF HINDUSTĀNĪ MUSIC

The question that now arises is how the performers in their respective roles, the melodic and metric concepts, and the performing mediums are put together in the creation of music. Part of the answer lies in what type of music is sung, what type of music is played, and on what instrument and by whom music is played. This chapter is devoted to the genres of Hindustānī classical music that can be heard on recordings readily available in the West.

VOCAL GENRES

Following the Indian order of priority, and also historical succession, let us discuss vocal music first. In North Indian classical music, three genres of vocal music are especially important: *dhrupad*, *khyāl*, and *ṭhumṛī*. Each consists of a brief composition and a great deal of improvisation. They are differentiated more by the nature of the improvisation associated with each than by the structure of their brief compositions.

Dhrupad is the oldest of the Hindustānī classical vocal genres heard today. Its direct forebear is thought to have been the *prabandha*, but there is no agreement on this—or on the components of the prabandha. Depending upon the time period or upon the source of information, prabandhas are thought to have consisted of several parts or just a few. Many classical treatises mention this ancient form of composition, but Indian musicologists and musicians do not know what prabandhas sounded like. The most common descriptions of them indicate that they consisted of four parts: an *udgrāha*, a *melāpaka*, a *dhruva*, and an *ābhoga*—in essence, a beginning section, a development and exposition-of-scale section, a fixed form, and an ending section. It is the dhruva that is supposed to be at the base of the development of dhrupad.

In the twelfth century, the last recorded exponent of the Gīta music, the great poet Jayadeva, composed his Gīta-Govinda in prabandha with just the dhruva and ābhoga sections, presumably because the first two sections of prabandhas had no text. Jayadeva has left compositions illustrating the rāga and tāla of each piece, but they are unintelligible to us today. Although there are no continuities that can be established, musicologists generally agree that prabandha were at first sung in the temples but later evolved into dhrupad in the North and kritis and kirtanas in the South. Further, they note that another development of the prabandha style occurred among the Vaishnavite poets of Bengal in North India, who wrote kirtans that were sung in accompaniment to dance in the temples. In kirtans the stress was on the emotional content of the songs.

Dhrupad was and still is performed by one or two male soloists, accompanied on tāmbūra and pakhāvaj. (Formerly, accompaniment was also provided by a bīn player.) Dhrupad is said to have been either a common type of temple music in the late fourteenth century or a regional variety of song associated with beggar minstrels.[1] It is also said to have been adapted for court performance in the reign of Rāja Man Singh Tomar (1496–1525), potentate of Gwalior (which is still a major musical center).

The majestic, dignified style of dhrupad appears to have been appropriate to the style of life in Mughal courts, where grandeur prevailed, martial heroes and loyalty were extolled, and prescribed rules of decorum and discipline were strictly observed. Mastery of dhrupad singing calls for developed breath control, strict adherence to rules of the rāgas, and meticulous rhythmic manipulation. Dhrupad texts blend noble sentiments with devo-

[1]B. R. Deodhar, "Evolution in Indian Music," *Music East and West* (New Delhi: Indian Council for Cultural Relations, 1966), p. 17; and O. Gosvami, *The Story of Indian Music* (Bombay: Asia Publishing House, 1957), p. 124.

tional feeling, eulogy of patrons with praise of deities. By the reign of the great Mughal emperor Akbar, the dhrupad had become the most important genre of music performed in the North and was sung in both Hindu and Muslim courts by both Hindu and Muslim musicians. The genre retained its preeminent position until the eighteenth century, when its popularity declined noticeably.

The name dhrupad is given to a type of song that, like other types of Hindustānī songs, is composed in a rāga and tāla and has a text, but is longer than other types of songs. A dhrupad is composed with four sections: *sthāī*, *aṅtarā*, *saṅchārī*, and *ābhog*. In contemporary practice, however, the saṅchārī and ābhog are rarely sung, so the composition is reduced to two parts—sthāī ("permanent, steady") and aṅtarā ("intermediate"). Today, a dhrupad is performed in a sthāī–aṅtarā–sthāī sequence.

The aṅtarā is composed so that melodically and rhythmically it can lead smoothly back to the sthāī. Example 7-1[2] is a dhrupad composition in a tāla that is particularly associated with dhrupad compositions. Chautāl has a cycle of 12 counts (2 + 2 + 2 + 2 + 2 + 2, marked × o २ o ३ ४), as explained in Chapter Six. In Example 7-1, both the sthāī and the aṅtarā take four cycles of the tāla; the final cycle is the return to the sthāī. The sthāī of this dhrupad begins on count 1 and ends on count 12 in order to connect smoothly with the aṅtarā, which also begins on count 1.

Dhrupad is also the name given to a performance that includes improvisation as well as the dhrupad composition. The sequence of the performance is as follows:

improvisation—dhrupad—improvisation
(sthāī–aṅtarā–sthāī)

The improvisation that precedes the dhrupad is related to it only by choice of rāga. Tāla and text become part of the performance when the dhrupad composition is sung, and they continue to be vital in the final improvisation. Accordingly, there is a progression in the performance from no meter to meter, and from no text to text.

The improvisation that precedes the dhrupad is called *ālāp*. Ālāp is an intense re-creation of all the things a rāga is, specifically the rāga in which the dhrupad is composed. The performance begins with the quiet sound of the tāmbūra intoning the drone. Then a prolonged madhya Sa by the vocalist focuses concentration at the beginning of the ālāp. Progressing very slowly, the singer gives thoughtful attention to each pitch, each turn of melody associated with the rāga, and establishes the mood of the rāga

[2] Transcribed by the author from Philips recording 6586003, *North India: Vocal Music: Dhrupad and Khyāl.* The dhrupad was sung by Ustads Mohinuddin and Aminuddin Dagar. Example 7-2 was also transcribed from this performance. Rhythmic durations notated in Example 7-2 are only relative, and are given the values ♪ ♩ 𝅗𝅥 𝅝.

EXAMPLE 7-1 Dhrupad: "Manusha ho to vohi"

Rāg Kāmbhojī

Chautāl

Sthāī *Very slowly and legato*

accordingly. The rhythm is free, ever changing, floating, gliding on the syllables na, re, de, ri, and so on. From Sa the few pitches around Sa, mostly down into the tetrachord below, are emphasized as the singer explores the low register (mandra saptak) and the descent of the rāga, as shown in Example 7-2. When the singer tires of the lower register and wants to dwell more in the middle register (madhya saptak), he finishes the segment with a brief melodic phrase called a mohṛā (bracketed in Example 7-2), and then begins to add pitches higher and higher. The ascent of the rāga is thereby made clear.

The mohṛā is the only element in the ālāp that makes one mindful of periodic temporal proportions. Although the rhythm of the melody is free, the melody as a whole is never aimless, and the return to the mohṛā provides a structure of a cadential sort.[3] Occasionally during the ālāp, the pakhāvaj player will quietly tap his drum just at the moment that Sa occurs in the mohṛā, thus inconspicuously underlining the periodicity. This action is called sam-ālāp. Since the drum is tuned to Sa and the tap is quiet, it is very subtle indeed. Otherwise, the drummer remains still in his place at the side of the singer, and listens to the music intently along with the audience.

EXAMPLE 7-2 Ālāp in Rāg Kāmbhojī

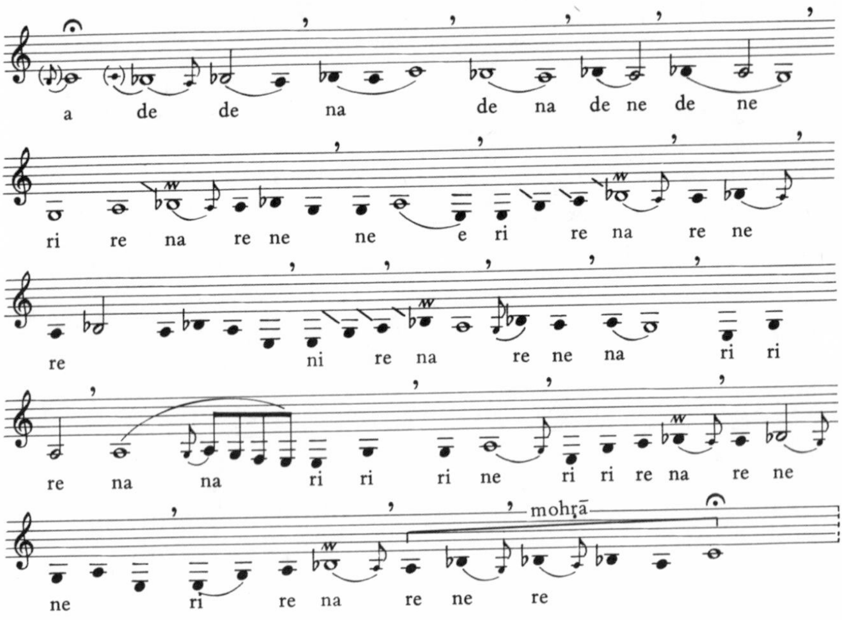

[3]In a recent study of the temporal units in ālāp, Shirish Korde of Brown University found more regular periodization between mohṛā than the free-floating rhythm of the melody would suggest. The study was based on his transcriptions, completed as part of an Independent Study with me at Brown University, 1974–75.

EXAMPLE 7-2 (Cont.)

The singer's goal in ālāp is to reach Sa of the upper register (tār Sa), then to go even beyond that into tār saptak. He prolongs his attainment of the goal by flirting with dha or ni, then withdraws, tantalizing the audience (who know what he is doing). At the finish of each melodic "thought" comes the mohṛā. If the artist is very good, his arrival at tār Sa can be extremely climactic.

Very gradually, the speed of the singing has been increasing, the melodic units becoming more extensive and including more pitches in a sweep. Then we realize that free melody is beginning to give way to melody with a more purposeful rhythm. By that time the rāga is firmly in our mind, if we have been listening carefully.

When the singer feels that the rāga has been explored sufficiently, he eases without pause into the second portion of the ālāp, called *nom-tom-ālāp*, Here, he initiates a definite rhythm by enunciating repeated pitches along with repeated vocables. Nom-tom-ālāp is demonstrated in Example 7-3, which is transcribed from a performance by Ustads Mohinuddin and Aminuddin Dagar on Bärenreiter BM 30L 2018.

EXAMPLE 7-3 Nom-Tom-Ālāp

Rāg Āsāvarī

(Ālāp→) Nom-Tom Ālāp (→Dhrupad)

EXAMPLE 7-3 (Cont.)

de ne ne ne de ne ne de ne ne de ne ne de ne ne na
de ne ne ne
de ne ne ne de ne ne ne
ri re na
de ne ne ne
de ne ne ne de ne ne de ne ne de ne ne de ne ne de ne ne de ne ne
etc.

Following the nom-tom-ālāp is the dhrupad. The drummer enters the performance now, since the dhrupad is metered. Example 7-4 is a partial transcription of a dhrupad composition in Rāg Bhairavī. This composition would be referred to by the first few words of the text—"Jagata jananī." The complete sthāī and aṅtarā texts are as follows:

Sthāī:

> Jagata jananī jvāla mukhī
> Mata Sarasvatī sharada vidya
> Deni dayānī dukha haranī/
>
> > O thou, who created the world, our
> > mother with a face of light, Sarasvatī,
> > from whom all knowledge flows, the
> > bestower of gifts, our shelter,
> > Thou takest away all our pain.

Aṅtarā:

> Jo hi jo hi mangata sohi
> Phala pavata mana ichha
> Purana karanī dukha haranī/
>
> > Everyone obtains from thee the fruits
> > he asks for. Thou fulfillest the desires
> > of our mind. Thou takest away all our
> > pain.

BAIJU BHAVARE (16th. c.)

"Jagata jananī" is in tīvra tāl of 7 counts—3 + 2 + 2 (♩♩♩♩♩♩♩). Tīvra tāl differs from rūpak tāl in that it begins with a tālī rather than a khālī. The portion of the performance transcribed in Example 7-4 includes sixteen cycles of sthāī and twenty-one cycles of aṅtarā. In the last cycle of Example 7-4, the singer returns to the sthāī. (This performance is on Bärenreiter Musicaphon 30L 2018.)

EXAMPLE 7-4 Dhrupad: "Jagata Jananī"

EXAMPLE 7-4 (Cont.)

Mata Sarasvatī sharada
sharada jagata jananī/
Mata Sarasvatī sharada jagata jana
Mata Sarasvatī sharada jagata jananī/
Mata Sarasvatī sharada
sharada (*3 times*)
Mata Sarasvatī sharada
sharada (*2 times*)
sharada jagata jana . . . . (*to* Aṅtarā.)

EXAMPLE 7-4 (Cont.)

so - - hi pha - la pa - - va - ta
ma - na - a ich - ha pu - ra - na ka - ra - nī
Sthāī
(Improvisation would continue)
du - kha ha - ra - ni / Ja - ga - ta ja - na - nī.

Rāg Bhairavī is an old rāga that was formerly a favorite for dhrupad compositions. It is now considered a "light" rāga, appropriate for ṭhumṛī compositions, and a good one with which to end a concert. Tradition classifies it as a late-morning rāga, but as it is sung to end concerts, it has become acceptable at night, too. Bhairavī is a sampūrṇa rāga, having seven pitches in ascent and descent, the same pitches, of course, as those of the ṭhāṭ by that name: Sa, Re, Ga, Ma, Pa, Dha, and Ni. Pitches Ma and Sa are said to be vādīs, but in this composition Pa seems much more a focal point than Ma. Two phrases that are particularly characteristic of Rāg Bhairavī and that enter into this dhrupad are Ni Sa Ga Ma Pa Dha Pa (see the beginning of the song) and Ga Ma Dha Ni Sa (with which the aṅtarā begins).

Most dhrupad compositions begin not on count one of the tāla cycle, but several counts before. The singer starts the sthāī at the speed he wants, and the drummer joins him at count one. That first phrase of the sthāī up to and including count one is used as a cadence phrase as long as the artist remains in the sthāī. In Example 7-4, that cadence phrase is "Jagata jananī," which also happens to be set to a characteristic Bhairavī melodic phrase. Since the cadence phrase recurs many times, a characteristic phrase of the rāga will be reiterated.

The artist(s) presents the entire composed sthāī and then, using the sthāī text, improvises melody. To say, "the artist is singing sthāī" in the process of improvisation does not mean that he is singing the composed sthāī melody; it means he is improvising, using the text of the composed sthāī.

After improvising in sthāī, the artist presents the second segment of the composition—the aṅtarā (as indicated in Example 7-4). The beginning of an aṅtarā is noticeable because it is a direct ascent from Ma or Pa to tār Sa (following, however, the pitches and shape of the particular rāga, as this aṅtarā does). While the aṅtarā is being presented and its text manipulated in improvised melody, the first phrase of that section is used as a temporary cadence—in Example 7-4, "Jo hi jo hi man." When the aṅtarā is finished, the first phrase of the sthāī resumes its role.

After the return to the sthāī, improvisation remains for the most part in the sthāī. It is rhythmically oriented, featuring mathematical subdivisions of the beats as well as subtle cross-rhythms. Acceleration usually does not take place except through increased rhythmic density. The text is stated clearly throughout the improvisation. The types of improvisation are called *bolbant*, "playing with the words," and *boltāns* (creating *tāns*, using the words for rhythmic purposes). Throughout, the rules of the rāga are strictly observed. On phonograph recordings, the ālāp–dhrupad sequence is usually allotted only the time of one side of a disc, but in live performance it lasts an hour or more. (The improvisation in the dhrupad recording transcribed in Example 7-4 scarcely gets under way, and little rhythmic manipulation is done.)

A genre very similar to dhrupad is *dhamār*.[4] Like dhrupad, dhamār is invariably preceded by a lengthy ālāp. Dhamār are songs about the playful Lord Krishna that are heard mostly at Holi Festival time, when spring is in the air. In the following text, "the dark skinned boy" is Krishna, the King of Vraja (Braj), the area where Krishna was born.[5]

> Come, my love, we are going to
> the King of Vraja!
>
> What are these rumoring voices to you?
>
> Someone will say, she has gone to
> the dark skinned boy,
>
> But that will be all they can say.

Dhamār are almost all in *dhamār tāl*, a cycle of 14 beats with irregular subdivisions—5 + 2 + 3 + 4—that lend the songs a rhythmic lilt.

Through the influence of Tansen, the great dhrupad gāyak (dhrupadīyā) who sang in Akbar's court, the dhrupad traditions were first associated with the area of Agra-Delhi. By the end of the eighteenth century, when the Mughal court was in decline, many musicians had left Delhi for the courts of other princes to the west and east. One dhrupad tradition came to be associated with a region in Southwest Bengal, and the other—that of the

[4]One other form, which I do not discuss here—mainly because it is seldom heard, especially outside of India—is a style of singing known as *tappā*. It is considered a rather difficult song style, and has been called a form akin to dhrupad. Tappā is supposed to have originated in a type of song sung by camel drivers. A fine—and rare—recording of a tappā sung by the famous Hindustānī vocalist Siddeshwari Devi can be heard on Bärenreiter-Musicaphone recording BM 30SL 2052, *An Anthology of North Indian Classical Music, Vol. II.*

[5]Krishna is often depicted as being blue. Scholars have suggested that he was a god of one of the pre-Aryan (possibly Dravidian) peoples. The dhamār whose text I have reproduced can be heard on (and read from the notes of) Bärenreiter-Musicaphon recording BM 30SL 2051, *An Anthology of North Indian Classical Music, Vol. I.*

Dagar family—with Rājasthān. Also, since the time of Tansen in the sixteenth century, most traditions of classical music in North India have been maintained by families of professional musicians, such as the Dagar family. These musicians are now frequently referred to as members of a *gharānā.*[6]

Members of the Dagar family are now the most prominent dhrupad singers. In recent decades, two sets of brothers have maintained the family traditions. Moinuddin and his younger brother Aminuddin first studied with their father, then with their mother's brother, then with their father's brother. They became inseparable and always performed together. In 1964, Moinuddin and Aminuddin toured Europe for UNESCO, and recordings of their singing have been released gradually by that organization. During that tour Moinuddin suffered a heart attack; he died two years later. Since then, his brother has lived in Calcutta and has concertized alone. The younger set of Dagar brothers, Nasiruddin and Faiyazuddin, also perform together. They live and teach in Delhi.

The second major genre of North Indian classical vocal music is khyāl, the most prominent vocal genre of Hindustānī classical music for the past two hundred years or so. The musical traditions that contributed to its evolution in the Mughal courts are somewhat of a mystery, It has been claimed that khyāl was a combination of qawwalī (a florid style of Muslim religious song) and dhrupad.[7] Khyāl found official acceptance at the eighteenth-century court of Muhammad Shah in Delhi. Legend relates that a bīn player at that court, Nyamat Khan, had rebelled against his subordinate position as an instrumentalist (which relegated him to sitting behind the vocalists at court) and had left his post. Nyamat Khan began training two young boys to sing an improvised type of khyāl that he had conceived. In time, the boys became master artists and sang the khyāls to numerous audiences. So artistically did they perform and so appealing were their voices that praise for their singing gradually filtered into the court of Muhammad Shah. The shah invited them to sing, and was so impressed that he asked them to be court musicians. Only later did he learn that the new musical creation the boys had rendered so beautifully was an innovation of Nyamat Khan. The reaction of the shah was to offer Nyamat a seat of honor and to relieve him from his subordinate position as an accompanist. Thereafter,

[6]A gharānā refers to a particular "house" or school of classical performance practice, as well as to a particular family of musicians. As we noted in Chapter Six, another term, *bāj*, refers to the manner of playing the instrument. To many Indian musicians, the two terms are interchangeable. Understandably, considerable confusion results. For a study of the gharānā as it is embodied in the family, see Daniel Neuman, *The Cultural Structure and Social Organization of Musicians in India* (Ann Arbor, Mich.: University Microfilms, 1974).

[7]Qawwalī is a song style that has existed in India since the earliest days of Muslim rule. It is characterized by rapid, florid, and lengthy passages up and down a male singer's range (similar to tāns) and male-chorus refrains repeating the main theme of the song. Qawwalī is sung particularly at tombs of Muslim saints, but it also enjoys widespread popularity today in North India, and particularly in Pakistan.

Nyamat played solos and for the first time gave the bīn a place of its own in court. He was given the honorific Sadarang, "ever gay."

The topics of khyāl texts range from praise of kings and praise or description of the seasons to the pranks of Lord Krishna, divine love, and sorrow caused by the absence of a beloved. The brief text lines contain rhyme, alliteration, and frequent plays on words. The most surprising thing about khyāl is that although it was developed by Muslim musicians in Mughal courts, most of its texts are on Hindu subjects, primarily Krishna. Khyāl offers proof that, at least in this musical instance, relations between the two communities were being ameliorated.

There are two types of khyāl performances: *baṛā* ("large") and *chhotā* ("small"). In either case, a khyāl consists of a composition (*chīz*) of two sections—sthāī and antarā—and extensive improvisation. It differs from dhrupad in one significant way: no lengthy unmetered ālāp precedes the singing of the composition, except in the Agra gharānā. Singers introduce the rāga for a few seconds, and occasionally, for as long as five minutes but the exposition of the pitches rarely exceeds pitch Pa of the middle octave and is often merely an anticipation of the melody of the chīz. Since the chīz is sung immediately, and since all chīz are metered songs, all of the improvisation in khyāl is metered and accompanied on tablā.

The two types of khyāl performance are distinguished primarily by the basic level of speed at which they are sung and by the type of improvisation that follows the chīz. Baṛā khyāl is sung in slow speed (*vilambit laya*) or medium speed (*madhya laya*). In slow speed, each count of the tāla is divided into four beats; this can be heard clearly in the tablā part.[8] In medium speed, each count of the tāla is either subdivided into two beats or receives one beat. Chhotā khyāl is always in fast speed. It receives one beat per tāla count but moves at a much faster clip than medium speed. Baṛā khyāl is usually in tīntāl, tilwāṛā tāl, ektāl, jhūmrā tāl, or jhaptāl; chhotā khyāl are almost invariably in tīntāl or ektāl.

Before discussing the differences in improvisation, between baṛā and chhotā khyāl, let us look more closely at the chīz. Example 7-5 is a chīz in madhya laya. The chīz is very short. It presents in song form the characteristics of the rāga and tāla in which it is composed. In particular, the first section of the chīz, the sthāī, states the melodic bundle of the rāga. The second section of most chīz, the antarā, are very similar in shape, ascending to tār Sa in a manner peculiar to the rāga, going higher into the upper octave, then descending to link with the sthāī again.

[8]The khyāl chīz in Example 3-2 is in slow speed. For readability in Chapter Three, I inserted a barline halfway through it, but the melody as transcribed there should all be in one tāla cycle. Each of the 12 counts in ektāl is divided into 4 counts, so a complete cycle is 48 pulses (each a ♩ there). This extremely slow speed is heard only in baṛā khyāl, and is a fairly recent phenomenon. Medium-speed performances of baṛā khyāl more closely resemble the old style. See the author's "Chīz in Khyāl: The Traditional Composition in the Improvised Performance," in *Ethnomusicology*, XVII, 3 (Sept. 1973), pp. 443–459.

"Bāje jhanana," the chīz transcribed in Example 7-5, is in Rāg Jaunpurī, which was supposedly named after the town Jaunpur (whose Sultan tried to popularize khyāl many years before it was accepted at other courts), and is particularly associated with khyāl.[9] Most chīz composed in Jaunpurī start with an initial rise to high in the middle octave—many to tār Sa, as this one does—and then descend. Pitch Ga is avoided in ascent, so the āroha and avāroha are as follows:

Sa Re Ma Pa Dha Ni Sȧ
Sȧ Ni Dha Pa Ma Ga Re Sa.

This can be seen by tracing Ga through the chīz in Example 7-5. Ga descends on beat thirteen (notated ३) of the first cycle of tīntāl, and again on sam (×) of the second cycle. It is avoided in the second segment of the second cycle (counts 5 to 8), in the ascent Sa Re Ma Pa Dha. It does not occur again until the next-to-last count of the third cycle. Here, it might appear to be in ascent Sȧ Rė Gȧ, but when a pitch is at the pinnacle of an ascent, followed by descending melody, it is considered descending. Ga is in descent in the remaining two tāla cycles in Example 7-5.

Rāg Jaunpurī is a late-morning rāga that is classified with Āsāvarī ṭhāṭ: Sa Re Ga Ma Pa Dha Ni. The vādīs of Jaunpurī are said to be Dha (and Ga), and in Example 7-5 Dha is indeed prominent. The role of Sa is also strong in this chīz, even though it is not strong theoretically. This is an example of the theoretical ambiguity surrounding pitch Sa in Hindustānī music.

Although pitch Ni is considered to be in the ascent of Rāg Jaunpurī, its treatment is particularized. As shown in Example 7-5, it does not occur in the ascent directly to tār Sa from below; rather, the melody goes directly from Pa to Sȧ (as in the mukhṛā), or from Dha to Sa (see text "dore" in the second tāla cycle). The usual occurrence is for Ni Sa to follow the ascent from Pa or Dha to Sa, as follows: (Pa) Dha Sa Ni Sa, with Ni a lower neighbor tone to Sa. It also recurs in the ascent Ni Sȧ Ṙi. In this chīz melody, the phrases that avoid Ni in ascent lend melodic contour. The first phrase of sthāī Pa Sȧ Dha is parallel to the frequent progression in the lower tetrachord Ri Pa Ga, but the ascent Ma Pa Dha Sȧ is not parallel to the lower tetrachord Sa Ri Ma Pa.[10] This chīz is constructed with considerable melodic interest.

In the performance transcribed in Example 7-5, the artist sang the sthāī, followed it immediately with the antarā, then returned to the sthāī for improvisation. Other artists might present the chīz in a different format:

[9]Transcribed by the author from a tape in a private collection.

[10]For an important theoretical idea concerning balanced and unbalanced tetrachordal structure in rāga, see Nazir Jairazbhoy, *The Rāgs of North Indian Music* (Middletown, Conn.: Wesleyan University Press, 1971). His example of Jaunpurī (p. 170) shows similar treatment of Ni in ascent.

EXAMPLE 7-5 Baṛā Khyāl Chīz

Hindustānī Rāg Jaunpurī, Tīntāl (Madhya Laya)

they might sing the sthāī, then improvise on it; sing the aṅtarā, then improvise on it; and return to the sthāī and begin the lengthy improvisation. The aṅtarā section of a chīz is frequently omitted altogether, which reduces the composed portion of the performance to one or two tāla cycles of sthāī. The entire presentation of the chīz takes a very small amount of time, usually no more than five minutes of the half-hour to forty minutes of performance time.

The text of this chīz follows:[11]

Sthāī:

Bāje jhananajhanana bāje pāyaliyā rājdulārī dole [dore] aṅganāvā meṅ //	The princess is moving about in the courtyard, her anklets jingling.

[11]Translation by B. D. Yadav. "Rājdulārī" ("princess") is an affectionate term for a young bride-to-be.

Aṅtarā:

Man mataṅg matvāro hī dore	The mind is unstable like
in nainan chhavi ati hī chhāī //	a love-mad elephant after
	seeing her; she is lovely
	to behold.

The first phrase of the sthāī, which is called the *mukhṛā*, is the most vital phrase in the chīz, it remains intact throughout the improvisation on the sthāī text, and is used at cadences. The sthāī mukhṛā in Example 7-5 is "Bāje jhana," When it occurs, the syllable "jha" falls on sam of the next cycle. When the aṅtarā text is referred to, the mukhṛā of that section serves as cadence, but less time is devoted to the aṅtarā than to the sthāī. The baṛā khyāl chīz melody is relatively unimportant after the initial statement; the most important contribution of the chīz to the total performance is the text, the tāla, and the mukhṛā.

Baṛā khyāl improvisation resembles the ālāp that precedes dhrupad: it begins slowly, explores the rāga in low register first, then moves upward. Although the tāla is kept by the tablā player, who repeats and repeats the theka, and although the singer certainly knows where (s)he is in the tāla cycle, the rhythm seems free and floating, as in unmetered ālāp. The recurrence of the mukhṛā functions as the mohṛā does in predhrupad ālāp. Rather than singing vocable syllables, as in dhrupad ālāp, the singer uses the chīz text (the improvisation using the text is then called *bolālāp* or *bolbant*) or vowels. (S)he is usually careful not to use the text rhythmically, however, so (s)he changes syllables off the counts, says the words indistinctly, and sings many pitches to a single syllable. As the performance progresses, (s)he begins to lean to rhythm by interspersing in the improvisation passages of boltān, tāns, and occasionally sargam.

Passages of sargam use the solfège syllables as text. As a pitch is sung, it is named, as in Example 7-6. The text enunciation emphasizes rhythm. Example 7-6 is in ektāl, the tablā tāla of twelve counts that is the same, structurally, as the pakhāvaj tāla, chautāl, in Example 7-1. It is in slow speed, and each count is subdivided, so each tāla count in this example is notated as one count.

Bolbānt is considered a carry-over into khyāl from dhrupad. It consists of a long phrase or sentence from the chīz text that is played upon to primarily rhythmic effect. The emphasis on the text in bolbānt provides marked contrast with the wide use of vowels only (*ākār*), in much khyāl improvisation. The transcription in Example 7-7 is one minute of a medium-speed performance of "Mhāre dere āo" in Rāg Desī by a musician of the Gwalior gharānā. In this example, ākār is contrasted with bolbānt.[12] Most

[12] If the slow improvisation in Example 7-7, which is sung to vowels, were sung to the text, it would be called *bolālāp*. Bolālāp differs from bolbānt in that it does not stress rhythm.

EXAMPLE 7-6 Sargam

Hindstānī Rāg Miyān kī Toḍī, Vilambit Laya Ektāl — Baṛā Khyāl Sargam

khyāl singers avoid enunciating the words clearly, except in bolbānt. This is often cited as a major difference between khyāl and dhrupad, in which every syllable must be clear. It can be frustrating to a Western listener not to be able to follow the text in a khyāl performance, but even Indian listeners experience this difficulty. This characteristic, and perhaps others, tends to make khyāl the most difficult classical vocal medium to interpret.

As a barā khyāl performance progresses, more and more *tāns* are sung. Tāns are very fast melodic figures that may (or may not) touch pitches not in the particular rāga. They are borne on the vowels of text syllables or on independent vowels, usually *ā*. Tāns are demonstrated in Examples 7-7 and 7-8.

Rāg Desī, shown in Examples 7-7 and 7-8, is a very popular rāga. It is sung with different characteristics by different artists. The materials used are Sa Re Ma Pa Ni [Ni] Sȧ, Sȧ Ni Dha [Dha] Pa Ma Ga Re Sa. It is classified in Āsāvarī thāt: Sa Re Ga Ma Pa Dha Ni. The vādīs are said to be Pa and Re; in Examples 7-7 and 7-8, Re stands out because it comes in the mukhṛā on sam. Ga comes in descent and frequently in the pakaḍ Ga Sa Re Ni [Ni] Sa, as in the second tāla cycle in Example 7-7, Dha comes between two Pas: Pa Dha Pa. In Example 7-8, Dha occurs only in descent.

Chhotā khyāl is rarely performed as a distinct entity. Usually, it follows a baṛā khyāl, in the same rāga but often in a different tāla, without break as a continuation of the acceleration of the baṛā khyāl. The chhotā khyāl chīz is presented quickly, and improvisation continues. Ālāp-type exploration of the rāga can be dispensed with since it was present in the baṛā khyāl. Chhotā khyāl improvisation is characterized by rapid passage work (tāns), many repetitions of the first phrase of the sthāī, a generally rhythmic orientation, and constant acceleration.

EXAMPLE 7-7 Baṛā Khyāl Ākār Improvisation and Bolbānt

Hindstānī Rāg Desī, Madhya Laya Tīntāl

EXAMPLE 7-8 Baṛā Khyāl Improvisation, Including Ākār Tān and Bolbānt

"Mhāre dere āo" *(continued)*

Most khyāl singers are "of a gharānā," and there are numerous khyāl gharānās. Gharānās are customarily named after a place where the family of musicians originated or where they developed their style—for example, Kirana, Agra, Jaipur, and Gwalior. A musical tradition is generally considered "of a gharānā" when at least three successive generations of able musicians have pursued a distinctive style of singing.[13] Part of the style is the quality of voice that is cultivated. Consequently, vocal training is developed to help successive members of the gharānā cultivate that vocal quality. Thus, "In Kirana the voice emerges from a deliberately constricted throat and has a nasal twang. An Agra voice is also nasal (*nakki*); in addition it has a gruff, grating quality. . . . On the other hand the Jaipur tradition emphasizes a natural, free and full-throated voice."[14]

Most performances of vocal music in North India today feature khyāl singing. If you were to attend a concert of dhrupad singing in India, chances are that you would say, "I'm going to hear dhrupad," or, "I'm going to hear the Dagar brothers," which would mean that you are going to hear dhrupad. But if you hear someone say "I'm going to a concert of vocal music," you can assume that the fare will consist of several khyāls, and a ṭhumṛī to end the program. If the concert is to consist of ṭhumṛī, that is specified, as dhrupad is. Such statements demonstrate how prominent khyāl is today in Hindustānī classical vocal music.

Occasionally, a khyāl singer will substitute another form for the chhotā khyāl; the sequence will be baṛā khyāl to tāranā. The major difference between chhotā khyāl and tāranā lies not in the composition, nor in the performance treatment, but in the text. Vocables are the major text rather than verse or prose, as in chīz. In the tāranā featured on Odeon MOAE 143 (sung by the Pakistani brothers Salamat Ali and Nakazat Ali Khan), the vocal phrase that constitutes much of the text is "Ta re da ni ta da ni." The initial syllable "ta" occurs on count 1 of a fast-speed cycle of tīntāl. The entire phrase takes one cycle of the tāla.

Having said that there is no verse in tāranā, I must make a retraction. Sometimes a tāranā will include a Persian couplet, but the couplet does not function as a chīz functions in khyāl. In the Odeon performance mentioned above, a couplet follows improvisation on the tāranā phrase, but the tāranā phrase is used at cadences, thus functioning as a chīz would.

One school of thought holds that the various combinations of vocables in tāranā are not just meaningless vocables but are Persian words. A sample of these words follows. Such poetry is said to be representative of the mystic school of poets, in which the beloved is the Almighty and the devotee is his lover. Thus, the poetry of tāranā is spiritual, though romantic.[15]

[13]Vamanrao H. Deshpande, *Indian Musical Traditions: An Aesthetic Study of the Gharanas in Hindustani Music* (Bombay: V. P. Bhagvat, 1973), p. 11.

[14]*Ibid.*, p. 16.

[15]Amir Khan, "The Tarana Style of Singing," in *Music East and West*, pp. 22–23.

Tanan dar ā	Enter my body.
O dani	He knows.
Tu dani	You know.
Ni dir dani	You are the complete wisdom.
Tom	I am yours, I belong to you.

Some sources on Indian music say that pakhāvaj bols are introduced into tāranā as text, and indeed that does happen, but not in this Odeon performance. The other vehicle for melody here is sargam (solfège syllables). The types of text in that performance, in the order they occur, are as follows:

Vocables:	ta re da ni ta da ni
	Couplet of poetry
Vocables:	ta re da ni ta da ni
	Sargam
Vocables:	ta re da ni ta da ni
	Sargam
Vocables:	ta re da ni ta da ni

In a different Odeon recording, MOAE 107, featuring music for Kathak dance, a tāranā begins with a sung verse (unmetered), and then the dancer enters. The main tāranā phrase of vocables is ta da re dim. Tablā bols and sargam are also used as text in that performance. Tāranā is thus both a vocal solo and dance genre.

Tāranā are usually performed by artists who specialize in them. Nissar Hussain Khan, the late Amir Khan, and Krishna Rao Shankar Pandit are particularly well known for performance of tāranā. To sing tāranā requires skill in rhythmic manipulation (*layakārī*) and the ability to sing syllables rapidly. The Karnatak version of tāranā, which is called *tillānā*, is very similar and is said to have developed at about the same time.

Ṭhumṛī is the most important "light classical" genre of North Indian music. It is performed in many contexts, from the sphere of dance, to the vocal concert stage, to performance on instruments. Ṭhumṛī is called "light classical," but the reasons for this are difficult to discover from Indian books on music. Possibly it is because the melodies are not always composed in a rāga, or because performers may break the rules in singing those that are. It has also been suggested that simpler tālas and less weighty rāgas are used for ṭhumṛī.[16] Yet another likely reason is that ālāp-type improvisation is not cultivated in ṭhumṛī, and ālāp is the real test of good musicianship. In addition, ṭhumṛī is traditionally accompanied by a harmonium, a small portable organ introduced by the British and referred to by Deva as "the bane" of

[16]The use of Bhairavī for dhrupad and ṭhumṛī throws this into question. Bhairavī, curiously enough, is rarely used for khyāl.

Indian classical music.[17] As the artist sings, he pumps a bellows at the back of the harmonium and reproduces the vocal melody on the keyboard with the other hand (see Plate 26). The fixed pitches that the harmonium is restricted to are considered a serious threat to traditional melodic flexibility. Whatever the reason, ṭhumṛī provides light, enjoyable music with which to end a vocal or instrumental concert.

Plate 26
Harmonium (left corner) Seen in Concert

Ṭhumṛi was cultivated primarily in Lucknow and Benares in the nineteenth century, and it is possible to pinpoint differences between the styles of ṭhumṛī from those two places. Other regional styles have developed as well—for example, that of Punjab. Nowadays, audiences prefer to hear female vocalists sing ṭhumṛī. A full performing ensemble includes harmonium, usually played by the vocalist, tāmbūra, tablā, and probably a sāraṅgī.

The texts of ṭhumṛī are romantic. They refer perhaps to Krishna and his amorous pranks, or to "the beloved," who may (or may not) be Krishna. Other texts are unequivocally romantic: they contain no allegorical suggestions. The text translated below is "Sāwana bīt jāye" as performed on Odeon MOCE 1084 by two female artists, Lakshmi Shankar and Nirmala Devi. One of the main tenets concerning ṭhumṛī is that the text is most important. Each word is pronounced clearly, and every bit of feeling the text might express is brought out musically. This is a major difference between ṭhumṛī and khyāl.

[17]B. Chaitanya Deva, *Indian Music* (New Delhi: Indian Council on Cultural Affairs, 1974), p. 285.

ṬHUMṚĪ TEXT

	Hindi	*English*
Sthāī:	Sajan wa	My husband. . . .
	Sāwana bīta jāye	The rainy season has gone [and you didn't come to me].
Aṅtarā 1:	Pīta ka rōta re	You don't know how to love.
	Karahūṅ na jāne	
	Muraka prīta na jāne	An insensitive heart doesn't know.
Aṅtarā 2:	Jaisi kara ni	Whatever *you* do, you shall reap.
	Esi barani	
	Ab kahe pacch tāye	Why are you now upset?

A ṭhumṛī is a brief composition consisting of sthāī and one or more aṅtarās with improvisation. Usually, the "more aṅtarās" are additional text, which is sung to approximately the same aṅtarā melody. Most ṭhumṛī, however, have only sthāī and aṅtarā. This structure cqn be seen in the transcription and description of "Sāwana bīt jāye" in Example 7-9. Since this is a performance by two singers (*jugalbandi*), this description provides an example of a jugalbandi type of performance as well.

The sthāī text in Example 7-9 is elongated in performance to "sajana wa sajana bīta jā [ye]." The sthāī phrase proper is used at cadences to close each singer's turn. After the several repetitions of the sthāī in variant forms, the amount of improvisation on the sthāī text increases gradually and the middle and upper registers are explored. In that respect, this performance is very similar to medium-speed khyāl. The aṅtarā is sung when the upper register has already been introduced in the improvisation, and it is presented partially at first, as a khyāl aṅtarā is likely to be.

After that point, the performance goes into a section that belongs specifically to ṭhumṛī. The singing stops, and melody making is left to the accompanying harmonium. The drummer takes the spotlight in a section called *laggī*. In laggī, the count will always be duple (4 or 8), no matter what the tāla cycle has been. The drummer doubles or quadruples the speed with a sudden splash of virtuosity.

Then the singing begins again, at the same speed (approximately) where it was before and in the old tāla. In this performance, the sthāī is heard for a short time, then a second aṅtarā is sung. (No khyāl has a second aṅtarā or laggī.) After a return to the sthāī and then another brief laggī, the performance ends with the sthāī.

The speed of this ṭhumṛī performance never increases beyond ♩ = 100. The gradual acceleration to a furious climax that marks khyāl is not usually a performance trait of ṭhumṛī.

EXAMPLE 7-9 Ṭhumṛī: "Sāwana Bīt Jāye"

Analysis of the performance beyond the portion notated above:

Change of singer (The two soloists sing in alternation.)
  4 cycles of the tāla

Change of singer
  9 cycles of the tāla (to 1 minute 48 seconds into the performance)
  Improvisation remains fairly close to the ṭhumṛī sthāī

Change of singer M.M. ♩ = 92
  11 cycles of the tāla (to 2 minutes, 30 seconds)
  Example of text treatment (slash indicates break for breath):
  sajan/ sajan/sajana wa/ sajan wa/sajan wa/ sajana bīta jā/
  Melody dwells between madhya Sa and Ma, then moves to madhya Ma to tār Sa.

Change of singer M.M. ♩ = 92–96
  10 cycles of the tāla (to 3 minutes, 8 seconds)
  Melody dwells between madhya Sa and Ma, then madhya Ma and Dha

Change of singer M.M. ♩ = 92
  13 cycles of the tāla (to 3 minutes, 57 seconds)
  Melody dwells between madhya Sa and Dha

Change of singer M.M. ♩ = 96
 $10\frac{1}{2}$ cycles of the tāla (to 4 minutes, 40 seconds)
 Melody dwells between madhya Ma and tār Sa. The artist plays with pitches Ni and Ni, which are not stressed otherwise.

Change of singer M.M. ♩ = 96
 13 cycles of the tāla (to 5 minutes, 28.5 seconds)
 Melody dwells between madhya Ma and tār Ma, and stresses tār Sa.

Change of singer
 Presentation of the first aṅtarā:

a pī - ta ka rī - ta re ka-ra - hūn na jā - ne

Followed by 11 cycles of the tāla
Improvisation mostly in upper register, on aṅtarā text.

Singers alternate
 12 cycles of the tāla
 Improvisation on aṅtarā text; then singer adds to the aṅtarā:

mu - ra - ka pri - ta na jā - ne

Sung four times, slightly varied

24 further cycles of the tāla

Laggī, with melody kept on harmonium

12 cycles of sung improvisation on sthāī text: sajana wa/sajana/ etc.

Second aṅtarā, given here in skeleton form:

♩ =100
Jai - si ka-ra ni
(Improvisation here)
e - si ba-ra - ni
(Improvisation here)
a - b ka - he pa - cch - tā - ye

Followed by 23 cycles of the tāla, including the second antarā and subsequent improvisation.

19 cycles of the tāla

Return to sthāī text.

Laggī

6 cycles of further improvisation; the performance then ends with sthāī.

The tāla most frequently used for ṭhumṛī are dīpchandi (14 counts), jat (16 counts), Panjābī (16 counts), kaharvā (8 counts), and dādra (6 counts). (Dādra tāl is usually associated with a light classical genre that is also called dādra.) The 16-count tālas jat and Panjābī have the same structural subdivisions as 16-count tīntāl, but the thekas with which they are drummed are very different, They can easily be distinguished in performance because the drummer keeps primarily to the theka. The three 16-count thekas are given in Example 7-10. Dīpchandi of 14 counts is the same as jat tāl, with one count removed in each half of the cycle (as indicated by the boxes in Example 7-10) so that the structure is 3 + 4 + 3 + 4. Bracketed strokes are played in one count.

EXAMPLE 7-10 Tīntāl, Jat Tāl, and Panjābī Tāl Thekas

Tīntāl

×				२				
Dha	dhin	dhin	dha	Dha	dhin	dhin	dha	
o				३				
Dha	tin	tin	ta	Ta	dhin	dhin	dha	/

Jat

×				२				
Dha	[—]	dhin	S	Dha	dha	tin	S	
o				३				
Ta	[—]	tin	S	Dha	dha	dhin	S	/

Panjābī

×				२				
Dha	[gadhi]	[S ga]	dha	Dha	[gadhi]	[S ga]	dha	
o				३				
Dha	[kati]	[S ka]	ta	Ta	[kadhi]	[S ga]	dha	/

The transcribed performance of "Sāwana bīta jāye" (Example 7-9) is in dādra tāla of 6 counts: $\overset{\times}{1}$ 2 3 $\overset{o}{4}$ 5 6. Since this tāla has such a brief cycle, the singers go through several cycles of it before singing a cadence. The principle of keeping the text at the same points in the tāla cycle and singing the full sthāī phrase for cadences is kept more consistently than it is in khyāl mukhṛā.

Dādra, another Hindustānī "light classical form," is very similar to ṭhumṛī in most respects. Its texts are equally amorous, and the text is sung clearly. It may be sung madhya laya or even faster. Frequently, singers follow a ṭhumṛī with a dādra, in a sequence like baṛā khyāl being followed by a chhotā khyāl. Dādra tāl is associated primarily with dādra singing. Theoretically, therefore, it is distinguished from ṭhumṛī by tāla. On occasion, kaharvā tāla of 8 counts is also used for dādra.

The same group of singers who cultivate ṭhumṛī as a specialty cultivate dādra as well. Among these performers, two particularly famous ones are Begum Akhtar and Rasoolan Bai.

With this discussion of ṭhumṛī and dādra, we can put "Sāwana bīta jāye" into proper perspective. The record says that this composition is a ṭhumṛī (and the singers noted that they were singing ṭhumṛī). Most Indians would know the performance as ṭhumṛī. However, it has two aṅtarās, which is characteristic of dādra, not of ṭhumṛī. It is in dādra tāla, which, theoretically, makes it a dādra. One explanation for this mixture of traits is that the piece was composed by Abdul Rehman Khan, who tends to compose his songs in this fashion. "Sāwana bīta jāye" is thus another example of the acceptable flexibility in Indian classical music.

One other light classical form flourishes throughout North India: *ghazal*. The poetry that is the heart of ghazal is distinct from that of the other light classical forms in one very obvious respect: it is in Urdu, the poetic language of Muslims in North India. Ghazal came into vogue in the nineteenth century in Lucknow. It carries the associations and romantic charm of the dancing girl tradition. The tālas used in singing ghazal are pushto and dīpchandi,[18] and laggī is featured in it. Accompaniment is provided on tablā, tāmbūra, harmonium, and/or sāraṅgī. An example of a ghazal text follows:

> What can we expect of faithfulness,
>   who do not know what faith is?
>
> What has happened to you?
>
> What is the remedy of this?
>
> And what is this all about?

Translated by B. D. YADAV

[18]Viney K. Agarwala, *Traditions and Trends in Indian Music* (Meerut, Uttar Pradesh: Rastogi and Co., 1966), p. 56.

One tāla closely associated with ghazal is dhumālī tāl, of 8 counts. It is essentially the same tāla as kaharvā of ṭhumṛī, but the theka is slightly different:

Kaharvā tāl				*Dhumālī tāl*			
× Dha	ge	na	ti	× Dha	trika	tin	tin
o Na	ka	dhi	na/	o Ta	trika	dhin	dhin/

Ghazals in dhumālī tāl sung by Begum Akhtar can be heard on Odeon S–MOCE 1153. The "trika" strokes in counts 2 and 6 are particularly clear in the performance of "Dard minnat kash-e-na hua." (On the same record are two ghazals in dādra tāl. Clearly, dādra tāl is not used only for dādra songs.)

INSTRUMENTAL GENRES

Several of the musical principles developed in ālāp, dhrupad, and khyāl are encapsulated in the ālāp–joṛ–jhālā–gat sequence of intrumental performance. The instrumental ālāp is much like the ālāp that precedes a dhrupad—unmetered, slow, and searching out the chosen rāga. Slight differences can be attributed to the differences in the performing medium. On a stringed instrument in particular, the prolonged, intense Sa with which a dhrupad ālāp begins cannot be produced because the string too quickly ceases to vibrate. Many instrumentalists begin their ālāp by running a finger down the sympathetic strings in glissando. They then play a couple of phrases in the middle and upper registers to show off the outlines of the rāga before settling into the traditional ālāp (see Example 7-11).

In addition, the exploration of the lower register is sometimes more prolonged in an instrumental performance than in a vocal one, again because of the nature of the medium. The ideal three-octave range of a vocalist is considerably easier to attain on sitār and sarod, where the range is provided on the strings. As in vocal ālāp, a single melodic figure functions cadentially to mark off segments in the melodic development.

The point in the instrumental ālāp where the performance begins to be more rhythm-oriented and where the speed accelerates noticeably is the *joṛ*. A pulsation becomes obvious, too, although it does not remain consistent. Later, toward the end of the unmetered portion of the performance, the artist refers constantly to the drone pitch (by using the drone/rhythm strings on stringed instruments) and maintains a rapid, constant pulsation by plucking (or tonguing, on a wind instrument) each pitch separately. This articulation and this section of the performance are called *jhālā*. The melody of the gat to follow is frequently foreshadowed in this jhālā, as melody pitches stand out from the drone pitches in the rhythmic drive. With a tremendous climax of speed and virtuosity, the performer brings the unmetered portion of the performance to an end with jhālā.[19]

Often, there is a short break between jhālā and the gat as the drummer and instrumentalist check their tuning. When all is ready, the instrumental soloist begins a composition, called a *gat*. Like the other types of Hindustānī compositions, most gats begin not on count 1 but on some previous count—perhaps at khālī, or on count 12 if in tīntāl. (Other gats begin right on count 1). When the drummer hears the gat beginning, he plays a fast flourish, which he times perfectly to meet the soloist at count 1. The metered portion of the performance has begun.

Occasionally, the soloist challenges his tablā player at this moment by refraining from telling him in advance which tāla the gat will be played in. Furthermore, the soloist has probably chosen a difficult or rare tāla, such as one with $11\frac{1}{2}$ counts or one with $13\frac{1}{2}$ counts. Challenges such as these are part of performance practice in Hindustānī instrumental music.

EXAMPLE 7-11 Beginning of Sitār Alāp

There are two basic types of instrumental gats: Masit Khani gats and Reza Khani gats. Masit Khani gats are in slow or medium speed, and Reza Khani gats are in medium or fast speed. In performances, they are often linked as a pair—slow to fast—as the two types of khyāl are linked. Most

[19]The jhālā section is frequently shortened or omitted on recordings. A second jhālā section at the end of the performance seems to take precedence over this one at the end of the ālāp.

gats are only one tāla cycle long and function both melodically and metrically in the performance. A gat's melodic shape is determined partly by the structure of the particular rāga being played, but various compositional means are employed to show off the structure of the tāla cycle, as well.

One of the compositional elements of sarod and sitār gats is stroking patterns—patterns of inward strokes (called da), outward strokes (ra), and a quick succession of in and out (dira). The ideal Masit Khani gat, for example, has the following basic pattern:

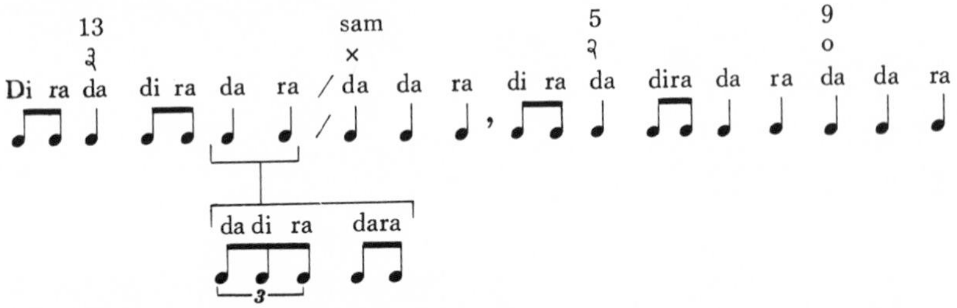

The stroking pattern divides the tāla cycle into two equal parts: counts 12 to 3 (past *sam*) and counts 4 to 11.

Other sitār gats with other stroking patterns are shown in Example 7-12. The rāgas are Āsāvarī, Bhairavī, and Mālkauns (or Mālkosh), which was discussed in Chapter Three. Each begins at a different place in the tīntāl cycle.[20]

The rhythm and melodic contour of a gat are additional compositional elements that may be used to delineate the tāla structure. In each of the gats in Example 7-12, the pitch on sam is the longest held pitch in the gat. In (b) and (d), a slight rhythmic displacement leads up to sam, and that is the only place in either gat where such rhythmic displacement occurs. Melodic contours in (c) and (d) are an especially important factor, because the subdivisions of the tāla have quite different pitch register. Note the means by which the two gats in Rāg Mālkauns are made similar, and yet very different.

Beyond the initial playing of the gat melody that begins the gat portion of the performance, the artists proceed quickly to improvisation. The improvisation resembles a combination of that portion of baṛā khyāl beyond the slow, searching ālāp and chhotā khyāl improvisation: ālāp and tān for melodic invention, and rhythmic elaborations like bolbānt of vocal music, which are called *toṛa* (or *toda*) here. The gat returns in part or in full at cadences.

A striking difference between a sarod or sitār gat performance and a khyāl performance is the amount of interplay between the melody soloist and the drummer. In one possible relationship, they alternate between the

[20]Bhagvat Sharan Sharma and Ravi Shankar, *Sitār Malika* (Hathras: Sangit Karyalaya, 1966), pp. 88, 87, 85, 84.

EXAMPLE 7-12 Sitār Gats

roles of soloist and timekeeper: either the drummer plays theka while the melody soloist improvises, or the melody soloist plays the gat while the drummer takes the spotlight. The melody soloist initiates the relationship.

In the gat portion of a performance, Western audiences in particular are likely to hear an exchange between drummer and melody soloist that is a challenge to imitation. This exchange is called *jawāb-sawāl* ("question-answer"). The melody soloist will play a phrase and challenge the drummer to reproduce it rhythmically and even melodically to some extent. (This is different from the exchange mentioned in the previous paragraph.) During this type of relationship, both musicians keep tāla in their head. The amount of attention that will be focused on the drummer depends on the performance custom of the melody soloist. Some prefer an accompanist-soloist relationship; others prefer a more equal partnership.

The speed accelerates throughout the gat improvisation, and the performance arrives finally at a breathtaking jhālā section for the ending. The jhālā is metered on this occasion, but the same driving rhythm heard in unmetered jhālā is obtained by constant articulation of pitch Sa.

This type of instrumental sitār and sarod ālāp–joṛ–jhālā–gat sequence is probably the best known of all Indian music to Western audiences, due to the popularity of some of India's finest instrumentalists: sitārist Pandit Ravi Shankar, sarodist Ustad Ali Akbar Khan, and drummers Alla Rakha and Chatur Lal. Sitārist Vilayat Khan is known for a somewhat different style of this type of performance. His style is said to be gāyakī ("vocal") style.

That is, he tries to reproduce on sitār the legato style of vocal music. This is difficult when one considers the idiom: strings from which sound decays quickly and on which the sharp attack of a stroke is unavoidable.[21]

The reason Nazir Jairazbhoy gives for this development of vocal style on a stringed instrument is a point that we noted in Chapter Four: "The voice is regarded in India as the most versatile of instruments and virtually without limitations, while all other instruments are restrictive."[22] Flute performances too are usually in gāyakī style. The difficulties of change of medium are perhaps not as great with flute as with stringed instruments because both flute and the voice are wind instruments.

The three major Hindustānī performance structures may be compared in Chart 13. The capitalized segments are unmetered; "*imp*" indicates improvisation; and dots separate the segments of a performance sequence.

1. ĀLĀP. NOM TOM ĀLĀP. dhrupad . . . *imp* with bolbānt

2. baṛa khyāl chīz . . . . ālāp . . . . *imp* with [bolbānt / tāns / sargam] . chhotā khyāl . . *imp*

3. ĀLĀP. JOṚ. JHĀLĀ . . . . medium gat. *imp* with [tāns / toda] . . fast gat . . *imp*

CHART 13. The Three Major Hindustānī Performance Structures

Ṭhumṛī, dādra, and dhun are "light classical" forms played by instrumentalists in North India. Instrumental ṭhumṛīs are supposedly based on vocal ṭhumṛīs, although the derivation is often difficult to trace. If the ṭhumṛī is well known, the melody reminds listeners of the sentiments of the texts. Ṭhumṛī and dādra have both been discussed at length in the section on vocal genres. As ṭhumṛīs are supposed to be based on vocal versions of ṭhumṛīs, so are instrumental dādras supposed to resemble their vocal versions. In each case, the relationship of instrumental ṭhumṛī and dādra to vocal ṭhumṛī and dādra has not been explored definitively. *Dhun* is the "lightest classical" of the Hindustānī instrumental forms. It is similar to ṭhumṛī but is based on folk or popular tunes. The performer of dhun is at liberty to mix rāgas or to play in whatever way he feels will appeal to his audience. Either a ṭhumṛī or a dhun is performed as the last item on a program in order to end a concert in a light, pleasant mood.

[21] For a more detailed discussion of this style, see Jairazbhoy, *Rāgs of North Indian Music*, pp. 186–89.

[22] Jairazbhoy, *Rāgs of North Indian Music*, p. 187.

EIGHT
PERFORMANCE GENRES OF KARNATAK MUSIC

In genres of Karnatak music, some of the same principles come into play that characterize Hindustānī genres: the contrast of unmetered with metered, the progression in some types of performances from free rāga to emphasis on rhythm, and the fusion of traditional compositions (generically called *kalpita saṅgīta*) with improvisation (*manodharma saṅgīta*). The structures within which these principles are carried out and the degree to which each is developed in the two traditions are quite different, however. One major difference is that dance concerts are frequent in South Indian cultural life. Consequently, several of the Karnatak genres have developed in variant forms appropriate for a dance or a musical concert. We shall give more attention to the concert versions, but shall briefly consider the dance versions as well.

VARṆAM

A concert in South India usually begins with a type of composition called a *varṇam*—in a music concert, a *tāna varṇam*; in a dance concert, a *pada varṇam*. A varṇam is similar to an étude, which in Karnatak terms is called the *abhyāsa gāna* category of composition. Varṇa are learned by students who are just about to move from the practice genres to learning concert music. They are good for training the voice and also for developing instrumental technique, partially because they are practiced at three different levels of speed. A varṇam is also considered an authoritative source for the correct rendering of a rāga. In concert, it is good for warming up, although it is entertaining in its own right. Since a varṇam is structured somewhat like other types of South Indian genres, it will serve as a good introduction here as well.

A varṇam has three basic sections: pallavi, anupallavi, and charaṇam. Other elements occur between these sections, or after a section.

first half [pallavi / anupallavi / muktāyi svara]

second half [charaṇa / ettugada svaras]

This format is shown in a tāna varṇam in Rāga Shankarābharana, Ādi tāla, in Example 8-1. It is transcribed in the middle speed, and two beats are given for each count of the tāla. Therefore, Ādi tāla of $4 + 2 + 2$ becomes $8 + 4 + 4$. Most varna are in the middle speed (*madhyamakāla*).

The sections of the composition are defined in terms of pitch register. Theoretically, a pallavi section delineates the lower tetrachord of the middle register and includes a few pitches in the low register. An anupallavi section consists, theoretically, of the upper tetrachord of the middle register and a few pitches of the upper register. However, as Example 8-1 demonstrates, practice does not always remain within theory.[1] The pallavi covers the entire

[1]Example 8-1 is from P. Sambamoorthy, *South Indian Music*, 5th ed., (Madras: Indian Music Publishing House, 1958), Book III, pp. 271–73. The text is in Telugu. A more literary rendering and translation was provided for me by Padmanabh S. Jaini, as follows.

Sami ninne kāri chala mārulu konndira.	O Lord, I desired you many times over.
Tāmamu seyaka dayecūdarāja gopala	Without delay show mercy to me, O king of the cowherds (Krishna).
Nirajākshi ni paini.	The lotus-eyed lady calls on you.

The Hindustānī sections sthāī and aṅtarā are said to delineate the registers in the same way. There too, practice does not always confirm theory.

middle register (here, middle C to B) and even touches Sa and Ri of the high register, not to mention descending into the low register. The anupallavi covers the whole middle register but does not go into the lower register; it does ascend higher into tār saptak.

The pallavi, anupallavi, and charaṇam are set to a literary text:

pallavi:	Sāmi ninne kōri chāla marulu kōnnadirā
anupallavi:	Tāmasamu seyaka dayajūdarā kumārā
charaṇam:	Nirajākshi ni pai

Varṇa texts may concern love or devotion to a deity, or they may praise a patron or even describe the varṇam itself.

Muktāyi svara and ettugada svara passages have no literary text; they are sung to the solfège syllables Sa, Ri, Ga, Ma, Pa, Dha, and Ni. As shown in Example 8-1, the muktāyi svara āvartas provide marked rhythmic contrast to the pallavi and anupallavi because of the text and its setting. In the svara passage, each pitch is enunciated with a syllable and there are few prolonged pitches. In the pallavi and anupallavi, the text is sparse and much of the melody is therefore sung to the vowels. When performed on an instrument, stroking (or tonguing) patterns achieve the same contrasting effects.

A varṇam will include several ettugada svara passages, which are based on the structural principle of ever increasing complexity and length. In Example 8-1, there are four of them: the first two are each one āvarta (cycle) long and the last two are each two āvarta long. The first ettugada svara is usually one cycle long, and each succeeding one must be equally long or longer. Even if they are the same length, the complexity must increase. This pattern of development, which is called *srōtōvaha yati*, is said to be like a river (*srōtōvaha*)—starting small and becoming larger. It is one of the basic structural principles of the Karnatak tradition of classical music.

In performance, the varṇam is lengthened by repetition. The repetition can be done smoothly because of the melodic "rhyme" at the end of each segment. Each āvarta of the first half is repeated, but at double speed. Therefore, it must be performed twice to fill the time cycle. In the second half, the charaṇam appears after each ettugada svara. In most Karnatak genres, the pallavi would occur after each section. The varṇam is unusual in that the pallavi does not appear in the second half at all. The structure of the varṇam in Example 8-1 is as follows:

first half:	pallavi anupallavi muktayi svara pallavi	second half:	charanam ettugada svara 1 charanam ettugada svara 2 etc.

EXAMPLE 8-1 Tāna Varṇam

|4 Charanam
0
0
nī - - ra - jā - - - - kshi nī pai
Ettugadu svara
1.
Pa Ma Pa Ga Ma Ri Ga Sa Ri Ni Sa Re Ga Ma
Repeat Charanam
2.
Pa Dha Pa Ma Ga Ma Pa Ma Ga Ma Ri Ga Ri Sa Ni Dha Ni Pa Dha Ni Sa Re Ni Sa Re Ga Ma
Repeat Charanam
3.
Ma Dha Pa Ma Ga Ma Pa Ga Ma Re Ga Sa Ni Sa Ma Ga Re Sa Ni Dha Ni Sa Re Ga Ma Pa Ga Ma
Pa Dha Ni Pa Dha Ni Sa Ri Sa Ga Re Sa Ni Dha Ni Sa Ri Ni Dha Pa Dha Ma Ga Re Sa Re Ga Ma
Repeat Charanam
4.
Pa Ma Pa Ga Ma Ri Ga Sa Ma Ga Re Sa Ni Pa Dha Ni Sa Re Sa Ni Sa Re Ga Ma Pa Dha Pa
Sa Ni Ri Sa Ma Ga Ri Ga Sa Ni Pa Dha Ni Sa Sa Ni Dha Pa Ma Ga Re Sa Re Ga Ma

A varṇam, then, is a type of composed music (*kalpita saṅgīta*). It is metered throughout. Most varṇa are in the same rāga throughout, but a few have a different rāga in each section. The latter are called *rāgamālikā* tāna (or pada) varṇa: tāna or pada varṇa in a garland (mālikā) of rāgas. The rāgamālikā idea is particularly South Indian and is utilized in various other genres as well as being a genre itself (as will be discussed later).

Dance varṇa are usually in slow speed (*chaukakāla*). When muktāyi svara and ettugada svara appear in the varṇam form, those svara are sung first, and then text is put to the same melody. (This replaces the repetition in double speed that occurs in tāna varṇam.) For the svara part, "pure dance" (*nṛitta*) is performed by the dancer. Then, when the text is sung, the dance expresses the mood of the text.[2] The texts of pada varṇa are longer and thus have fewer extended vowels than the texts in tāna varṇa. Pada varṇam is not to be confused with another dance genre, pāḍam.

KRITI

A large part of every South Indian musical concert is devoted to a major genre of Karnatak classical music, kriti. Since the eighteenth century, the kriti has been the most vital song-type of Karnatak music. The theme of a kriti text may be heroic, romantic, or narrative, but whether jocular or serious, most texts are devotional in nature (see the text given below). Kritis can be metered or prose. The majority of the texts are in Telugu, Sanskrit, and Tamil. Kritis can be performed in slow, medium, or fast speed, and in ghana rāgas as well as in rakti rāgas (those that express a particular sentiment). They are written in a variety of tālas. Thousands of kritis have been composed by a number of composers.

Tyāgarāja: "RĀMA SĪTĀ RĀMA"

> O Sītā Rāma! My mind feels as though snakes had coiled round it. Pray, have mercy on me and take me by the hand. Just as a chaste wife delights in serving her Lord, my mind rejoices in celebrating your festivities. Just as a creeper twines round the Kalpaka tree, my mind is inseparably attached to you and will not leave you even for ages. This is the nature of Advaitic realization, real detachment, and salvation itself. This is the essence of the Vedas. Pray accept all this from me and be happy.[3]

[2]*Ibid.*, p. 128. Indian classical dance is categorized into two types: nṛitta ("pure dance"), which has no interpretive elements, and *nṛtya* (interpretive dance), which uses the gestural vocabulary of mime (*abhināya*).

[3]C. Ramanujachari and V. Raghavan, *The Spiritual Heritage of Tyāgarāja*, 2nd ed. (Madras: Sri Ramakrishna Math, 1966), p. 422.

Performers usually precede the singing or playing of a kriti with an ālāpana (comparable to the Hindustānī ālāp). This helps the performer as well as the listener to prepare for the kriti and to establish the identity and mood of the rāga. The ālāpana should be no longer than the kriti.

Most kriti have three sections: pallavi, anupallavi, and charaṇam. Many have multiple charaṇa, which are set either to the same melody or to different melodies, like a series of through-composed verses. All the charaṇa should be of the same length so that the proportions are kept in balance. Example 8-2 is a kriti with only one charaṇa. It has been transcribed from a performance (not from notation) and is reduced to skeletal form here. Example 8-3 is the same kriti in fuller form.[4] The kriti is "Bruhi Mukundeti," composed by Sadasiva Brahmendra. It is in Rāga Kurañji and Ādi tāla. In the Sanskrit text, a saint calls upon his tongue to continue uttering the many sacred names of the Lord—Keshava, Madhavam, Govinda, Krishna, Ananta, and so on.

EXAMPLE 8-2 Kriti: "Bruhi Mukundeti" (Skeletal Melody)

Karnatak Rāga Kurañji, Adi Tāla

[4]Example 8-2 was transcribed with the assistance of Smt. Kamala Vedanthan from World Pacific recording WPS 21440: "Sounds of Subbulakshmi."

Example 8-2 demonstrates several points. First, it is transcribed so that each count of Ādi tāla gets one beat (fast speed). Thus each cycle is of eight beats. The pallavi section takes two cycles, as do the anupallavi and the charaṇam. Thus, each section of this kriti begins at the same point in the tāla cycle—here, a half count past sama. The point in the cycle where melody begins is called the eḍuppu, so here the eḍuppu of the sections are the same. In many kritis, however, the eḍuppu are different.

The pallavi returns after the anupallavi and also after the charaṇam. It must return at the same place in the tāla cycle in which it originally appeared. The pallavi is thus a kind of cadence, just as the beginning phrases of the Hindustānī dhrupad and khyāl sthāī were. In Karnatak music, however, the compositional structure does not necessarily aim toward count 1 (sama) as the demarcation point for phrases; in "Bruhi Mukundeti" it certainly does not.

This kriti also demonstrates a principle of repetition: the charaṇam repeats the melody of the anupallavi. It is not unusual to find repetitions of whole sections of melody in kriti. On the other hand, many kritis are through-composed. Clearly, the sectional structure of kriti can vary from composition to composition. A kriti may even have only two sections—pallavi and a *samashti charaṇam*, which substitutes for the usual anupallavi and charaṇam.

The pallavi, anupallavi, and charaṇam are the basic elements of a kriti. This structure can be stretched to include several other elements: *sangati*, *citta svara*, *svara sāhitya*, *kalpana svara*, and *niraval*. Sangati are composed variations developed on a musical theme. The greatest of all kriti composers, Tyāgarāja, introduced these into the form. When present, they are integral to the composition and not an optional feature. The fuller form of "Bruhi Mukundeti" (Example 8-3) includes the sangati composed for all three sections of this kriti. The principle of variation is one of gradual change within the basic theme, to a point where the last sangati may be totally different from the original theme. Each new sangati is repeated. With the relatively few sangati in Example 8-3, the pallavi is expanded to six cycles of the tāla (after the mṛdañga enters) and the anupallavi to nine cycles, the pallavi repetition is three more cycles, the charaṇam is twelve cycles, and the final return of the pallavi is again three cycles. Frequently, the "pallavi repetition" is a repetition of the last pallavi sangati rather than of the "original" pallavi. The original placement of the text is retained throughout.

Citta svara are composed passages sung to solfège syllables that may appear at the end of the anupallavi or at the end of the charaṇam. These passages are sometimes added to kritis by someone other than the original composer. They can be in the same speed as the kriti melody, or in a faster speed (double or quadruple the original speed). Theoretically, citta svara should present an aspect of the rāga that is not covered by the kriti itself. Thus, a citta svara can be sung only with the one kriti for which it was composed. Unlike Hindustānī dhrupad or khyāl chīz, which theoretically encapsulate the entire essence of a rāga, a kriti may present only one aspect of the rāga. One would need to learn a number of compositions in the same rāga in order to obtain its gestalt.

Svara sāhitya are citta svara passages for which a text has been composed. The text presumably continues the sense of the anupallavi and charaṇam texts. When a kriti includes svara sāhitya, the solfège version (citta svara) is sung after the anupallavi and the text version (svara sāhitya) is sung after the charaṇam.[5] Another great kriti composer, Syāma Śastri, introduced this element into kriti.

EXAMPLE 8-3 Kriti: "Bruhi Mukundeti" (As Performed)

[5]Sambamoorthy, *South Indian Music*, Book III, p. 142.

EXAMPLE 8-3 (Cont.)

Kalpana svara passages are also sung to solfège, but they are improvised rather than composed. They can occur in pallavi, anupallavi, and charaṇam. Frequently less than one cycle long, they replace one or two words in a phrase of the original theme. The svara passage may then be expanded gradually in srōtōvaha fashion. Another possibility is to begin with a long kalpana svara, then reduce it gradually in a shape called *gopuccha yati* ("like the cow's tail"). Whatever form the artist improvises kalpana svara in, it must tie back into the composition smoothly, both melodically and at the proper place in the tāla cycle. An example of kalpana svara is given in Example 8-4. Only a snatch of a pallavi returns at the end of each passage.

EXAMPLE 8-4 Kalpana Svara

Niraval is the remaining type of improvisation that can appear in kriti. Here, the performer improvises melodic variations, keeping the text of the anupallavi or charaṇam, in basically the same relationship to the tāla as it originally had been.

Kriti has a special heritage, for it stems from *kirtana*, a genre of the fourteenth, fifteenth, and sixteenth centuries. During these times, many great musicians of South India were bhaktas, individuals who expressed their religious devotion through song. One of the greatest was Purandara Das, a sixteenth-century saint who composed many kirtanas in order to make his religious preaching more appealing to the masses. Purandara Das is often referred to as the "father of Karnatak music," both because he initiated the methodical study of music and because he established a precedent by composing songs in the vernacular rather than in Sanskrit. Kirtanas remain in currency today.

In many sources on Indian music, references to kirtana and kriti are quite confusing. Indeed, some kirtana and kriti are difficult to distinguish from each other as types. For the most part, however, kriti are musical compositions valued for their aesthetic contents.[6] The portrayal of the rāga is of primary importance in kriti, but is only incidental in kirtana. Only common, well-known rāgas are used for kirtana; not only well-known but also scholarly, even rare, rāgas are featured in kriti. Kirtana have been composed with pallavi, anupallavi, and charaṇa since the fifteenth century, but their melody and rhythm are simpler than those of kriti. The words are most important in kirtana, whereas in kriti they are the vehicle for melody.

In the eighteenth and nineteenth centuries, kriti attained prominence through the works of three of South India's most famous composers, Tyāgarāja, Syāma Śastri, and Muttuswāmi Dīkshitar, all of whom were born in the same village, Tiruvarur in Tanjore. Their works still dominate the

[6]Sambamoorthy, *South Indian Music*, Book III, pp. 131–35, notes these contrasts. Not all his points have been presented here.

Karnatak musical scene. Tyāgarāja's life (1759–1847) was devoted to the worship of God, particularly Lord Rāma. He subsisted only by singing and begging.[7] He spurned the proferred patronage of royalty, rejected the gifts of the Mahārāja of Tanjore, and refused even to compose a song in the ruler's name. The famous musician became a saint and is remembered with reverence. Indeed, his compositions predominate in the average South Indian recital.

In Tyāgarāja's compositions, the kriti evolved from the kirtana to its present form. Placing emphasis more on the music than on the words, he kept text to a minimum. However, he followed the example of Purandara Das and wrote in a vernacular prose (Telugu) rather than in the more traditional Sanskrit poetry. As we noted, Tyāgarāja introduced sangati into the kriti form. About 700 of Tyāgarāja's texts remain, but it is impossible to know if all of their musical settings are his or if some were composed by his students (none of whom ever became famous).

Syāma Śastri (1762–1827) was a devout Brahmin. Like his contemporary, Tyāgarāja, he was well educated, knew Sanskrit, and lived a life of devotion. Since his father had received large gifts of land from Tanjore's mahārāja, Śastri could devote all of his time to music. He became famous both as a performing musician and as a composer of kritis. Although he composed about 300 pieces, only 30 of them have been popularized. Many were lost because he did not teach them to his disciples, just as Tyāgarāja and Dīkshitar did not. But whereas his two great contemporaries performed widely outside Tanjore, Śastri remained near home.[8] He wrote in Sanskrit, Telugu, and occasionally Tamil, and composed intricate passages of solfège syllables. His kritis are of a very scholarly nature and are very demanding in their use of tāla. For these reasons, they cannot be learned as easily as Tyāgarāja's kritis.

Muttuswāmi Dīkshitar (1776–1835) was a scion of a distinguished musical family. For five years he lived with his two wives in Benares, North India, holy city of the Hindus, where he studied yoga. There he was attracted very much to Hindustānī music, especially the slow singing of dhrupad, and the influence of this experience can be seen in some of his kritis. Upon his return to South India, he achieved fame as a performer and composer and enjoyed royal patronage for the rest of his life. Though Tamil was his native tongue, Dīkshitar wrote texts only in Sanskrit. His verse is technically complex and contains many references to ancient mythology in a context of praise of God. His musical style is dignified, his form through-composed without sectional repetition, and his purpose to explore the rāga thoroughly. His songs move at a slow tempo and are heavily ornamented. Dīkshitar was also skilled at tāla, and at the end of one or more sections of his composi-

[7] L. Isaac, *Theory of Indian Music* (Madras: Shyam Printers, 1967) pp. 206–25.
[8] *Ibid.*, pp. 225–34.

tions there is often a passage in dvikāla or catuskāla for rhythmic contrast. Like Śastri's kritis and unlike Tyāgarāja's, the kritis of Dīkshitar require repeated hearing to be understood.

The flexibility inherent in the basic kriti form has attracted many composers. Moreover, kriti has been incorporated intact into solo instrumental performance. Since kriti is a musical composition rather than a textual composition, its performance on instruments is seen as posing no difficulty. Stroking patterns are faithful to "text" enunciation and the rhythm of solfège passages.

RĀGAM-TĀNAM-PALLAVI

A kriti with a long preceding ālāpana is the featured selection in most South Indian performances of classical music. Some performers, however, cultivate another major form as the featured selection: rāgam-tānam-pallavi. This form is performed either vocally or instrumentally. The following description is of a vocal performance. The full ensemble would include the vocalist, a violinist, a mṛdaṅga player and probably another percussionist(s), and someone to keep the drone. The violin complements the vocal part. Frequently the vocalist and violinist pair off with the mṛdaṅga player and the other percussionist (on kanjīra or ghaṭam), respectively. The composition of the performance ensemble is flexible.

The soloist begins the rāgam (or rāga ālāpana) with short, fairly slow phrases that reveal and explore the details of the rāga in a deliberate fashion. The violinist joins the soloist in the improvisation, repeating the soloist's phrases and thereby forming a bridge to the next phrase. He may repeat the phrases exactly, or render them only approximately with the "nutshell" of the idea, but near the beginning of the performance he repeats them as closely as possible. Gradually, the soloist lengthens the lines and sings fast phrases around one pitch in the rāga. The length of time he leaves between his phrases determines how much the violinist will play alone, but the violinist may begin the repetition even before the soloist has completed the phrases.

After the soloist has completed his rāga ālāpana, the violinist takes his turn. He usually takes approximately the same amount of time that the soloist has taken.[9] This contrasts strikingly with Hindustānī ālāp practice, in which the creation of the melody is the responsibility of one performer only.

In tānam, the second portion of the rāgam-tānam-pallavi sequence, rhythmic pulsation is established. As in Hindustānī nom-tom-ālāp and joṛ,

[9]L. Shankar, *The Art of Violin Accompaniment in South Indian Classical Music* (Ann Arbor, Mich.: University Microfilms, 1974), pp. 50–51.

the pulsation comes and goes; it is not always consistent. In a vocal tānam (on meaningless syllables), the placement of a syllable on each pitch articulation, particular types of ornamentation, and much pitch repetition create the pulsation. Melodic and rhythmic contrast is provided by slurred, nonenunciated pitches. In instrumental tānam the resources consist of plucked (therefore "enunciated") pitches, contrasting with pitches obtained by pulling or sliding along a string ("nonenunciated" pitches), and pitches obtained by the striking of the drone strings. At first, there are lapses into the free rhythm of rāgam style. Once pulsation becomes consistent, the speed is increased by doubling. All of this takes place without reference to a meter.

With the pallavi, the metered portion of the rāgam-tānam-pallavi sequence begins. "Pallavi" refers to a brief composition and also to a complete composition-plus-improvisation movement. According to at least one writer, the first evidence of the pallavi form appeared about 250 years ago, in the work of a famous composer of that time, Pachimirian Adiappier.[10] It is a form that seems always to have contained the element of musical challenge in it, not only challenge to the soloist to perform well, but also the context for challenge by the soloist to the other members of the ensemble: solo singer to violinist, mṛdañga player, and secondary percussionists, such as ghaṭam and kanjīra players.

The pallavi itself is one line of composed melody—a traditional pallavi melody, a line from some portion of a kriti (not necessarily the pallavi), or a newly composed melody. If a soloist decides to have the accompanist hear the pallavi not in advance but only during the performance, the challenge can begin at the outset. In this case, the contest of memory is already in motion, because it is the duty of the accompanists to reproduce the soloist's pallavi perfectly after one hearing. This may sound simple for one line of melody, but it is probable that the one line is composed in an old and complex tāla[11] and in slow speed, that each count is subdivided, and that pitches of the melody fall at odd places within the subdivision. The primary orientation of the composed pallavi is rhythmic, and the primary orientation of the improvisation that follows is similarly rhythmic. It is a "highly technical rhythmic exercise."[12]

Pallavis are from one to six cycles long. They are constructed so that the point of principal rhythmic weight is not the first beat, but rather the halfway point in the tāla cycle. This is demonstrated in Example 8-5, a pallavi in Karnatak Rāga Bhairavī, in Ādi tāla, which is said to be taken from a Tyāgarāja kriti. It is in slow speed, and consequently, there are four commas

[10] *Ibid.*, p. 108.

[11] Robert Brown comments that tālas of unusual length and complexity dating from the so-called medieval period are often used in pallavi (*The Mṛdañga: A Study of Drumming in South India* (Ann Arbor, Mich.: University Microfilms, 1965), Vol. I, p. 5).

[12] Shankar, *Art of Violin Accompaniment*, p. 116.

in the notation for every tāla count. The point of rhythmic weight, which is called *arudi*, is marked with an asterisk. While improvising in a pallavi, one may tamper with virtually every element of it except the location of the arudi.[13]

EXAMPLE 8-5 Pallavi

```
                                          *
|| , , P , D  N , Ṡ , N D P , D , , N , , | Ṡ , , , , , , D |, N Ṡ , , N D P ||
       Tā-ma-ra- sa da-  ḷa nē-            tri            tyā- ga-rā-  ju-ni- mi-
|| D M-
   tri
```

The starting point of the pallavi is called the eḍuppu. The melody must fill the tāla cycle so that it ends just before the eḍuppu, to allow for the repetition of the pallavi in a cyclical manner.

To begin the pallavi performance, the soloist sings the line and then repeats it once or twice. The violinist then tries to reproduce the line exactly, even bowing so as to "enunciate" the text. The mṛdaṅga player then joins the violinist in attempting to reproduce the rhythm exactly. Then, niraval improvisation begins. As in kriti, niraval means that the text remains the same but the melody is varied. The text must also remain at the same place in the tāla cycle. In niraval, the soloist and accompanist create variations to higher and higher pitches until they reach a climax. Then they descend to the beginning point and repeat the pallavi.

The next type of improvisation shows the pallavi melody in different levels of speed: *dvigun*, *tiśra naḍai* (triple speed), *caturaśra naḍai* (quadruple speed), and even sextuple speed. After this rhythmic play comes svara kalpana, in which the solfège syllables (svara) are fit into parts of the cycle and sung at different levels of speed. (This can all be followed on the Nonesuch recording from which the pallavi of Example 8-5 was transcribed.)

Rāgamālikā can be fit into the pallavi from in the svara kalpana portion of the improvisation. At the conclusion of each new rāga, the pallavi line must be restated, either "transposed" to the new rāga in the chain or left in the original rāga. At the conclusion of the chain, the pallavi must be in the original rāga.

Pallavi improvisation may also be extended to include tālamālikā, rāga tāla mālikā, and tani āvartam. Tani āvartam is solo improvisation by the percussionists in the performing ensemble. All melody disappears as the singer devotes himself only to keeping the tāla visibly. Each percussionist

[13] I am indebted to David Schonfeld for this transcription from Nonesuch recording HS-72023 *Ramnad Krishnan: Vidvan*, a superb performance of pallavi. However, the pallavi melody does not actually conform to the kriti melody, as the record notes suggest.

tries in turn to outdo the one before him in rhythmic intricacy and technical skill. This is the epitome of the interest in rhythm and meter that is so prominent in Karnatak classical music. Then a short section of fast vocal variations concludes a performance full of musical variety. Indeed, the variety possible within pallavi is one reason the form is so significant.

Tānam, the second "movement" in the rāgam-tānam-pallavi succession, is an instrumental form in its own right when it is combined with the rāgamālikā idea. More specifically, it is a vīṇā form that frequently treats the *pancharāgamālikā* (chain of five [*pancha*] rāgas) succession of the five ghana rāgas Nāṭa, Gauḷa, Arabhī, Varāḷi, and Shrī.

Many compositions group rāgas in rāgamālikā fashion. Some of these compositions are groups of varṇa, some groups of kritis. The principle is to string together rāgas that share one or more common pitches and are in approximately the same mood, but are definitely distinct. They should not, for example, be janya rāgas of the same mela. The change in rāga should not be veiled discreetly, but should be enunciated through the citta svaras or, in the case of vocal music with text, by working the name of the rāga into the text.

LIGHT CLASSICAL GENRES

After a long rāgam-tānam-pallavi in a Karnatak music concert, or near the end of a dance concert, a *tillānā* may be sung in order to provide a contrast in mood. A tillānā is a lively composition and lasts only four or five minutes. It comprises three sections (pallavi, anupallavi, and charaṇa) and features successively greater increases in speed in the now familiar mathematical proportions. Drum syllables, solfège, and brief passages of poetry provide the text. In dance tillānās, the rhythmic passages are composed so as to correspond with footwork, and drum syllables provide the only text.

Another "light classical" form that may end a concert of Karnatak music is jāvali. Jāvali are dance and music concert pieces and are either played or sung. They too have the traditional three sections. The anupallavi may be omitted, however. If there are multiple charaṇa, all are sung to the same melody. Many composers have written jāvalis, including the famous Svāti Tirunāl Mahārāja of Tanjore, one of the greatest patrons of the arts in the nineteenth century.

Jāvalis have bright, catchy melodies and are composed in well-known rāgas, such as Rāga Khamās. Liberties may be taken with the rendition of the rāga that are not allowed in any other form of Karnatak vocal music. Indeed, phrases from other rāgas are sometimes introduced. The texts concern love, and not necessarily religious love. Most jāvalis are sung in the Telugu or Kannada language.

The major genres discussed in this chapter are varṇam, kriti, and rāgam-tānam-pallavi. Varṇam is kalpita saṅgīta, composed music. Through varṇam, the tripartite structure (pallavi-anupallavi-charaṇam) was introduced, as well as the inclusion of solfège passages within that form, and the srōtōvaha principle of melodic and rhythmic development.

Kriti is the major kalpita saṅgīta genre in the Karnatak classical tradition. It can be a combination of both kalpita saṅgīta and manodharma saṅgīta (improvised music), because it can include kalpana svara and niraval. If kriti is preceded by even a brief ālāpanam, then the progression from unmetered to metered is present. Otherwise, both varṇam and kriti are entirely metered. We noted the possibilities for flexibility of formal structure and expansion within the kriti, and its effective manipulation of prose or poetry text in contrast with solfège. The prominence of the tāla, since it is tied so closely to the text throughout, and the ever present contrasts in speed through mathematical proportions are also basic principles.

Rāgam-tānam-pallavi is the *pièce de résistance* of Karnatak classical music because it is entirely manodharma saṅgīta, with the exception of the short pallavi composition. Improvisation is the challenge taken up by the best musicians: to be a pallavi vidvan is to be a musician's musician. The progression from unmetered to metered, and from free rāga to emphasis on rhythm in general and complex rhythmic manipulation in particular, are in full play here, and all members of a performing ensemble must prove their musical mettle.

Another organizational principle mentioned here is rāgamālikā, which may appear in various genres. In one varṇam or kriti, each section is in a different rāga. In groups of varṇam, kriti, or tānam, each composition in a chain is in a different rāga. Rāgamālikā can also be utilized in pallavi improvisation if a performer so desires. Also possible, (but, like the seventy-two-melakarta rāga-classification system, not so frequently done) is tālamālikā, a "garland of tālas" operating on the same principle as rāgamālikā.

Although Karnatak classical music has a much larger repertoire of composed pieces than Hindustānī classical music, and although composed pieces take a much larger share of Karnatak concert time, the underlying principle of both traditions is the same: basic structures within which there are a host of possibilities for making music. These structures, but also the repretoire of possibilities that they embrace, contribute to distinguishing one genre from another in both the Karnatak and Hindustānī traditions.

NINE

MUSICIANS AND MUSICIANSHIP: THE PERFORMANCE AND THE AUDIENCE CONTEXTS

Returning to the concert stage where artists are assembled to perform, we can now view the ensemble with better educated eyes. At stage center will be the soloist(s)—either vocalist or instrumentalist. To this person falls the major responsibility for the music making to come. The composition of the remainder of the ensemble will depend on what type of music is to be performed. (See Chart 14, which shows both Hindustānī and Karnatak classical-music performance ensembles. Brackets indicate optional instruments.)

The constant factors in an ensemble are clear. A melody-producing soloist is joined by some drone-producing instruments and by one or more percussion instruments. In most cases there is also a second melody-producing instrument, which supports the soloist. In Hindustānī vocal music, this means a sāraṅgī for khyāl, and sāraṅgī and harmonium for ṭhumṛī. In Karnatak music, a violin will usually fill this role. Among Hindustānī instrumental ensembles, the shehnai group frequently includes a second melody-producing shehnai, which supports the soloist. Likewise, Karnatak vocal performances include a supporting vocalist. In Hindustānī dhrupad, where there is now no accompanying melodic instrument, it is common for two singers to perform together; they share the solo role. This can happen with khyāl and ṭhumṛī as well. The solo-sharing role for melody making in the North is also found in frequent instrumental *jugalbandi* performances, such as sitār-sarod, shehnai-violin, sarod-violin, and sitār-*surbahār* (a large sitār). The performance practice remains the same: one line of melody at a time.

KARNATAK			HINDUSTĀNĪ	
Vocal			*Vocal*	
Voice			Dhrupad	Khyāl
Tāmbūra			Tāmbūra	Tāmbūra
Mṛdañga			Pakhāvaj	Tablā
Violin			[formerly, Bīn]	Sāraṅgī
[Ghaṭam, Kanjīra]				[or Violin]
			Ṭhumṛī	Harmonium
			Tāmbūra	Svarmandal
			Tablā	
			Harmonium	
			[Sārangī]	
Instrumental			*Instrumental*	
Flute	Vīṇā		Sitār, Sarod	Flute, Sāraṅgī,
Tāmbūra	[Tāmbūra]		Tāmbūra	and Jaltarang
Mṛdañga, etc.	Mṛdañga [Ghaṭam]		Tablā	Tāmbūra
Violin	[Violin]			Tablā
[Flute]	[Vīṇā]			
Violin	Nagasvaram	Nagasvaram	Shehnai	
Tāmbūra	Ottu or	Tāmbūra	Sruti shehnai	
Mṛdañga, etc.	Tavil	Mṛdañga	Naghāṛa [or tablā]	
[Violin]		Violin	Shehnai	

CHART 14. Performance Ensembles

Ensembles in the South are rather flexible in their choice of instruments to fulfill the traditional roles, but the roles remain clear. A solo flute may be accompanied by mṛdañga alone, or by mṛdañga together with ghaṭam or kanjīra, or by one of the latter without the mṛdañga. For melodic support, the flute may be joined by a violin or by another flute. The same type of flexibility is found also with vīṇā, violin, and especially vocal-solo ensembles. The role of the supporting melodic instrument approaches one of partnership with the soloist.

Within the established ensembles of North India, however, the musical roles of the respective instruments differ from performance genre to performance genre. In vocal genres, for example, the drum is assigned different tasks. In dhrupad, the pakhāvaj player tries to match the rhythm of the song in a supportive partnership. In khyāl, the drummer is a timekeeper: he is supposed to repeat the theka of the particular tāla again and again. He can perhaps insert a mukhṛā or mohaṛā at cadences, but he must not be assertive. This same role is also maintained in gāyakī-style instrumental performances. In ṭhumṛī, the drumming is less restricted in that the laggī section gives the drummer a chance to play in the spotlight.

Only in Hindustānī solo instrumental performance does the drummer participate in anything approaching a partnership with the melody-producing soloist. But the length and the frequency of such opportunities depend on the will of the melody soloist. Sensing that American audiences enjoy hearing drumming on the tablā, Indian artists tend to give drummers more opportunities to solo when they play in the United States. During such tablā solos the instrumental soloist repeats the gat melody over and over, and thus assumes the role of timekeeper. In addition, American audiences respond enthusiastically to the clear (rather than subtle) challenge between soloist and drummer (jawāb-sawāl) that has been a feature of Ravi Shankar–Chatur Lal performances. A tablā player's best opportunity to show his skill is when he is the soloist. It requires an extremely talented durmmer and sensitive musician to build rhythmic and aesthetic climaxes of sufficient artistry to hold the attention of audiences who, for the most part, cannot really understand the finer details of their drumming.

In Hindustānī ensembles, the role of accompanying stringed instrument is more constant. The role of the sāraṅgī (and harmonium) is to shadow and thus support the melody of the soloist. The sāraṅgī is used precisely because it is deemed most suitable for imitating the display of virtuosity, even the tonal quality, of a voice. Sāraṅgī players must be excellent musicians in their own right, and must have a firm knowledge of rāgas and an excellent musical memory in order to follow the soloist's phrases a split second behind and to remember them for repetition while the soloist rests after sam.

Onstage, the tāmbūra player just keeps plucking, keeping the drone steady. (S)he, too, will respond to a finely turned phrase. (There is a dreadful feeling of having missed something precious when (s)he responds and you have not!) The accompanying stringed instruments join the soloist right from the beginning. When the drummer is not playing in the unmetered portions of a performance, he will also listen attentively; the soloist looks for his responses.

Throughout a Hindustānī or a Karnatak performance, the musically educated audience listens closely, keeping tāla with their hands or in their head when a tāla is being played.[1] The audience follows closely and reacts

[1]That is, under optimum conditions all in the audience listen carefully. When concerts are held outdoors under tents, a more casual audience attitude prevails. Those seriously interested sit in the front or at the side, close to the stage, and take the role of the intimate concert audience. The less knowledgeable and more socially oriented members of the audience wander at the rear of the tent or sit and talk. At Western-style indoor concerts, the audience adjusts to Western-style restricted movement and sound.

audibly and visibly when a fine phrase has been made. Reactions flow back and forth throughout a lengthy selection. A feeling of intense mutual enjoyment prevails when the artist knows that he has done something exquisite, the audience knows that he has, and he knows that the audience knows that he has. There is no tradition here of a listener sitting absolutely quiet until the last note dies away!

The interrelationships among performers in Karnatak ensembles are more explicitly partnerships: "It should be the sacred duty [of a Karnatak artist] to give solo chances to the violinist and the mṛdañgam player and encourage them by applauding them when they play extraordinarily well."[2]

The rāgam-tānam-pallavi sequence in Karnatak music is structured according to this principle of partnership. In rāgam, a vocal soloist first sings ālāpana, and the violinist then follows suit. In pallavi, the portion referred to above, the tani (thani) āvartam portion is entirely percussion, since the melody-producing soloist turns to keeping the tāla. Keeping the tāla is by no means simple when the drumming intricacies begin to develop. There have been instances of eminent musicians in the past who hesitated to count time when an expert mṛidañgam player began to give a solo display.

For the most part, however, the Karnatak performance partnership is not a partnership in the sense of equal responsibility. Mṛdañga players in an accompanying role used to cultivate a more independent style of cross-rhythmical counterpoint with the soloist than they do today. That former style is used more often now with the vīṇā, but the tone of the mṛdañga has become sharper and more penetrating during the last few decades, which causes a problem with the vīṇā. This problem is exacerbated when microphones are used (as they are, more and more frequently). Nowadays, the drum is more likely to reinforce and embellish the melodic line in close rapport.[3]

As a South Indian violinist stated, the first demand placed on any accompanist is an immediate grasp and a flawless repetition of the soloist's ideas. "Constant tension is felt while the accompanist plays back the patterns, and satisfaction is experienced only after a successful repetition. This satisfaction is transient, however, because the soloist will have already begun a new variation."[4] The role of the accompanist is not, however, just to echo what the soloist has done. It is more to lend support by focusing on the ideas of the soloist, by connecting one idea to the next, by choosing a pitch register (unison or an octave above or below) that will emphasize or enhance tonal color, by adjusting the playing style to reproduce the style of the solo melody, and so forth. Even when the violinist is imitating exactly what has come

[2]L. Isaac, *Theory of Indian Music* (Madras: Shyam Printers, 1967), p. 163.

[3]Robert Brown, *The Mṛdañga: A Study of Drumming in South India* (Ann Arbor, Mich.: University Microfilms, 1965), Vol. 1, p. 284.

[4]L. Shankar, *The Art of Violin Accompaniment in South Indian Classical Music* (Ann Arbor, Mich.: University Microfilms, 1974), p. 26.

before, his performance should be viewed not as a "parasitical representation of an original," but as an active reconstruction of the soloist's music.[5]

Stated plainly, "the accompanist is defined by his duty to the soloist, whereas the soloist has more freedom."[6] The hierarchy in the performance ensemble, whether Hindustānī or Karnatak, is defined by the degree of freedom in the music making, and by that definition the soloist reigns supreme.

The type of support lent to the soloist, however, fosters a spirit of competition among the members of the performance ensemble and contributes to that partnership. The risk involved in attempting to produce someone else's music, either a split second behind or after the phrase has ended, causes tension between melodic accompanist and soloist. The challenge thrown by the soloist to the drummer to repeat the rhythm of the passage just played, in jawāb-sawāl, and the contest between percussionists in tani āvartam are just two other examples of such "battles." Then, too, there are the shifts of dependence if a soloist should falter and an accompanist have to cover up for him. A knowledgeable and sensitive listener is aware of the tension, is able to judge the "winner of the battle," and in this sense is a partner in the interaction. The tension is a lively and anticipated part of the music making. Reviewing a percussion performance in 1970, a critic commented on this very process:

> Each [player] showed his individual artistry with an astounding variety of patterns. Specially absorbing were those final moments of speed when the players vied with one another and rhythms moved in a crescendo, now jostling, now shuffling to create an intense mood of evocation in the auditorium: they compelled inward delight into open applause.[7]

In improvisatory performance, it is the responsibility of each artist to balance the various musical elements. A soloist must develop melody to the best of his creative ability and must be equally at home with rhythmic exploration. He must pace the improvisation so that it remains imaginative, and must go on to something else when the imagination runs out. One performance in good balance drew the following remarks:

> Mention must first be made of the vocal *jugalbandi* [duet] from the duo from Delhi, the Kichlu Brothers. Harmony of style and exemplary teamwork combined to make their recital an enjoyable experience. The brothers gave an exhaustive treatment to Bihag which they rendered in ālāp followed by

[5] *Ibid.*, p. 32.

[6] *Ibid.*, p. 33.

[7] "Maestros, Prodigy Produce Thrilling Music," *Times of India* (Delhi), January 11, 1970.

khyāls in vilambit and drut in the typical Agra manner. The rendering showed meticulous attention to form and a correct insight into model proportion.[8]

The most delicate balance is between virtuosic display and sensitive musicality. Said a reviewer of a flute concert, "A sedate opening piece by [the artist] . . . held promise of musical excellence. But soon came [Rāga] Kapi in which instrumental dexterity got the better of musical sense and notes were played recalling the chirping of birds in the woods."[9] A later piece, however, was deemed good: "The concert touched its best in Kambhoji with [the artist] achieving intense and profound melodic flow. . . . The interpretation of the piece was absolutely chaste."[10]

In every musical culture, a few artists stand out from all the rest. Among the thousands of artists in North and South India, a few meet the highest standards of musicianship that their culture demands. We in the West are fortunate that those whom we have been able to hear, whether on tour or on recordings, are among those few great musicians. This book has been written partially on their behalf and partially for their audiences, in hopes that both will experience in the West the give and take that is at the heart of Indian classical music.

[8]"Enjoyable 'talavadya Kachvi'at sammelan,' " *Times of India* (Bombay), November 24, 1969.

[9][T.R.] at His Best," *The Hindu* (Madras), March 14, 1969.

[10]*Ibid.*

APPENDIX

A GUIDE TO SOURCE MATERIALS

BIBLIOGRAPHY

Two organizations that disseminate basic source materials on Indian cultures and Indian classical music are the Information Service of India (3 East 64th Street, New York, N.Y., 10021) and the Government of India Tourist Offices. These offices issue catalogues of materials available on India—mostly film—and maintain free, postage-païd only, distribution of these materials for temporary use. Music materials feature prominently in this service.

The best single source of up-to-date materials on Indian classical music is *Ethnomusicology*, the journal of the Society for Ethnomusicology. Published three times a year since 1956, it regularly features a comprehensive bibliography and discography of music materials, and from time to time includes a filmography section. Almost every issue contains an article or a review of a book, record, or film related to Indian classical music.

The *Journal of Asian Studies* (formerly known as the *Far Eastern Quarterly*) is the major organ of the Association for Asian Studies. Every year, its entire fifth number (usually September) is given over to materials on Asia, from Afghanistan to the Pacific, including a sizable section on India. This issue is subdivided according to specific subjects and disciplinary interests, including music.

Several institutions in the United States and in Europe have collections not only of books, other printed matter, recordings, and films, but also of materials compiled from field work. The best-known such institution in the United States is the Archives of Traditional Music, housed at Indiana University. The New York Public Library, the Museum of Fine Arts in Boston, the University of Pennsylvania's museum, and the Library of Congress also house considerable materials on music, as do the archives of the former Institute of Ethnomusicology at the University of California, Los Angeles, and the Regenstein Library of the University of Chicago. In Canada, the Museum of Man (Ottawa) is the central clearing agency for non-Western music materials. In the British Isles, there is the British Museum collection (London); in Germany, the International Institute for Comparative Music Studies and Documentation (Berlin) and the Berlin Museum; in France, the Musée de l'Homme (Paris).

An excellent source of materials on Indian culture and Indian classical music is J. Michael Mahar's *India: A Critical Bibliography* (Tucson: University of Arizona Press, 1964) (which should be updated). Xerox University Microfilms Dissertation Abstracts consists of a growing list of sources that reflects the growth of interest in Indian music.

The sixth edition of Grove's *Dictionary of Music and Musicians* (London: Macmillan, forthcoming) devotes a large portion to non-Western, folk, popular, and hybrid musics. It contains a sizable number of entries on Indian music by several scholars.

Two other very useful publications are easily available: Elise B. Barnett's substantial but selective "Special Bibliography: The Art Music of India," *Ethnomusicology*, 14, no. 2 (May 1970), 278–312 (in which there are some notable omissions); and her useful and fairly comprehensive *A Discography of the Art Music of India*, Society for Ethnomusicology, Special Series No. 3 (1975). In addition, Harold S. Powers, "Indian Music and the English Language: A Review Essay," *Ethnomusicology*, 9, no. 1 (January 1965), 1–12, is a useful short article.

Among surveys of Indic civilization, its cultures and musics, and its land and peoples, relatively few are substantive. *The Cambridge History of India* (Cambridge: Cambridge University Press, 1922), under the general editorship of Henry Dodwell, and *The History and Culture of the Indian People* (Bombay: Vidya Bhavan, 1951–1960), publised in England by Allen & Unwin under the general editorship of Ramesh C. Majumdar, both multi-volume works, are the best comprehensive studies yet available. An indispensable, comprehensive, and scholarly survey of Indic civilization up to the time of the Mughals is A. L Basham, *The Wonder that was India* (New York: Grove Press, Evergreen Books, 1954, 1959; London: Hawthorne Books, 1963; New York: Taplinger Press, 1968). This is the best single introduction to pre-Mughal Indic civilization. William Theodore De Bary's *Sources of Indian Tradition*, 2 vols. (New York: Columbia University Press, 1964) is a good chronological and topical collection of primary and secondary source materials on Indic civilization.

Recent general overviews of Indic society and cultures include David G. Mandelbaum's *Society in India*, 2 vols. (Berkeley and Los Angeles: University of California Press, 1972); Bernard Cohn's excellent book, *India: The Social Anthropology of a Civilization* (Englewood Cliffs, N.J.: Prentice-Hall, 1971), a succinct, solid, and readable introduction to Indic civilization; Milton Singer's *When a Great Tradition Modernizes* (New York: Praeger, 1972); and William Lannoy's *The Speaking Tree* (Chicago: University of Chicago Press, 1971).

Several American universities have centers for South Asian Studies—among them, the University of California at Berkeley, the University of Chicago, and the University of Pennsylvania. These and other institutions publish materials on India of a general and a specific nature.

For an excellent introduction to the world view of Indians, and the land they inhabit, see Louis DuMont's *Homo Hierarchicus: The Caste System and its Implications* (London: Weidenfeld & Nicolson, 1970), probably the best definition yet of stratification, its theory, and its practice in India. McKim Marriott's *Village India: Studies in the Little Community* (Chicago: University of Chicago Press, 1955), a pioneering work on various facets of Indian life at its most important level, the village, is still a major study. Other insightful studies of importance to the scholar of Indian musical culture are L. Renou and J. Filliozat's *L'Inde classique*, 2 vols. (Paris: Payot, 1947 [Vol. I]; Hanoi, 1953 [Vol. II]); Milton B. Singer and Bernard S. Cohn, eds. *Structure and Change in Indian Society* (Chicago: Aldine, 1968); and Mysore N. Srinivas, *Caste in Modern India and Other Essays* (Bombay: Asia Publishing House, 1962).

Indian-authored surveys and introductions to Indian music abound, under such titles as *Glimpses Into . . .*, *Studies in . . .*, *A History of . . . .* Unfortunately, most are confusing to the Western reader attempting to understand Indian music, for the reasons discussed in Chapter Three.

Indian-language written and oral treatises date back through millenia. The oldest source in English is Sir William Jones's *On the Musical Modes of the Hindoos* (1784), now available in Sourindo Mohun Tagore's *Hindu Music From Various Authors*, 3rd ed. (Varanasi, India: Chowkhmaba Sanskrit Series Office, 1965), pp. 125–60, and in Sir William Jones and N. Augustus Willard, *Music of India*, 2nd rev. ed. (Calcutta: Susil Gupta, 1962).

Tagore's *Hindu Music* contains, in addition to Jones's essay, other items of the oldest English-language literature on Indian music. Jones's essay is important primarily for its historical curiosity, but Jones and Willard's work is good on Hindustānī forms and in its glossary materials.

B. R. Pingle's *History of Indian Music*, 3rd ed. (Calcutta: Susil Gupta, 1962), first published in 1894, is important for several reasons. For one, it is the first English source to elaborate North Indian musical practice. Also, it is the first step toward a Western-ology of Indian music and a combination of Indian and Western approaches to music.

Pingle was followed by K. B. Deval, *The Hindu Musical Scale and the Twenty-Two Shrutees* (Songli, 1910). Deval carried Pingle's initial effort much further, emphasizing a scientific approach and the matter of intonation in Indian music.

South India has not been neglected. Charles R. Day produced an elaborate book, lavishly illustrated with photographs, *The Music and Musical Instruments of Southern India and the Deccan* (London: Novello, 1891; New York: Ever, 1891; reprinted in 1974, with an added index, by B. R. Publishing, Delhi). This book contains the first in-depth research in English of the South Indian musical system. It includes seventeen beautiful plates of Indian musical instruments; biographical sketches of famous South Indian musicians; and a descriptive, current bibliography of Indian music and Sanskrit manuscripts.

The next phase in the English-language historiography of Indian music consists of the several works of the Indian Civil Service officer Ernest Clements. He offers the interested reader three tomes. The first, *Introduction to the Study of Indian Music* (London: Longmans, Green, 1913; Allahabad: Kitab Mahal, 1967), is a theoretical introduction to Indian scales and intervals and reflects Clements's interpretation of such materials from old Indian sources—the *Nāṭya Śāstra* and the *Saṅgīta Ratnākara.* In his *The Rāgas of Hindustan* (Poona, 1918), Clements expanded his examples of compositions on rāgas and recast his theory. In his *The Rāgas of Tanjore* (London: Dharwar Gayan Samaj, 1920) he tried the same format and applied his theory to South Indian music.

Not the least of the early English-language studies is A. H. Fox-Strangways's perceptive (for its time) *The Music of Hindostan* (Oxford: Clarendon Press, 1914; reprinted 1967). This volume includes a "Musical Diary" of a trip through India, as well as copious detail on Indian music, particularly of the North.

Many Indian scholars write in English. Most are as repetitious of one another in this language as those who write in the Indian languages. This is probably because more value is placed on reiteration (therefore reaffirmation) of the tradition than is placed on entirely fresh scholarship. I shall note the more Western-type Indian-authored studies available in English.

A major early music treatise is still one of the best: V. N. Bhatkhande's *A Comparative Study of Some of the Leading Music Systems of the 15th, 16th, 17th, and 18th Centuries* (a series of articles in the journal *Saṅgīta* [Lucknow], 1930–31). This is an attempt to connect Sanskrit treatises to the earlier *Nāṭya Śāstra* and *Saṅgīta Ratnākara.* Fine complementary summaries of Sanskrit musical literature appear in V. Raghavan's numerous articles, first published in the *Journal of the Madras Music Academy*, 3 (1932) and 4 (1933), and later reissued in the Sangeet Natak Akademi *Bulletin*, No. 5 (December 1956) and No. 6 (May 1957). See also the same *Bulletin*, No. 17 (July 1960) 1–24 and no. 18 (April 1961) 1–18 for "Later Sangita Literature."

General studies of Indian musical history include O. C. Gangoly's *Ragas and Raginis* (Bombay, 1935, with a second volume of plates promised but never published; reprinted in 1948). This is a very good general discussion that combines art history and music history in focusing on the history of rāgas and on general treatise materials.

Swami Prajnananda has written several books and articles, which often overlap. As Powers has noted elsewhere ("Indian Music," p. 9), he is at his best when the reader has access to published editions of major treatises, since he has pinpointed several major ancient items from, among other sources, Matanga's *Bṛihaddeśī* (Trivandrum, 1928) and Bharata's *Nāṭya Śāstra.*

O. Gosvami's *The Story of Indian Music* (New York: Asia Publishing House, 1957; reprinted 1961) is a very good introduction to the appreciation of Indian music. However, it requires more acquaintance with Indian music than most Western readers possess.

No study of Hindustānī music by an Indian in English is comparable to P. Sambamoorthy's *South Indian Music*, 6 vols. (Madras: Indian Music Publishing House, multiple editions; see from 1960 to 1969). The only survey in English for Hindustānī music is V. N. Bhatkhande's *A Short Historical Survey of the Music of Upper India* (Bombay, 1934).

A recent general survey of South Indian music is R. Rangaramanuja Ayyangar's *History of South Indian (Carnatic) Music: From Vedic Times to the Present* (Madras: R. Rangaramanuja Ayyangar, 1972). It must be used cautiously and in conjunction with other materials on South Indian music, for it is highly anecdotal.

A general view of North Indian music is Alain Danielou's *Northern Indian Music*, 2 vols. (London: C. Johnson, 1949 [Vol. I]; Halcyon Press, 1954 [Vol. II]). Volume I discusses music theory and technique; Volume II discusses major rāgas and offers a discography on Indian music. This source should also be used with care and in conjunction with other authorities on North Indian music. In particular, see Arnold A. Bake's fine review of Danielou's *Traité de musicologie comparée* in Ethnomusicology, 5, no. 3, 231–37) for a good general assessment of the problems the reader should be aware of when working with Danielou's materials.

Europeans have produced some important works, both in their own languages and in English, either original or in translation. Danielou has published several pieces in his native French. For a compilation of these, see Barnett, "Special Bibliography," p. 284. Arnold A. Bake was one of the best authorities on Indian music. See, for example, his "Indische Musik," in *Die Musik in Geschichte und Gegenwart*, ed. Friedrich Blume (Kassel: Allemeine Enzyclopädie der Musik, Band 6, 1957), and "The Music of India," in *The New Oxford History of Music*, Vol. I, (London: 1957; reprinted 1960, 1966).

The reader should consult both of B. C. Deva's general works on Indian music: *Introduction to Indian Music* (New Delhi: Government of India, Publications Division, 1973) and *Indian Music* (New Delhi: Indian Council for Cultural Relations, 1974). The latter supersedes the former and is oriented more to a non-Indian reading audience.

Indian journals available in English and substantial in coverage include the *Bulletin* of the Sangeet Natak Akademi in New Delhi, the government institution for Fine arts in India, and the *Journal of the Madras Music Academy* (Madras), especially good in its coverage of South Indian materials. Other useful journals include the *Indian Music Journal* (New Delhi), *Journal of the National Centre for Performing Arts* (Bombay), and the *Journal of the Indian Musicological Society* (Baroda). The last stems from a Hindi-Marathi journal, the *Sangeet Kala Vihar*, of which it is the English supplement. The *Sangeet Kala Vihar* was the progenitor of the Indian Musicological Society, which was established early in the 1970's under Dr. R. C. Mehta, head of the Department of Music at the University of Baroda.

Now that we have surveyed the general sources—both institutions and materials—on Indian music and culture, let us turn to materials pertinent to the specific chapters in this book. In Chapter One we discussed the setting of Indian music, the relationship between listener and performer, rasa, and diversity and unity in Indian music. The chapter is geared to creating an atmosphere for appreciating Indian music. Among important works that consider these topics are S. K. De's *Sanskrit Poetics as a Study of Aesthetics* (Berkeley and Los Angeles: University of California Press, 1963), and V. Raghavan's *The Number of Rasa-s* (Madras: Adyar Library and Research Centre, 1967). John Brough's *Poems from the Sanskrit* (Baltimore: Penguin, 1968) is a beautiful collection in translation of later Sanskritic poetry. Other fine collections of literature include Arthur W. Ryder's translation of Kalidasa's *Shakuntala and Other Writings* (New York: Dutton, 1959), which contains an excellent introduction; J. A. B. van Buitenen's *Tales of Ancient India* (New York: Bantam, 1961), a superb scholarly anthology of mostly Sanskritic and some Buddhist stories on secular life during the heyday of the Guptas in the fourth and fifth centuries A.D.; and a condensed metrical version of *The Rāmāyana and the Mahābhārata*, trans. R. C. Dutt (London: J. M. Dent, 1910; last reprint, Dutton, 1972). Van Buitenen has already produced one volume of the *Mahābhārata* (University of Chicago Press), and this work promises to stand for some time as the definitive translation with scholarly textual treatment.

Two major collections on South India are Malladi R. Balakrishna Mudaliyar's *The Golden Anthology of Ancient Tamil Literature*, 3 vols. (Triunveli, Madras: South India Saiva Siddharta Works, 1959–1960), and S. Vaiyapuri Pillai's *History of Tamil Language and Literature* (Madras: New Century Book House, 1956). One other major source of information on music and dance in ancient Tamilnadu is the 2nd Century A.D. Tamil Classic, *Cilappatikaaram*. A convenient edition is the paperback version *Shilappadikaram* (The Ankle Bracelet) by Prince Ilangro Adigal, trans. Alain Daniélou (N.Y: New Directions Books, 1965).

Bengali literature is one of the richest of India's literary traditions. In addition to the innumerable works by Rabindranath Tagore, including *A Tagore Reader*, ed. Amiya Chavravarty (New York: Macmillan, 1961), there are the excellent translations by Edward C. Dimock, *The Thief of Love; Bengali Tales from Court and Village* (Chicago: University of Chicago Press, 1963) and *In Praise of Krishna: Songs from the Bengali* (New York: Doubleday, Anchor Books, 1967). See also the works of Deben Bhattacharya.

For a substantive listing of Hindi-Urdu and other Indian vernacular literatures, see Mahar, *India*, pp. 106–8. A new and excellent collection of the best that India has to offer is Edward Dimock and others, *The Literatures of India* (Chicago: University of Chicago Press, 1974).

On art and architecture, see Heinrich Zimmer, *The Art of India Asia*, 2 vols., ed. Joseph Campbell (New York: Pantheon, 1955); Benjamin Rowland, *Early Indian and Indonesian Art* (Newton, Mass: University Prints, 1938) and *The Art and Architecture of India* (Baltimore: Penguin, 1956); and Ananda Coomaraswamy, *History of Indian and Indonesian Art* (New York: E. Weyhe, 1927; Dover, 1965). See especially Stella Kramrisch, *The Art of India Through the Ages* (New York: Phaidon, 1954), a superb book. Other works of importance on this subject include Kramrisch's *The Hindu Temple*, 2 vols. (Calcutta: University of Calcutta, 1946); her translation of *Vishnudharmottara* (Calcutta: University of Calcutta, 1924), the oldest and most complete treatise on painting; and Willam G. Archer's *Indian Miniatures* (Greenwich, Conn: New York Graphic Society, 1960). See also Waldschmidt, Ernst and Rose, *Miniatures of Musical Inspiration*, 2 vols., in the Collection of the Berlin Museum of Indian Art (Wiesbaden: Harrassowitz, 1967).

Melody—rāga theory and melody instruments—is the dominant topic of much of the literature on Indian music. Powers ("Indian Music," pp. 4–6) succinctly discusses the hypothetical connections between ancient Indian theory and modern Indian practice that have been postulated by scholars. Probably the best studies on acoustics are by B. C. Deva. See in particular his *Psychoacoustics of Music and Speech* (Madras: The Music

Academy, 1967). On science in music, see M. Roychaudhuri, *Studies in Artistic Creativity* (Rabindra Bharati University, 1966).

Three major studies concerning rāga in North Indian music have appeared in recent years. Walter Kauffman's *The Rāgas of North India* (Bloomington, Ind.: Indiana University Press, 1968) is a detailed survey of the rāgas of Hindustānī music. It is a valuable compendium and source book. However, it should be read in conjunction with Harold S. Powers's exacting review essay in *Ethnomusicology*, 13, no. 2 (May 1969), 350–64. Alain Danielou's *The Rāga-s of Northern Indian Music* (London: Barrie & Rockliff, Cresset Press, 1968) also should be on the reading list of the student of North Indian music. (For careful critiques of the prolific production of Danielou, consult the index of *Ethnomusicology*). Nazir A. Jairazbhoy's The *Rāgs of North Indian Music* (Middletown, Conn.: Wesleyan University Press, 1971) is a major treatise, rich in ideas and suggestive of new avenues for research in the study of rāga. It might be read in conjunction with a review essay by B. C. Wade in *Ethnomusicology*, 17, no. 2 (May 1973), 331–34.

Walter Kauffmann's *The Rāgas of South India* (Bloomington, Ind.: Indiana University Press, 1976) is a companion volume to his study of North Indian rāgas. South Indian rāga is also treated in Harold S. Powers's "The Background of the South Indian Rāga-System" (Ph.D. dissertation, Princeton University, 1958), and in B. Subba Rao, comp., *Raganidhi* (Madras: The Music Academy, 1965), a compendium of Karnatak and Hindustānī rāgas.

Three excellent monographs on meter (tāla) and rhythm are available. Robert Brown's *The Mṛdañga: A Study of Drumming in South India*, 2 vols. (Ann Arbor, Mich.: University Microfilms, 1965) is an unsurpassed introduction to the major rhythmic instrument of South Indian music and its function in the performance. Rebecca Stewart's *The Tablā in Perspective* (Ann Arbor, Mich.: University Microfilms, 1974) is a very welcome addition to the literature on Indian drumming. It is the first major treatment in English of that important percussion instrument in Hindustānī music, and its relationship to other North Indian drum traditions. In addition, the solo tradition of the Benares tablā bāj is treated by Frances Shepherd in *Tablā and the Benares Gharānā* (Ann Arbor, Mich.: University Microfilms, 1976). An accessible article on the same family's tradition is David Roach's "The Benares Bāj—The Tablā Tradition of a North Indian City," in *Asian Music*, Vol. 3, No. 2 (1972) 29–40.

On notational systems, consult Walter Kaufmann, *Musical Notations of the Orient* (Bloomington, Ind.: Indiana University Press, 1967), pp. 183–261. See also Howard Boatwright, *A Handbook on Staff Notation for Indian Music* (Bombay: B. H. Bhavan, 1960), which consists of exercises and notated examples of traditional Hindustānī pieces. For South India, see the collections noted in Chapter Two of the present text.

Studies on melodic and rhythmic instruments are scarce. The best and most accessible sources are S. Krishnaswamy, *Musical Instruments of India* (New Delhi: Government of India, Publications Division, 1967); Claudie Marcel-DuBois, *Les Instruments de musique de l'Inde ancienne* (Paris: Presses Universitaires de France, 1941); the Sangeet Natak Akademi volume, *Indian Folk Musical Instruments* (New Delhi: Sangeet Natak Akademi, 1968); and P. Sambamoorthy, *Catalogue of Instruments in the Government Museum* (Madras, 1962). Less accessible but beautiful is the collection of plates in Day's *Music and Musical Instruments of Southern India and the Deccan*. A useful older study is Curt Sachs, *Die Musikinstrumente Indiens und Indonesiens* (Berlin and Leipzig: Walter de Gruyter, 1923). Also consult B. C. Deva's *Indian Music*, Chap. Seven. A recent addition to the literature is L. Shankar's *The Art of Violin Accompaniment in South Indian Classical Music* (Ann Arbor, Mich.: University Microfilms, 1974), a useful analysis by a performing Indian musician. Another recent book is Manfred Junius's *The Sitār: The Instrument and Its Technique* (Wilhelmshavan: Heinrichskofen Verlag, 1974).

Monographs on forms and styles in Indian classical music are even scarcer. Two of the few are Bonnie C. Wade's *Khyāl: A Study of Hindustānī Classical Vocal Music*, 2 vols. (Ann Arbor, Mich.: University Microfilms, 1971), which is in the process of revision for press publication, and Indurama Srivastava's *Dhrupada: A Study of its Origin, Historical Development, Structure and Present State* (Utrecht: Drukkerij Elinkwijk B. V., 1977).

For South India, see Ranganayaki Ayyangar's "Analysis of the Melodic, Rhythmic and Formal Structure of Karnatic Kriti as Exemplified in the Kritis of Sri Syāma Śastri, Sri Muttuswāmi Dīkṣitar and Sri Tyāgarāja" (Master's thesis, University of Hawaii, 1965). See also T. Viswanathan's *Rāga Ālāpana in South Indian Music* (Ann Arbor, Mich.: University Microfilms, 1975). Jon B. Higgins's *The Music of Bharata Nāṭyam* (Ann Arbor, Mich.: University Microfilms, 1973) is a fine study of the music accompanying an Indian dance form. The author is an accomplished American performer of Karnatak vocal music.

Studies of and by musicians are more readily available. Ravi Shankar's fine *My Music, My Life* (New York: Simon & Schuster, 1968) is an exceptionally readable volume. On performers in groups, see Daniel M. Neuman's *The Cultural Structure and Social Organization of Musicians in India* (Ann Arbor, Mich.: University Microfilms, 1974).

DISCOGRAPHY

By far the single most important published listing of phonorecorded music of the Indian subcontinent is Elise B. Barnett's *A Discography of the Art Music of India*, Society for Ethnomusicology, Special Series no. 3

(Ann Arbor, Mich., 1975). It claims to list "the phonorecorded music of the Indian subcontinent . . . to January 1 1973." But in fact it lists primarily $33\frac{1}{3}$-rpm discs of Indian art music, and omits numerous records listed in the Schwann catalogues. It is organized according to several criteria, and it can be particularly helpful for Hindustānī music. Perhaps of major importance is that Barnett cites the published reviews of the records. Information on recordings of Indian music released after January 1, 1973 is available in the various Indian and Western journals cited earlier.

I have chosen to list recordings that are easily accessible to the reader and the listener. Most of these recordings are also listed in the Barnett discography, and in such cases I have supplied the entry number from Barnett (in parentheses) for easy reference. I have also annotated some of the entries. Barnett cites the distributing company from which the recordings are available.

Taped collections of Indian music are most easily available at the Archives of the defunct Institute of Ethnomusicology at the University of California, Los Angeles. The Archives of Traditional Music, Indiana University, also has some taped material.

Indian classical music, once the purview of the courts and now the art music of the cities, is one of the most-recorded types of Indian music. This reflects the interest of Indian elites, who by and large are little concerned with other types of Indian music—an attitude not unlike that of many cosmopolitan Westerners (but an attitude not shared by the recording companies nowadays). Instrumental classical music, particularly Hindustānī music, is the variety of Indian music heard most often in the West, despite the preeminence of vocal music in India. This is because Indian classical music was first brought to the West by Indian instrumentalists.

The quality of recorded Indian music and its performance is variable, as listeners will come to appreciate as they become more sensitive to the intricacies of Indian classical music. We should bear in mind that the performances on these recordings are not necessarily like live performances. Time restrictions and, perhaps most important, the reluctance of artists to record the essence of their art make recordings a shadow of the reality. Accordingly, learning from these recordings is only a step in the process of learning how to listen to Indian music.

Section I of the discography comprises recordings of the rāgas discussed in the text. The rāga names are listed in alphabetical order (*H* indicates Hindustānī and *K* indicates Karnatak). The Barnett entry number appears before each record. In Section II the listing is by performance genre, with subdivisions as appropriate. For example, under instrumental ṭhumṛī, subdivisions are made for sitār, sarod, sāraṅgī, shehnai, flute, and violin.

For the sake of economy, I have selected wherever possible recordings that may serve multiple functions—those, for example, featuring two rāgas that are discussed, or two performance genres. Cross-references to such recordings are provided in such cases; all references to previously mentioned recordings are made by Barnett entry number, thus: See also B 180 and B 60. Recordings were also selected to include diverse performers within the same speciality, for example, several sitārists and sarod players.

Section I: Rāgas

(*H*) Rāg Ahīr Bhairav

(B 4) *Music of India, Vol. II.* Angel (ANG 35468). Ravi Shankar, sitār; Chaturlal, tablā. Originally issued by Gramophone Company of India (GCI ALPC 7). Also released in America as:

(B 28) *Three Ragas.*
Capitol (DT 2720).

(B 283) *Three Ragas.*
World Pacific (WPS 21438).

(B 52) *Ustad Ali Akbar Khan: Predawn to Sunrise Ragas.* Connoisseur Society (CS 1967). Ali Akbar Khan, sarod; Mahapurush Mishra, tablā.

(B 118) *Ustad Vilayat Khan: Sitar.* Odeon (MOAE 109). Vilayat Khan, sitār; Mohammad Ahmad, tablā; Shamta Prasad, tablā.

(B 232) *Shehnai Nawaz Bismillah Khan.* Odeon (MOCE 1171). Bismillah Khan, shehnai and ensemble. A brief selection, one of twelve rāgas included on this recording. Good for demonstration purposes.

(*K*) Rāga Ananda Bhairavī

(B 34) *Carnatic Music of India Sung by Jon Higgins.* Capitol (ST 10501). Jon Higgins, vocalist; V. Thyagarajan, violin; T. Ranganathan, mridañgam; V. Nagarajan, kanjīra. Originally issued by Gramophone Company of India (GCI ECLP 2339). Performance of a Dīkshitar kriti, "Tyāgarāja Yoga." Jon Higgins is an American who is well known and respected in India as a performer of Karnatak music. He was one of the first Americans to make an impact on the Indian music scene in this country. He is an ethnomusicologist, and is presently teaching at Wesleyan University in Connecticut. The members of this ensemble are well known in America; they were among the first Indian artists to teach here for a prolonged time.

(B 294) *N. Ramani, Flute.* World Pacific (WPS 21456). N. Ramani, flute; A. Alagiriswami, violin; V. Ramabhadran, mridañgam. Originally issued by Gramophone Company of India (GCI EASD 1333). Performance of a Syāma Śastri kriti, "Mariveragathi."

(*H*) Rāg Āsāvarī (see also *Rāg Komal Re Āsāvarī*)

(B 67) *Earth Groove: Pandit Prannath, the Voice of Cosmic India.* Douglas (SD 784). Prannath, vocalist; no tablā player credited, as is all too frequently the case on recordings of Indian classical music. Prannath (a singer of the Kirana gharānā) has been living in America, teaching in New York and in California. He is known for his sustained style of singing, particularly in the lower and middle registers.

(B 156) *D. V. Paluskar.* Odeon (MOAE 161). D. V. Paluskar, vocalist; noncredited tablā accompaniment. The late D. V. Paluskar was one of the foremost performers of the Gwalior style of singing. He was the son of the great V. D. Paluskar of that school of singing. This recording is a collection of ten khyāl chīz, one in Āsāvarī.

(B 259) *Imrat Khan.* Tower (ST 5154). Imrat Khan, sitār and surbahār; Shamta Prasad, tablā. This performance is ālāp-joṛ-jhālā-gat on surbahār. It is a rather rare performance, since few surbahār performances are available on record. Imrat Khan has taught in England and performed widely. His popularity is increasing in India as well.

(*H*) Rāg Bhairav

(B 147) *Shehnai Nawaz Bismillah Khan of Banaras.* Odeon (MOAE 151). Bismillah Khan, shehnai; ensemble. This is an ālāp-joṛ-jhālā-gat by the artist who has almost single-handedly placed the shehnai on the concert stage. He has toured America numerous times.

(*H*) Rāg Bhairavī

(B 20) *A Musical Anthology of the Orient, India III: Dhrupads in Ragas of the Morning.* Bärenreiter-Musicaphon (BM 30L 2018). N. Mohinuddin Dagar and N. Aminuddin Dagar, vocalists; Chhatrapati Singh, pakhāvaj. This is a gorgeous performance of ālāp by the "older Dagar brothers."

(B 31) *Duets from India.* Capitol (ST 10483). Vilayat Khan, sitār; Bismillah Khan, shehnai; Shamta Prasad, tablā. This performance of Bhairavī is an instrumental ṭhumṛī and a good example of a jugalbandi (duet).

(B 123) *The Magic Shehnai of Bismillah Khan.* Odeon (MOAE 122). Bismillah Khan, shehnai; ensemble. A prolonged ālāp-gat sequence.

(B 130) *Ustad Faiyaz Khan Sahib.* Odeon (MOAE 131). Faiyaz Khan, vocalist; noncredited tablā accompaniment. One of the ten selections on this record is a brief vocal ṭhumṛī by the late leading artist of the Agra gharānā.

(B 152) *Surshri Kesar Bai Kerkar.* Odeon (MOAE 156). Kesar Bai Kerkar, vocaliste, with tablā accompaniment. One of nine khyāl chīz, therefore a short selection by a leading singer of the Itrauli gharānā.

(B 164) *Sitar Nawaz Ustad Vilayat Khan.* Odeon (MOAE 169). Vilayat Khan, sitār; Shamta Prasad, tablā. An instrumental ṭhumṛī.

(B 187) *Amjad Ali Khan.* Odeon (MOAE 185). Amjad Ali Khan, sarod; Shamta Prasad, tablā. A dhun in Bhairavī.

(B 211) *Sharan Rani, the Great Sarod Virtuoso.* Odeon (MOCE 1070). Sharan Rani, sarod; Manikrao Popatkar, tablā. Sharan Rani is a female sarod player. This performance of Bhairavī is a prolonged one.

(B 248) *Traditional Music of India.* Philips (PR 7402/PTG 7545). Ali Akbar Khan, sarod; Sashi Bellari, tablā. A prolonged performance by India's greatest sarod player.

(*H*) Rāg Bhīmpalāsī (Bhīmpalāshrī)

(B 61) *Bangala Desh: Ali Akbar Khan, Sarod.* Connoisseur Society (CS 2042). Ali Akbar Khan, sarod; Mahapurush Mishra, tablā.

(B 142) *Khansahib Abdul Karim Khan.* Odeon (MOAE 144). Abdul Karim Khan, vocalist; tablā accompaniment. A brief presentation of a khyāl chīz. The late Abdul Karim Khan was a leading figure in the Kirana gharānā.

(B 180) *Padma Bhushan Bade Ghulam Ali Khan.* Odeon (MOAE 5004). Bade Ghulam Ali Khan, vocalist; tablā accompaniment. A brief khyāl chīz, one of eleven on this record. Ustad Bade Ghulam Ali Khan was a much beloved singer of the Patiali (Punjabi) gharānā.

(B 204) *Prof. Gajananrao Joshi, Violin.* Odeon (MOCE 1059). Gajananrao Joshi, violin; tablā accompaniment.

(B 286) *Ravi Shankar at the Monterey International Pop Festival.* World Pacific (WPS 21442). Ravi Shankar, sitār; Alla Rakha, tablā. A prolonged performance of the rāg.

(*H*) Rāg Bihāg

(B 39) *The Shenai Artistry of Bismillah Khan.* Capitol (ST 10513). Bismillah Khan, shehnai; ensemble.

(B 262) *Treasures in Sound.* United Artists International (UNS 15532/UN 14532). Spoken analysis of Rāg Bihāg by Deben Bhattacharya.

(*H*) Rāg Chandrakant (Chandrakauns)

(B 108) *Ram Narain, Sarangi.* Odeon (EMOE 8). Ram Narain, sāraṅgī; noncredited tablā accompanist. Ālāp-gat sequence by the person who has done the most to make the sāraṅgī a classical solo instrument.

(B 158) *Shehnai Nawaz Bismillah Khan and Prof. V. G. Jog: Jugalbandi, Shehnai and Violin.* Odeon (MOAE 163). Bismillah Khan, Shehnai; V. G. Jog, violin; Mahadev Indorkar, tablā. The Chandrakauns performance ends in a dhun.

(*H*) Rāg Darbārī Kanaṛā (Kānaḍā, Kānhṛā)

(B 40) *Ustad Vilayat Khan, India's Master of the Sitar.* Capitol (ST 10514). Vilayat Khan, sitār; Shankar Ghosh, tablā. A long, superb performance by the sitārist who is as well known in India as Ravi Shankar is in America and in India.

(B 114) *Hindustani Classical Music: Ustad Amir Khan, Indore.* Odeon (MOAE 103). Amir Khan, vocalist; tablā accompaniment. The late Amir Khan was respected as one of India's finest singers of khyāl. He was from Indore.

(B 134) *Dagar Brothers.* Odeon (MOAE 135). N. Mohinuddin Dagar and N. Aminuddin Dagar, vocalists; S. V. Patwardhan, pakhāvaj. An ālāp-dhamār by the "older Dagar brothers."

(B 136) *Ustad Bade Ghulam Ali Khan.* Odeon (MOAE 137). Bade Ghulam Ali Khan, vocalist; tablā accompaniment. A long khyāl performance.

(B 195) *Sharan Rani Plays Raga Darbari Kanada and Raga Nat Bhairav.* Odeon (MOCE 1039). Sharan Rani, sarod; Chaturlal, tablā.

(B 278) *Ali Akbar Khan, North Indian Master of the Sarod.* World Pacific

(WPS 21433). Ali Akbar Khan, sarod; Shankar Ghosh, tablā. Ālāp in Darbārī Kanhṛā.

(*H*) Rāg Desh (Desī)

(B 45) *The Genius of Ravi Shankar.* Columbia (CS 9560/CL 2760). Ravi Shankar, sitār; tablā accompaniment.

(B 82) *Dr. B. R. Deodhar Presents the Ragas of India.* Folkways (FI 8368). B. R. Deodhar, vocalist, instrumentalist, and commentator. Includes lecture with demonstration.

(B 146) *Sitar: Pandit Ravi Shankar.* Odeon (MOAE 150). Ravi Shankar, sitār; Alla Rakha, tablā.

(B 148) *Shehnai Nawaz Bismillah Khan: Raga Malkauns, Raga Des, Tilak Kamod.* Odeon (MOAE 152). Bismillah Khan, shehnai; ensemble.

(B 178) *Amjad Ali Khan.* Odeon (MOAE 185). Amjad Ali Khan, sarod; Shamta Prasad, tablā. Also includes a dhun in Bhairavī.

(B 228) *Music of India, Flute Recital: Hariprasad Chaurasia.* Odeon (MOCE 1152). Hariprasad Chaurasia, flute; Manikrao Popatkar, tablā.

See also B 130, B 152, and B 204.

(*K*) Rāga Devagāndhāri

(B 295) *Man from Madras: S. Balachander.* World Pacific (WPS 21457). S. Balachander, vīṇā; T. K. Upendran, mṛdangam; R. Gurumurty, ghaṭam. The trio perform an instrumental kriti, "Vinaradha na Manavi." The record also includes a percussion selection featuring the two drums.

See also B 34.

(*H*) Rāg Hansnārāyanī

See B 232 for a brief look at the rāg by Bismillah Khan.

(*H*) Rāg Jaunpurī

(B 155) *Jugalbandi, Shehnai and Violin: Shehnai Nawaz Bismillah Khan and Prof. V. G. Jog.* Odeon (MOAE 160). Bismillah Khan, shehnai; V. G. Jog, violin; Shamta Prasad, tablā.

See also B 130 and B 232.

(*H*) Rāg Kāfī

(B 240) *Ravi Shankar, Music of India: Ravi Shankar, India's Master Musician, Recorded in London.* Odeon (ASD 463/ALP 1893). Ravi Shankar, sitār; Kanai Dutta, tablā. This performance of Kāfī is a dhun. Kāfī is frequently chosen for dhun.

See also B 262.

(*H*) Rāg Kāmbhojī

(B 245) *Musical Sources: Modal Music and Improvisation, Northern India, Vocal Music.* (*UNESCO Collection Musical Sources: North India Vocal Music, Dhrupad and Khyal*). Philips (6586 003). N. Mohinuddin Dagar and N. Aminuddin Dagar, vocalists; Chhatrapati Singh, pakhāvaj. This is a valuable record because it includes both dhrupad and khyāl (one side devoted to each).

(*H*) Rāg Kedār (Kedārā)

(B 238) *A Tribute to Ustad Abdul Karim Khan.* Odeon (PCLP 1514). Roshan Ara Begam, vocaliste; Allah Dutta, tablā. A performance by a singer of the Kirana gharānā devoted to her gūrū.

See also B 156, B 158, and B 180.

(*K*) Rāga Khamās

(B 97) *Dhyanam, Meditation: South Indian Vocal Music.* Nonesuch (H-72018). K. V. Narayanaswami, vocalist; Palghat Raghu, mridañgam; V. V. Subramanium, violin. Jāvali "Marulukonnadira" by R. S. Iyengar in Rāga Khamās. This trio of musicians are among the finest in South India today.

(B 105) *Ramnad Krishnan: Kaccheri (A Concert of South Indian Classical Music).* Nonesuch (H-72040). Ramnad Krishnan, vocalist; V. Thyagarajan, violin; T. Ranganathan, mridañgam; V. Nagarajan, kanjīra. Jāvali "Modi Jesevelara" by T. Pattabhiramiah in Rāga Khamās, also performed by excellent musicians.

(B 177) *T. R. Mahalingam.* Odeon (MOAE 184). T. R. Mahalingam, flute; T. S. Sankaran, mridaṅgam. Again a jāvali, "Appa Durko." Mahalingam is a somewhat controversial musician, capable of very fine performances.

(B 313) *V. Doreswamy Iyengar (Mysore Veena, Doreswamy Iyengar).* Odeon (MOCE 1207). Doreswamy Iyengar, vīṇā. Kriti in Khamās, "Brochevarevarura" by Vasudevacharya of Mysore.

(*H*) Rāg Komal Re Āsāvarī

(B 151) *Sitar: Nikhil Banerjee.* Odeon (MOAE 155). Nikhil Banerjee, sitār; Kanai Dutta, tablā. A fine performance of the ālāp-gat sequence. Nikhil Banerjee was among the first sitārists to tour the United States and has made prolonged returns to teach, particularly in California.

(B 167) *Shehnai Nawaz Bismillah Khan.* Odeon (MOAE 172). A clear exposition of the rāga.

See also B 20 for a superb ālāp (and dhrupad) sung by the Dagar brothers.

(*H*) Rāg Lālit

(B 176) *Sarangi Solo: Pandit Ram Narain.* Odeon (MOAE 183). Ram Narain, sāraṅgī; Sashi Ballari, tablā.

See also B 130, B 152, B 156, and B 232.

(*H*) Rāg Mālkosh (Mālkauns)

(B 154) *Pandit Omkarnath Thakur.* Odeon (MOAE 159). Omkarnath Thakur, vocalist; tablā accompaniment. This is a brief khyāl performance (one of five on the record) by one of the leading artists in the Gwalior gharānā. He was respected both as a musicologist and as a performer.

(B 157) *Late Pandit Yeshwantrai Purohit.* Odeon (MOAE 162). Yeshwantrai Purohit, vocalist; tablā accompaniment. A fine khyāl performance.

(B 160) *Khan Sahib Abdul Karim Khan.* Odeon (MOAE 165). Abdul Karim Khan, vocalist; tablā accompaniment. A brief khyāl performance. This recording has five such khyāls and three ṭhumṛīs.

See also B 148, B 152, B 156, B 180, and B 232.

(*K*) Rāga Māyāmālavagaula

See B 105 for a Tyāgarāja kriti, "Merusumana," sung by Ramnad Krishnan.

(*H*) Rāg Miyāṅ kī Toḍī

(B 128) *Bhimsen Joshi.* Odeon (MOAE 129). Bhimsen Joshi, vocalist; tablā accompaniment. A fine one side of the record-long performance of khyāl by one of the leading artists of the Kirana gharānā. His style is thought to be distinctive within that gharānā, however.

(B 129) *Ustad Ali Akbar Khan.* Odeon (MOAE 130). Ali Akbar Khan, sarod; Shankar Ghosh, tablā. Ālāp-gat sequence by this superb musician.

(B 241) *Music of India: Vilayat Khan.* Odeon (ASK 498/PALP 1946). Vilayat Khan, sitār; Imrat Khan, surbahār; Shamta Prasad, tablā.

(*H*) Rāg Sāraṅg

(B 182) *The Magic Flute of Pannalal Ghosh.* Odeon (MOAE 5006). Pannalal Ghosh, flute; tablā accompaniment. One of five selections on this recording by the late P. Ghosh, one of India's most respected musicians.

(*K*) Rāga Sarasvati

(B 101) *The Ten Graces Played on the Vina: Music of South India.* Nonesuch (H-72027). M. Nageswara Rao, vīṇā; V. Thyagarajan, violin; T. Ranganathan, mridañgam; V. Nagarajan, kanjīra. Instrumental performance of a Tyāgarāja kriti, "Anurāgamuleni." (See the transcriptions of this kriti in Chapter Two.)

(*K*) Rāga Sāveri

(B 189) *Sanskrit Recitation, Devotional: M. S. Subbulakshmi.* Odeon (MOCE 1009/MOAE 1009). M. S. Subbulakshmi, vocaliste; R. S. Gopala Krishnan, violin; T. K. Murthy, mridañgam. Sāveri occurs as one of the rāgas in a rāgamālikā. M. S. Subbulakshmi is considered one of the premier singers of Karnatak music. She was one of the first Indian musicians to perform in the United States. She also performed in a concert at the United Nations (see Rāgamālikā in Section II).

(*K*) Rāga Shankarābharana

(B 21) *A Musical Anthology of the Orient: Karnatic Music (South India) (UNESCO Collection: India, IV).* K. S. Narayanaswami, vīṇā; Semmangudi Srinivasa S. Aiyar, vocalist; Kedarnathan, vocalist; Palghat Raghu, mridañgam. Performance of a Dīkshitar kriti, "Dakshinamurti."

(B 145) *Classical Indian Music.* Odeon (MOAE 147, 148, 149), Disc I: M. S. Subbulakshmi, vocalist; P. M. S. Gopal Krishnan, violin; T. K.

Murthy, mridañgam; K. S. Narayanaswami, vīṇā; Palghat Raghu, mridañgam. Performance of a Syama Sastri kriti, "Saroja Dala Netri."

See also B 105.

(*K*) Rāga Shrī

(B 103) *The Pulse of Tanam: Ragas of South India.* Nonesuch (H-72032). M. Nageswara Rao, vīṇā. Shrī is the fifth rāga in the frequently performed rāgamālikā in tānam of the five ghana rāgas: Naṭa, Gauḷa, Ārabhi, Varāḷi, and Shrī.

See also B 21.

(*H*) Rāg Toḍī

(B 121) *Shehnai Nawaz Bismillah Khan of Banaras.* Odeon (MOAE 120). Bismillah Khan, shehnai; ensemble.

See also B 45, B 130, B 152, B 154, B 232.

(*K*) Rāga Toḍī

(B 64) *Music of India, V. V. Subramaniam and Group: Vadya Ghoshti, Raga Music of South Indian Ensemble.* Decca (DL 75102) V. V. Subramaniam, violin; T. Shankaran, flute; Ramakrishna Naidu, clarinet; T. K. Murthy, mridañgam; C. K. Shyam Sunder, kanjīra. A Tyāgarāja kriti, "Endu Dagi Nado."

(B 281) *Sounds of the Veena: Balachander (Featuring the Flute of Ramani).* World Pacific (WP 1436/WPS 21436). S. Balachander, vīṇā; N. Ramani, flute; V. T. G. Ramabhadran, mridañgam. Kriti "Kaddanuvariki." Balachander is often described by South Indian musicians as "unorthodox."

(B 291) *Carnatic Music, The Music of South India: The Voice of K. V. Narayanswamy.* World Pacific (WPS 21450). K. V. Narayanswamy, vocalist; V. V. Subramaniam, violin; Palghat Raghu, mridañgam. An excellent performance of rāgam-tānam-pallavi in Rāga Toḍī.

(B 299) *In Concert from her American Tour: M. S. Subbulakshmi.* World Pacific (WPS 21463). M. S. Subbulakshmi, vocaliste; R. Subbulakshmi, accompanying vocaliste; V. V. Subramaniam, violin; T. K. Murthy, mridañgam; T. H. Vinayakaram, ghaṭam. Varṇam, "Era Napai" by Patnam Subrahmanya Aiyar.

See also B 101 and B 145.

(*H*) Rāg Vilas Khani Toḍī

See a brief vocal exposition by D. V. Paluskar, B 156.

(*H*) Rāg Yaman

(B 113) *Late Pannalal Ghosh.* Odeon (MOAE 102). Pannalal Ghosh, flute; tablā accompaniment. One side of the record is devoted to Yaman.

(B 199) *Srimati Hirabai Barodekar.* Odeon (MOCE 1050). Hirabai Barodekar, vocaliste; Shamsuddin Khan, tablā. Hirabai Barodekar is one of the outstanding singers of the Kirana gharānā.

(B 203) *Ustad Niaz Ahmed Khan and Ustad Fayyaz Ahmed Khan.* Odeon (MOCE 1058). Niaz Ahmad Khan and Fayyaz Ahmed Khan, vocalists; Mohammad Ahmad, tablā. It is less usual to hear two singers perform khyāl together than to hear dhrupad or the instrumental sequence performed by two artists.

Section II: Performance Genres

Ālāp-Dhrupad and/or Dhamār (*H*)

(B 174) *Nasir Zahiruddin Dagar; Nasir Faiyazuddin Dagar.* Odeon (MOAE 181). N. Zahiruddin Dagar and N. Faiyazuddin Dagar, vocalists; Bithal Das Gujrati, pakhāvaj. The "younger Dagar brothers" perform Rāg Jaijaivantī and Rāg Ābhogi Kanhṛā.

An Anthology of North Indian Classical Music, Vol. I. Bärenreiter-Musicaphon (BM 30SL 2052). N. Mohinuddin Dagar and N. Aminuddin Dagar, vocalists. Vol. I also has a khyāl sung by Yunus Hussain Khan of the Agra gharānā and a vocal ṭhumṛī sung by Dipali Nag, also of the Agra gharānā.

See also B 20, B 130, B 134, and B 245.

Ālāp-Joṛ-Jhālā-Gat (*H*)

(B 35) *The Sitar Genius of Nikhil Banerjee.* Capitol (ST 10502). Nikhil Banerjee, sitār; Kanai Dutta, tablā. Side 1; Rāg Mālkauns; Side 2; Rāg Hem Lālit.

(B 145) *Classical Indian Music.* Odeon (MOAE 148). Ravi Shankar, sitār; Alla Rakha, tablā; Ali Akbar Khan, sarod; Sashi Bellari, tablā. Rāgs Jhinjhoti, Bahār, and Yaman Kalyān.

(B 218) *Sitar and Flute: Jaya Bose (Sitar) and Himangshu Biswas (Flute).* Odeon (MOCE 1090). Afaq Hussain Khan, tablā. Rāgs Alaiyā Bilāval and Desh.

(B 279) *The Sound of the Sitar, Ravi Shankar.* World Pacific (WPS 21434). With Alla Rakha, tablā. Rāgs Mālkauns and Pahārī (dhun).

For other sitār performances, see B 4, B 40, B 45, B 118, B 146, B 151, B 240, B 241, and B 259.

(B 60) *Ali Akbar Khan: Ragas of India, Homage to Tagore.* Connoisseur Society (CS 2020). Ali Akbar Khan, sarod; Mahapurush Mishra, tablā. Rāgs Madhavi and Khamāj.

(B 188) *Introduction to the Music of India.* Odeon (MOCE 1006). Radhika Mohan Moitra, sarod; Kalyani Roy, sitār; Shankar Ghosh, tablā; A. T. Kanan, vocalist; Malavika Kanan, vocaliste; Jnan Prakash Ghosh, tablā. Rāgs Bhairav and Darbārī Kānhṛā.

For other sarod performances, see B 52, B 61, B 129, B 145, and B 178.

For shehnai performances, see B 39, B 145, B 147, B 148, B 155, B 158, B 167, and B 232.

(B 169) *Late Pandit Chaturlal, Pandit Ram Narain.* Odeon (MOAE 174).

Ram Narain, sāraṅgī; Chaturlal, tablā; Niazmuddin Khan, tablā. Rāgs Patdip and Misra Khamāj (ṭhumṛī).

For other sāraṅgī performances, see B 108 and B 176.

(B 209) *Himangshu Biswas.* Odeon (MOCE 1068). Himangshu Biswas, flute; Shankar Chatterjee, tablā. Rāgs Nārāyanī and Khamāj (ṭhumṛī).

(B 217) *Vijay Raghav Rao, Flute.* Odeon (MOCE 1089). With Manikrao Popatkar, tablā. Rāgs Ābhogi, Amritavarsini; and Misra Pīlū (ṭhumṛī).

(B 260) *Vijay Raghav Rao.* Tower (ST 5155). Vijay Raghav Rao, flute; D. K. Thakar, flute; Manikrao Popatkar, tablā. Rāgs Hamsdhvanī, Sivrañjanī (dhun), and Mālkauns.

For other flute performances, see B 113, B 182, B 218, B 228.

(B 32) *Ragas, Midnight and Spring.* Capitol (ST 10494). Bismillah Khan, shehnai; V. G. Jog, violin; Mahapurush Mishra, tablā. Rāgs Jaijaivantī, Bahār, Misra Khamāj (dhun).

(B 171) *Shehnai and Violin: Shehnai Nawaz Bismillah Khan and Prof. V. G. Jog.* Odeon (SMOAE 178). Bismillah Khan, shehnai; V. G. Jog, violin; Kanai Dutta, tablā. Rāgs Toḍī and Durgā.

For other violin performances, see B 155 and B 158.

Chanting of Vishnu's names (*K*).

(B 187) *Smt. M. S. Subbulakshmi: Bhaja Govindam and Vishnu Sahasranamam.* Odeon (MOAE 5011).

Dādra (*H*)

(B 223) *Begum Akhtar.* Odeon (MOCE 1147). Begum Akhtar, vocaliste; Mohammad Ahmad, tablā. Ṭhumṛī and dādra.

For other vocal dādra, see B 130.

(B 44) *The Sounds of India: Ravi Shankar, Sitar.* Columbia (CS 9296/CL 2496/WL 119). With Chaturlal, tablā. Rāg Pancam se Gārā dādra and other selections.

(B 243) *Flute Recital: Pannalal Ghosh.* Odeon (EALP 1354). With tablā accompaniment. A dādra among several other selections.

(B 265). *Musique Classique Indienne: Ustad Ghulam Hussein Khan, Sitar.* Vogue, Disques International (CLVLX 260). With Nizamuddin Khan, tablā. Rāg Pancam se Gārā dādra.

For other instrumental dādras, see B 155 and B 158.

Dhun (*H*)

For dhun performances, see B 39, B 155, B 158, B 178, B 182, and B 240.

Ghazal (*H*)

(B 229) *Begum Akhtar Sings Ghalib (Urdu).* Odeon (MOCE 1153). Eight ghazals by the poet Ghalib. The late Begum Akhtar is considered among the best performers of light classical music in North India.

(B 230) *Ghalib, Portrait of Genius.* Odeon (MOCE 1154). Begum Akhtar, vocaliste; Mohammad Rafi, vocalist.

Jāvali (*K*)

(B 19) *A Musical Anthology of the Orient: Music of the Dance and Theatre of South India* (*UNESCO Collection: India II*). Bärenreiter-Musicaphon (BM 30L 2007). Jāvali in Rāga Harikāmbhojī.

(B 89) *Classical Indian Music.* London (CS 6213/CS 9282). K. S. Narayanaswami, vīṇā; Narayana Menon, vīṇā; Palghat Raghu, mridañgam; Yehudi Menuhin, commentator. Jāvali in Rāga Señcuruṭṭi by Subbarayar Dharmapuri.

(B 197) *Vidwan S. Balachander: Veena Maestro of India.* Odeon (MOCE 1044). S. Balachander, vīṇā; Guruvayur Dorai, mridañgam. Jāvali in Rāga Kāpi, "Sarasamulade," by Ramnad Srinivasa Iyengar.

(B 292) *South Indian Flute: T. Visvanathan.* World Pacific (WPS 21451). T. Visvanathan, flute; V. Thyagarajan, violin; T. Ranganathan, mridañgam; V. Nagarajan, kanjīra. Jāvali in Rāga Behāg, "Saramaira," by Swati Tirunal. T. Viswanathan, although he considers himself first and foremost a performer, has completed a Ph.D. in ethnomusicology at Wesleyan University. He has lived and taught in the United States for a number of years, but continues to perform regularly in India.

For other performances of jāvali, see B 97, B 105, and B 177.

Khyāl (*H*)

(B 116) *Hindustani Classical Music: Ustad Bade Ghulam Ali Khan.* Odeon (MOAE 105). Bade Ghulam Ali Khan, vocalist; tablā accompaniment. Rāgs Gunkalī and Mālkauns.

(B 192) *Bhimsen Joshi.* Odeon (MOCE 1029). Bhimsen Joshi, vocalist; tablā accompaniment. Rāgs Mālkauns and Māru Bihāg.

For other khyāl performances, see B 114, B 128, B 130, B 142, B 152, B 154, B 156, B 157, B 160, B 180, B 199, and B 245.

Kriti (*K*)

(B 68) *Anthologie de la Musique Classique de l'Inde.* Ducretet-Thomson (320 C 096, 097, 098) Three-disc set; kritis scattered throughout.

For other kriti performances, see B 21, B 34, B 64, B 97, B 105, B 145, B 189, and B 299.

Rāgam-Tānam-Pallavi (*K*)

(B 190) *S. Balachander.* Odeon (MOCE 1017). S. Balachander, vīṇā; U. K. Sivaraman, mridañgam. Rāga Varāḷi.

See also B 291.

Rāgamālikā (*K*)

(B 179) *Music Recital by M. S. Subbulakshmi at the United Nations on Sunday, 23 October 1966.* Odeon (MOAE 5001, 5002, 5003). M. S. Subbulakshmi, vocaliste; Radha Viswanathan, vocaliste; V. V. Subramaniam, violin; T. K. Murthy, mridañgam; T. H. Vinayakaram, ghaṭam. Three-disc set; Rāgamālikā "Vadavaraiyai" by Ilango Adigal on disc III.

See also B 21, B 68, B 177, B 189, B 197.

Tānam (*K*)

See B 103.

Tāranā (*H*)

(B 117) *Sitara Devi: Kathak Dance of India.* Odeon (MOAE 107). This is a dance type of tāranā.

(B 141) *Nazakat Ali and Salamat Ali: Pakistan.* Odeon (MOAE 143). Nazakat Ali Khan and Salamat Ali Khan, vocalists; Alla Rakha, tablā. Rāgs Madhuvantī (with ṭhumṛī) and Purvī. The khyāl performance on Side 2 ends in a tāranā. This pair concertize together and have made a number of recordings. They live in Pakistan and are of the Samchaurasi gharānā.

Ṭhumṛī (*H*)

(B 181) *Ustad Bade Ghulam Ali Khan: Eleven Thumris.* Odeon (MOAE 5005). Bade Ghulam Ali Khan, vocalist; tablā accompaniment. Some of these ṭhumṛīs are in dādra tāl!

(B 212) *Nirmala Devi and Lakshmi Shankar: Sawan Beeta Jaye.* Odeon (MOCE 1084). Nirmala Devi and Lakshmi Shankar, vocalistes; Nizamuddin Khan, tablā. Jugalbandi performances of ṭhumṛīs, as well as solos. Songs composed by Abdul Rehman Khan.

(B 213) *Nirmala Devi and Lakshmi Shankar.* Odeon (MOCE 1085).

For other performances of vocal ṭhumṛī, see B 128, B 130, B 141, B 142, B 157, B 160, and B 223.

(B 2) *Indian Sitar Music.* ABK Productions (ABK 2001). Debrata Chaudhuri, sitār; Shyamal Bose, tablā Rāgs Rāgeshrī and Pīlū (ṭhumṛī).

(B 242) *Music of India: Vilayat Khan, Vol. II.* Odeon (PASD 539/ASK 539). Vilayat Khan, sitār; Imrat Khan, surbahār; Shamta Prasad, tablā. Rāgs Sūhā Sughrāī and Pīlū (ṭhumṛī).

For other sitār ṭhumṛīs, see B 31, B 45, B 118, and B 151.

For sarod ṭhumṛīs, see B 60 and B 129.

For shehnai ṭhumṛīs, see B 147, B 148, and B 164.

(B 102) *Sarangi, the Voice of a Hundred Colors: Instrumental Music of North India.* Nonesuch (H-72030). Ram Narain, sāraṅgī; Mahapurush Mishra, tablā. Rāgs Nand Kedār, Jogiya (ṭhumṛī), and Khamāj (dhun).

For another sāraṅgī ṭhumṛī, see B 169.

For flute ṭhumṛī, see B 182, B 209, and B 217.

For a violin ṭhumṛī, see B 204.

Tillānā (*K*)

(B 36) *India's Lalgudi Jayaraman Trio.* Capitol (ST 10503). Lalgudi Jayaraman, violin; N. Ramani, flute; R. Venkataraman, vīṇā; V. Sivaraman, mridaṅgam; T. K. Murthy, mridaṅgam. Tillānā in Rāga Behāg.

(B 70) *Classical Ragas of India: The National Raga Company of India.* Everest (SDRR 3217). Mrinalini Sarabhai's troupe; the Southern India Darpana Company of Dancers and Musicians. Tillānā in Rāga Behāg.

See also B 19, B 97, B 291, and B 313.

Varṇam (*K*)

See B 19, B 34, B 68, B 292, B 294, and B 299.

FILMOGRAPHY

Films dealing with India are of two basic types: those about the culture and the commercial films produced by India's Hollywood-like film industry (India has the second largest film industry in the world). Erik Barnouw and S. Krishnaswamy's *Indian Film* (New York: Columbia University Press, 1963) is a good study of the social implications, the origins, and the development of this industry. The films produced in the various regions of India are fascinating sources, because music and dance are as integral a part of them as they have been in Indian drama through the centuries.

A useful source about films of various types produced in India, Pakistan, Bangladesh, and Sri Lanka is Winifred Holmes's *Orient: A Survey of Films Produced in Countries of Arab and Asian Culture* (London: British Film Institute, 1959). An excellent guide with periodic supplements is the Asia Society's *Films on Asia*, which provides a select list of recommended films and film sources, a brief summary of each film, information on rentals, purchase, and cost, and a list of distributors (The Asia Society, 18 East Fiftieth Street, New York, N.Y. 10022).

Some films on Indian musical culture are discussed below.

Asian Earth. Color. 22 minutes. UC Media Center.
This film shows the life of a peasant family in northern India and includes scenes of a village fair with dancing and shehnai.

Baba. B & W. 20 minutes. Government of India Information Service.
The life story of Ustad Allauddin Khan, a great sitārist who taught some of India's greatest instrumentalists, including his son, sarodist Ustad Ali Akbar Khan, and sitārist Pandit Ravi Shankar (who is also Allauddin Khan's son-in-law).

Bharat Natyam. B & W. 12 minutes. Government of India Information Service.
This film explains the unique features in the technique of this classical dance of South India.

A Bridge in Music. B & W. 20 minutes. Contemporary/McGraw-Hill.
Yehudi Menuhin compares Eastern and Western music with emphasis on the music of India. (Annotation: E. May).

Bismillah Khan. B & W. 29 minutes. Creative Person Series.
Extension Media Center. University of California, Berkeley. A beautiful, delicate portrait of the most famous shehnai player in India. The film includes a demonstration of learning to play by rote, provides glimpses of Khan's native Benares and its culture, and ends with a concert by the artist.

Classical Music of North India. Color. 33 minutes. University of Washington Press.
This film presents a sarod performance by Ustad Ali Akbar Khan, accompanied by Pandit Mahapurush Misra on tablā. Filmed in studio.

Discovering Indian Music. Color. 22 minutes. BFA. Made under the auspices of the American Society for Eastern Arts and Wesleyan University. T. Viswanathan, advisor.
The film includes a discussion of the structure of Indian music. It presents Karnatak and Hindustānī music separately, introducing instruments and music typical of each. A dance, with explanation of the hand gestures, is presented. Study guide included.

God With a Green Face. Color. 25 minutes. American Society for Eastern Arts.
This film deficts India's most famous dance-drama performed by the famous Kerala Kalamandalam Kathakali troupe.

Kathakali. Color. 20 minutes. Consulate General of India.
This is a documentary by famous Kathakali dancers on make-up procedures, costuming of actors, training, basic dance poses. A segment of a dance drama is included.

Kathakali. Color 22 minutes. American Society for Eastern Arts.
This is another performance of one of India's most famous theater tradition from India's southwest coast, in Kerala. The film shows daily life, and portrays the vigorous training of the dancers, the intricate art of make-up, and actual performances.

Moments with Maestro. B & W. 17 minutes. Government of India Information Service.
Ravi Shankar plays different rāgas, and speaks briefly on the guru-ṣisya method of learning.

Music of India (Drums). B & W. 12 minutes. Association-Sterling Films.
Features the drums pakhāvaj, tablā, and mṛdaṅga.

Music of India (Instrumental). B & W. 11 minutes. Association-Sterling Films. (It appears that this film is also distributed by the Government of India Information Service.)
This film is a brief introduction to the music of North India featuring Ravi Shankar, sitār; Ali Akbar Khan, sarod; Ram Nayaran, sāraṅgī; and Mohammed Khan, vīṇā.

Music of India (Vocal). B & W. 19 minutes. Government of India Information Service.
A film which provides a variety rāgas of classical vocal music.

Ravi Shankar. B & W. 27 minutes. Government of India Information Service.
A film portrait of the sitār great, done in a series of interviews and recitals.

Ustad Alla Rakha. B & W. 13 minutes. Government of India Information Service.
The art and life of the famous tablā player.

Therayattam. B & W. 18 minutes. Radim.
Dances of North Malabar in South India, is badly filmed, but features traditional material.

The following films are currently available from the Information Service of India, 3 East 64th Street, New York, N.Y. 10021, free of charge except for return postage.

Ustad Amir Khan. B & W. 18 minutes. In Hindi.
This is the story of one of India's greatest vocalists, recently killed in an automobile accident. Born in 1912, Amir Khan rose to national and international fame particularly as the master of *Tāranā*, a form of classical music. This film discusses his life and shows some musical performances.

Vadya Vrinda. B & W. 25 minutes.
This film is about the National Orchestra built by All-India Radio. The role of each of the major instruments is explained.

The following color video-tapes, each 28 minutes, are available from the New York State Educational Department, 99 Washington Avenue, Albany, New York, 12219. Each tape focuses on a master of either instrumental or vocal traditions and in training or performance contexts.

Amjad Ali Khan. Color. 28 minutes. On sarod.
Vijay Raghav Rao. Color. 28 minutes. On flute.
Pandit Jasraj. Color. 28 minutes. Vocal music.
Bhiṁsen Joshi. Color. 28 minutes. Vocal music.

GLOSSARY

NOTE: (H) indicates Hindustānī, (K) indicates Karnatak

Abhināya dance miming expressing the poetic meaning of song

Ābhoga (H) last section of *prabandha* or *dhrupad* composition

Abhyāsa gāna (K) category of song composed for learning music

Aḍavu (K) coordination of hands, torso, feet in Bhārata Nāṭyam

Ādi tāla (K) cycle of 8 counts (4 + 2 + 2); *tṛipuṭa tāla caturaśra jāti*

Aerophone instrument in which a vibrating column of air is the primary sound-producing medium; *sushira vādya*

Ākār (H) vowel "ā" used as "text" for singing

Akṣara (K) a single count

Alankāra (K) graded musical exercises

Ālāp [*ālāpana*] improvised melody structured to reveal a *rāga*

Ālāp-dhrupad (H) vocal genre featuring unmetered *ālāp*, followed by a metered *dhrupad* with text- and rhythm-oriented improvisation

Ālāp-joṛ-jhālā-gat (H) instrumental genre featuring unmetered melodic improvisation that gradually gains rhythmic pulsation, then procedes to metered improvisation on a *gat*

Aṃśa predominant pitch

Andolan (K) undulating vibrato

Aṅga a subdivision, part

Aṅtarā (H) second section of a composition

Anudrutam (K) one-count subdivision in a *tāla*

Anupallavi (K) second section of a composition

Ārohana ascent

Arudi (K) point of rhythmic weight in a melody
Aṭa tāla (K) cycle of *laghu-laghu-drutam-drutam* (10, 12, 14, 18 or 22 counts)
Auḍava five
Avanaddha vādya instrument in which a membrane is the primary sound-producing medium; membranophone
Avārohana descent
Āvarta (H) a cycle of the *tāla*

Bāj (H) style of playing
Baṛā khyāl (H) *khyāl* performance in slow or medium speed, featuring the *chīz* and improvised *bolālāp*, *bolbānt*, *sargam*, *boltān*, and *tān*
Bāyāṅ (H) left hand head or drum; hemispherical-shaped drum of metal or pottery, in a *tablā* set
Bhakta individual experiencing intense religious devotion
Bhārata Nāṭyam (K) style of classical dance
Bhāshāṅga rāga (K) *rāga* in which a foreign tone is permissible
Bīn (H) plucked zither-type stringed instrument, with frets fixed in wax, without sympathetic strings
Bīnkār (H) player of *bīn*
Bolālāp (H) *ālāp*-type improvisation on text, featured in *khyāl*
Bolbānt (H) rhythm-oriented improvisation on text, featured in *dhrupad* and *khyāl*
Boltān (H) improvised *tān* on text, featured in *khyāl*

Cāpu tāla (K) type of *tāla* with cycle of assymetrical subdivisions, a shorter one followed by a longer one
Caturaśra naḍai (K) quadruple speed
Cauka (K) slow speed
Chakra (K) subdivision of six *rāgas* in the *melakarta rāga* classification system
Chakradar tukṛa (H) *tablā* composition in which a *tukṛa* is repeated three times, calculated to end on *sam*
Charaṇa (K) third section in a composition of *pallavi-anupallavi-charaṇa*
Chaturaśra (K) four; four counts in a *tāla* subdivision
Chatuskāla (K) quadruple speed
Chaugun (H) quadruple subdivision of a count; quadruple speed
Chautāl (H) cycle of 12 counts (2 + 2 + 2 + 2 + 2 + 2)
Chhotā khyāl (H) *khyāl* performance in fast speed featuring a *chīz* and improvised *tāns*
Chikāri (H) drone/rhythm string on instruments
Chīz (H) *khyāl* composition of two sections (*sthāī* and *aṅtarā*)
Citta svara (K) composed passage of *solfège*, featured in *kriti*
Cordophone instrument on which a vibrating string is the primary sound-producing medium; *tāta vādya*

Dādra (H) genre of light classical music; *tāla* of six counts (3 + 3)
Dāhinā (H) right-hand head or drum
Damaru yati structural design of large to small to large, or fast to slow to fast, featured in compositions and improvisation
Dāyāṅ (H) right-hand head or drum
Dhama (H) larger, metal drum of a pair of *naghāṛa* drums
Dhamār (H) genre featuring text on springtime and Krishna, structurally similar to *dhrupad*; *tāla* of fourteen counts (5 + 2 + 3 + 4)
Dholak barrel-shaped double-headed wooden drum used in folk music and in Hindustānī *qawwalī*
Dhrupad (H) vocal composition of four parts (*sthāī*, *aṅtarā*, *sanchārī*, *ābhog*), which is the basis for primarily text- and rhythm-oriented improvisation, including *bolbānt*
Dhrupadīyā (H) singer of *ālāp-dhrupad*
Dhruva (H) "fixed form"; section of a *prabandha* composition
Dhruva tāla (K) cycle of *laghu-drutam-laghu-laghu* (11, 14, 17, 23, or 29 counts)
Dhumālī tāl (H) cycle of 8 counts (4 + 4)
Dhun (H) light classical instrumental genre featuring improvisation on a folk-like melody
Dīpchandi tāl (H) cycle of 14 counts (3 + 4 + 3 + 4)
Druta fast speed
Drutam (K) two-count subdivision of a *tāla*
Dūggī (H) hemispherical-shaped single-headed drum with variable pitch, of the Delhi area
Dugun (H) duple subdivision of a count; double speed
Dvayānugam accompaniment to dance with vocal music
Dvigun (K) double speed

Dvikāla (K) duple subdivision of a count; double speed

Eḍuppu (K) starting point in a *tāla* for section or main phrases in a composition

Eka tāla (K) cycle of *laghu* (3, 4, 5, 7, or 9 counts)

Ektāl (H) cycle of 12 counts (2 + 2 + 2 + 2 + 2 + 2)

Ettugada svara (K) passages sung to *solfège* syllables, featured in *varṇam*

Gamaka (H) generic word for "ornament"; to some artists, a particular ornament, as well

Gat (H) instrumental composition, usually one or two *tāla* cycles long, played with extensive metered improvisation

Gāyakī style (H) singing style, often referring to playing an instrument in vocal music style

Ghana rāga (K) *rāga* expressing universal rather than particular emotion

Ghana vādya instrument with solid vibrating body; instrument whose parts are struck against each other; idiophone

Ghaṭam (K) clay pot drum

Gharānā (H) musically affiliated group with a distinctive traditional style of singing or playing

Ghazal (H) genre of light classical vocal music, with Urdu text

Gita singing; song

Gitānugam accompaniment to voice

Gopuccha yati structural design of large to small, or fast to slow, featured in compositions and improvisation

Graha (K) pitch on which a composition or section of a composition in a particular *rāga* should begin

Grama scale in ancient Indian music theory

Idiophone instrument in which the solid body of the instrument itself is the primary sound-producing medium; *ghana vādya*

Jaltarang instrument consisting of a set of porcelain bowls filled with water to different levels to produce the pitches of a *rāga*

Janaka rāga (K) *rāga* from which others can be generated

Janya rāga (K) *rāga* derived from a *janaka rāga*

Jat tāl (H) cycle of 16 counts (4 + 4 + 4 + 4)

Jāti (K) type or group; in *tāla*, type of *laghu* subdivision

Jāvali (K) vocal and instrumental genre of "light music," performed near the end of a recital

Jawāb-sawāl (H) interplay between two instrumentalists, a challenge to exact repetition

Jawari (H) secondary bridge on a sarod

Jhālā (H) unmetered or metered portion of instrumental performance sequence in which constant repetition of pitches, including drone, creates driving rhythm

Jhampa tāla (K) cycle of *laghu-anudrutam-drutam* (6, 7, 8, 10, or 12 counts)

Jhaptāl (H) cycle of 10 counts (2 + 3 + 2 + 3)

Jhil (H) smaller, metal or wooden drum in a *nagharā* pair

Jhūmrā tāl (H) cycle of 14 counts (3 + 4 + 3 + 4)

Jīva svara (K) "life-giving pitch" in a *rāga*

Joṛ (H) unmetered portion of instrumental performance sequence, after *ālāp* when rhythm becomes emphasized

Jugalbandi (H) performance in which the solo role is shared equally between two performers

Kaharvā tāl (H) cycle of 8 counts (4 + 4)

Kāla (K) speed

Kalpana svara (K) improvised passages of *solfège*, featured in *kriti* and *pallavi*

Kalpita saṅgīta (K) generic term for composed music

Kampita (K) ornamental shake of a definite interval

Kanjīra (K) single-headed frame drum; in the West, tambourine

Kaṭapayadi (K) syllable formula system coordinated with numbers of *melakarta rāgas*

Kathak (H) style of classical dance

Kāyadā (H) *tablā* composition, the basis for a succession of variations (*palta*)

Khālī (H) a non-stressed count marking the beginning of a *tāla* subdivision, frequently at the mid-point of the cycle, shown in *krīya* by a wave of the hand

Khaṇḍa five

Khaṇḍa cāpu tāla (K) cycle of 5 counts (2 + 3)

Khyāl (H) vocal genre, featuring a composition (*chīz*) of two parts (*sthāī* and *aṅtarā*) followed by melodic and rhyth-

Khyāl (cont'd)
mic improvisation, including *bolālāp*, *bolbānt*, *boltān*, *sargam*, and *tān*

Kirtana (K) Hindu religious song-type, predecessor of *kriti*

Komal (H) "lowered," referring to pitch

Kriti (K) vocal genre, featuring a composition of three parts (*pallavi*, *anupallavi*, *charaṇa*), possibly complemented by composed *citta svara* and *svara sāhitya*, and improvised *kalpana svara* and *niraval*

Krīya hand motions used to count out the *tāla* cycle

Laggī (H) drum solo sections in the vocal genres *thumṛī* and *ghazal*

Laghu (K) type of *tāla* subdivision with 2, 3 4, 5, 7, or 9 counts

Laya H) speed

Layakārī (H) rhythmic manipulation

Lute cordophone-type instrument on which the strings run over both a resonating chamber and a neck

Madhya laya (H) medium-speed; middle "level" of speed

Madhyamakāla (K) medium speed; middle "level" of speed

Madhya saptak middle pitch register; middle "octave"

Mandra saptak low pitch register; low "octave"

Manodharma saṅgīta (K) generic term for improvised music

Mātrā (H) a single count; (K) a half count

Mela (K) scale-type

Melakarta rāga (K) named scale-type in the classification chart (*karta*) for *rāgas*

Melāpaka (H) section in *prabandha* featuring the exposition and development of the mode

Membranophone instrument in which a vibrating membrane is the primary sound-producing medium; *avanaddha vādya*

Mīnd [*meend*] (H) glide from one pitch to another, touching the intervening pitches in the *rāga*

Miśra seven; "mixed"

Miśra cāpu tāla(K) cycle of 7 counts (3 + 4)

Moharā (H) brief *tablā* composition, including a *tihāī*, used at the end of a musical phrase

Mohṛā (H) in pre-*dhrupad ālāp*, a brief melodic fragment marking the end of a segment of improvisation

Mōrā (K) a cross-rhythmic drumming structure repeated three times at the end of a musical phrase, timed to end on *sama* or *eḍuppu*

Mṛdaṅga (K) double-headed, externally barrel-shaped wooden drum (similar to Hindustānī *pakhāvaj*), the predominant percussion instrument of South India

Mukhṛā (H) the first musical/textual phrase of each section of a *khyāl chīz*, restated to end musical phrases in improvisation

Muktāyi svara (K) passages sung to *solfège*, in *varṇam*

Nāda sound, conceived in metaphysical terms

Nagasvaram (K) double-reed aerophone

Nagharā (H) single-headed conical drum used in *naubat khana*; pair of drums (*dhama* and *jhil*) used to accompany *shehnai*

Naṭak drama

Naṭṭuvanar (K) dance master

Nāṭya dance

Nāṭya Śāstra ancient Sanskrit treatise on dramaturgy, expounding on music and dance which are integral to drama

Naṭya tāla (K) cycle of *laghu-drutam-laghu* (8, 10, 12, 16, or 20 counts)

Naubat khana (H) ensemble of wind and percussion instruments associated with royal courts, used to signal arrival of visitors, mark off time of day, accompany processions, and stir troops to battle

Niraval (K) improvised melody on a given text, featured in *kriti* and *pallavi*

Nom-tom-ālāp (K) second portion of unmetered *ālāp* in *ālāp-dhrupad* performance, with emphasis on rhythm

Nṛtta "pure dance" without poetic interpretive content

Nṛittānugam accompaniment to dance

Nṛtya dance with poetic interpretive content

Nyāsa (K) ending, usually referring to the pitch in a *rāga* on which a phrase, section, or composition should end

Ottu (H) double-reed aerophone used with *shehnai* for drone

Pāḍam (K) vocal genre of multiple sections (*pallavi*, *anupallavi*, multiple *charaṇa*) with romantic and devotional texts

Pakaḍ (H) distinctive melodic phrase that characterizes a *rāga*

Pakhāvaj (H) double-headed, modified barrel-shaped wooden drum (similar to Karnatak *mṛdaṅga*) used to accompany *dhrupad* and *bīn*

Pallavi (K) first section of a composition; third portion of the vocal or instrumental performance sequence *rāgam-tānam-pallavi*, featuring the brief composed *pallavi* and rhythmic and melodic improvisation including *kalpana svara*, *niraval*, and *tani āvartam*

Palta (H) improvised variation of a *tablā kāyadā*

Pancharāgamālikā (K) a series of five *rāgas* performed in succession

Pandit a learned man; in some parts of North India, a surname

Panjābī tāl (H) cycle of 16 counts (4 + 4 + 4 + 4)

Paran (H) structure for *tablā* or *pakhāvaj* composition or improvisation, consisting of a rhythmic passage and a *tihāī*

Pashto tāl (H) cycle of 7 counts (3 + 2 + 2)

Peshkar (H) *tablā* composition and variations on it, each in a particular form

Poorvāṅga lower four pitches (tetrachord) in a *saptak*: Sa Re Ga Ma; *rāga* emphasizing the lower tetrachord pitches

Prabandha (H) performance genre of multiple sections (at least *udgrāha*, *melāpaka*, *dhruva*, *ābhoga*) which preceded *dhrupad* in time

Prati Ma (K) "sharp" or "raised" pitch Ma

Purvāṅga (see *Poorvāṅga*)

Putra "son"; designation used in one classification system to group secondary *rāgas*

Qawwalī (H) Muslim devotional song

Rāga modal system of Indian classical music; a melodic mode distinguished from others by a potential variety of elements: selection of pitches (scale-type), melodic shape, melodic motive, pitch hierarchy, pitch register, ornamentation, mood

Rāgam (see *Ālāp*)

Rāgamālikā (K) "garland" of *rāgas*, a series of *rāgas* performed in succession, as part of the structure of *kriti*, *tānam*, *pallavi*, or other contexts

Rāgam-tānam-pallavi (K) vocal and instrumental genre featuring unmetered melodic improvisation that gradually gains rhythmic pulsation, then procedes to metered improvisation on a *pallavi*

Rāga tāla mālikā (K) a series of *rāgas* and *tālas* performed in succession, as part of metered performance genres

Rāginī (H) female *rāga*; a designation used in one classification system to group secondary *rāga*s

Rakti rāga (K) *rāga* expressing a particular feeling

Rasa theory of aesthetic bliss; nine primary emotions felt by all human beings: love, humor, pathos, violence, heroism, fear, loathsomeness, wonder, peace; mood

Rasika person of aesthetic taste who responds to expressions of *rasa*

Rebāb lute or zither-type bowed stringed instrument, considered the predecessor of *sarod*

Rela (H) structure for *tablā* composition and variations on it, each conceived in two halves, the second a slight change from the first

Rudra vīṇā (H) zither-type plucked stringed instrument, otherwise known as *bīn*

Rūpak tāl (H) cycle of 7 counts (3 + 2 + 2)

Rūpaka tāla (K) cycle of *drutam-laghu* (5, 6, 7, 9 or 11 counts)

Sādra (H) generic name for any composition in a *tāla* of 10 counts (usually *jhaptāl*)

Sāhitya text

Sam [*sama*] count 1 of a *tāla* cycle that functions as a final count of a musical phrase

Sam-ālāp (H) a "*sam*-like" moment that occurs in the *mohṛā* of unmetered *ālāp*

Samashti charaṇam (K) combined *anupallavi* and *charaṇa* in a two-section *kriti*

Sāma Veda the one of the four sacred "books" of the Aryan religion, which is chanted tunefully and is thus considered the basis of Indian classical music

Sampūrṇa seven; "full"

Samvādī (H) term used by some scholars to refer to the second most important pitch in a *rāga*

Sanchāra (K) distinctive melodic pattern of a *rāga*

Sanchārī (H) third section in a *dhrupad* composition

Sandhi prakash rāga (H) *rāga* associated with the juncture of day and night, i.e., sunrise and sunset

Sangati (K) composed melodic variations, featured in *kriti*

Saṅgīta generic term encompassing three arts: singing, playing of instruments, dancing

Sankīrṇa (K) nine

Saptak group of seven basic pitches encompassing (in Western terms) an octave: Sa Re Ga Ma Pa Dha Ni

Sāraṅgī (H) bowed lute-type stringed instrument, with sympathetic strings; considered voice-like, thus appropriate for accompanying vocal music

Sargam (H) *solfège* syllables for the seven basic pitches in a *saptak*

Sarod (H) plucked lute-type stringed instrument, without frets, with sympathetic strings

Shadava six

Shehnai (H) double-reed aerophone used in folk and classical music

Shuddh svara (H) "natural" pitch, considered by some musicians to be the low form of a pitch, considered by others the "half step" above the low form

Sitār (H) plucked lute-type stringed instrument, with movable frets and sympathetic strings

Solkattu (K) generic term for syllables that name drum strokes

Srōtōvaha yati structural design of small to large or slow to fast, featured in compositions and improvisation

Śruti pitch; interval; intonation

Śruti box organ-like instrument which sounds the drone pitch

Sthāī (H) first section of a composition

Suddha (see *Shuddh svara*)

Sur svara; (H) drone-producing double-reed aerophone

Surbahār (H) plucked lute-type instrument with movable frets and sympathetic strings, frequently described as a large *sitār*

Surnai (see *Shehnai*)

Sushira vādya wind instrument; aerophone

Sushkam solo playing

Svara pitch; (K) term for *solfège* syllable

Svara sāhitya (K) new text composed for *citta svara* passages, featured in *kriti*

Svarmandal (H) strummed zither-type stringed instrument with metal strings, played by some vocalists to provide further drone and other pitch support

Sympathetic strings metal strings placed underneath the playing strings on *sitār*, *sarod. surbahār*, and *sārangī* that sound in response to the vibrations of the playing strings, adding a shimmering effect to the total sound

Tablā (H) pair of drums (*tablā*—right hand—and *bāyāṅ*—left hand), the primary percussion instrument in Hindustānī classical music

Tāla metric system of Indian classical music; a metric cycle distinguished by a recurring pattern of subdivisions

Tālam (K) drone and rhythm strings on *vīṇā*; small cymbals used in dance accompaniment

Tālamālikā (K) "garland of *tālas*," series of different metric cycles performed successively as part of the structure of metered genres

Tāla vādya kacceri percussion ensemble performance, usually featuring rhythmic challenge among players

Tālī (H) a count marking the beginning of a *tāla* subdivision, shown in *krīya* by a "clap" of the hands

Tāmbūra plucked lute or zither-type stringed instrument played open strings only to produce drone pitches

Tān (H) fast (at least double-speed) melodic figure, featured in *khyāl* and instrumental improvisation

Tānam (K) second portion of vocal or instrumental *rāgam-tānam-pallavi* sequence, when rhythmic pulsation begins to be regular in an unmetered context; independent *vīṇā* performance genre, usually structured as *rāgamālikā*

Tani āvartam (K) portion of *pallavi* improvisation, when melody ceases but *tāla* continues as the percussion players vie with one another

Tarab (H) sympathetic strings on *sarod*

Tāranā (H) rhythm-oriented vocal genre featuring vocables and sometimes poetry, *sargam*, or drum syllables as text, frequently performed after *khyāl* in medium or fast speed but occasionally sung slow speed; counterpart of Karnatak *tillānā*

Tār saptak highest of three vocal pitch registers; high octave

Tāta vādya stringed instrument; cordophone

Tavil (K) double-headed, approximately

Tavil (cont'd)
barrel-shaped wooden drum, used to accompany *nagasvaram*

Tetrachord grouping of four pitches

Ṭhāṭ (H) tuning for *sitār*; scale-type by which Bhaṭkhande suggested classifying Hindustānī *rāgas*

Theka (H) one-cycle long drumming pattern identified with a particular *tāla* and used for keeping time

Ṭhumṛī (H) genre of light vocal music, featuring a composition of two parts (*sthāī* and *aṅtarā*) followed by melodic improvisation that emphasizes text meaning, and solo section(s) for *tablā* (*laggī*)

Tihāī (H) a cadential pattern repeated three times in succession and calculated to end on *sam*

Tillānā (K) vocal genre in music or dance concert, prominently featuring drum syllables as text; counterpart of Hindustānī *tāranā*

Tilwāṛā tāl (H) cycle of 16 counts (4 + 4 + 4 + 4)

Tīntāl (H) cycle of 16 counts (4 + 4 + 4 + 4)

Tiśra three

Tiśra naḍai (K) triple speed

Tivra (H) raised; usually referring to the higher form of a pitch, as in pitch Ma *tivra*

Tīvra tāl (H) cycle of 7 counts (3 + 2 + 2)

Toṛa (H) instrumental counterpart of vocal *tān*

Transcription process of transferring music from aural to written form

Transnotation process of transferring music from one written form to another written form

Trikāla (K) three levels of speed presented: first speed, double, and quadruple

Tripuṭa tāla (K) cycle of *laghu-drutam-drutam* (7, 8, 9, 11 or 13 counts)

Trītantri vīṇā (H) three-stringed *vīṇā*, a possible predecessor of *sitār*

Tukṛa (H) structure for *tablā* composition or improvisation consisting of a rhythmic passage and *tihāī*

Udgrāha (H) initial section of *prabandha* composition

Upāṅga rāga (see *Uttarāṅga rāga*)

Uttarāṅga rāga a *rāga* which emphasizes the upper tetrachord pitches: Pa Dha Ni Sa or Ma Pa Dha Ni

Uthān (H) in Benares *bāj tablā* solo, improvised or composed piece that follows the introduction; ends in *tihāī*

Vādī (H) term used by some scholars to refer to the most important pitch in a *rāga*

Vādya generic term for "instrument"; playing of an instrument

Vādya Vrinda (H) ensemble of melody and percussion instruments, usually referred to as an "Indian orchestra"

Vaiṇika (K) player of *vīṇā*

Vakra "crooked," referring to non-scalar melodic motion featured in a *rāga*

Valandalai (K) right-hand head on *mṛdaṅga*

Varika (K) style of singing or playing with each pitch ornamented

Varṇam (K) composed vocal genre for initiating a dance (*tāna varṇam*) or music (*pada varṇam*) concert, featuring a composition of three sections (*pallavi, anupallavi, charaṇa*) complemented by passages of *ettugada svara* and *muktāyi svara*

Venu flute

Vibhāg (H) subdivision in a *tāla* cycle

Vichitra vīṇā (H) recent plucked zither-type stringed instrument without frets, with sympathetic strings; piece of glass rather than finger slid over string to attain a pitch

Vidvan (K) accomplished musician-scholar

Vikrita svara (K) all forms of a pitch but the lowest

Vilambita slow speed

Vīṇā (K) plucked lute-type stringed instrument with frets set in wax, without sympathetic strings

Viśrāntisthan (H) note in a *rāga* on which one may pause

Vocable syllable without semantic meaning

Yati (K) shape, as in *damaru yati, gopuccha yati, srōtōvaha yati*

Zither cordophone-type instrument in which the strings run over a resonating chamber the length of the body of the instrument (with no appreciable neck)

INDEX